Frommer's®

SPAIN'S
BEST-LOVED
DRIVING
TOURS

Wiley Publishing, Inc.

Written by Mona King

Revised eighth edition published 2008
Revised seventh edition published 2006
Revised sixth edition published 2004
Revised fifth edition published 2002
Revised second edition 1996, published in this format 1998
First published 1992

Edited, designed and produced by AA Publishing.

Published by AA Publishing

Published in the United States by
Wiley Publishing, Inc.
111 River Street, Hoboken, NJ 07030

Find us online at Frommers.com

Frommer's is a registered trademark of Arthur Frommer. Used under license.

ISBN 978-0-470-22690-2

Color separation: Daylight Colour Art, Singapore

Printed and bound by G. Canale & C. S.P.A., Torino, Italy

Right: *Templo de la Sagrada Família, Barcelona*

A03367

CONTENTS

ABOUT THIS BOOK

This book is not only a practical guide for the independent traveller, but is also invaluable for those who would like to know more about the country.

It is divided into 5 regions, each containing between 3 and 6 tours which start and finish in major towns and cities which we consider to be the best centres for exploration.

Each tour has details of the most interesting places to visit en route, plus panels catering for special interests – for those whose interest is in history, wildlife or walking, and those who have children. There are also panels which highlight scenic stretches of road along the route and which give details of special events, crafts and customs. The route directions are accompanied by an easy-to-use map at the beginning of each tour, along with a simple chart showing intermediate distances in kilometres and miles. This can help you to decide where to take a break and stop overnight, for example. (All distances quoted are approximate.)

Before setting off it is advisable to check with the tourist information centre (addresses are given after the symbol $\boxed{i}$ at the end of town entries) at the start of the tour for recommendations on where to break your journey and for additional information on what to see and do, and when best to visit.

Tour Information
See pages 169–176 for addresses, telephone numbers and opening times of the attractions mentioned in the tours, including the telephone numbers of tourist offices.

Hotels and restaurants
See pages 160–168 for a list of recommended hotels and restaurants en route for each tour.

Business Hours
Banks: savings banks, mostly offering exchange facilities, are called *cajas*. They are generally open: Monday–Friday 9–2, Saturday (October–May, main branches only) 9–1.
Exchange facilities are also available outside these hours.
Post offices: generally open Monday–Saturday 9–2, but major branches have longer hours on weekdays. Mail can be sent addressed to you at *Lista de Correos*. You will need to take personal identification with you when collecting. Post boxes are yellow and some have different sections for different destinations. *Sellos* (stamps) can be bought at *estancos* (tobacconists).
Shops: open Monday–Saturday 10–1.30, 4–8 (large stores 10–9). Tourist-oriented shops may open on Sunday.

Credit Cards
Major credit cards are widely accepted, but check first for the card sign. Cash can be obtained from banks and certain cash dispensers. Note your credit card numbers and emergency telephone numbers in case of loss. Advise the company immediately if your card is lost or stolen.

Currency
The unit of currency in Spain is the euro (€). There are 100 cents to 1 Euro. Coins are in denominations of 1, 2, 5, 10, 20 and 50 cents, and €1 and €2. Notes are in denominations of €5, €10, €20, €50, €100, €200 and €500.

Customs Regulations
Visitors from EU countries can bring in items for their personal use without paying any duty. For tobacco products, alcohol and perfume, officials have guidelines as to what is an acceptable amount for personal use. Customs duties are leviable on amounts exceeding their limits. Wines, spirits and cigarettes are generally cheaper in Spain than in many countries.

Electricity
220/230 volts AC 50HZ and 110/125 in some bathrooms and older buildings. Plugs have two round pins, so an adaptor is required.

Embassies
Australia: Plaza Descrubidor Diego de Ordás 3, Madrid, tel: 913 53 66 00.
Canada: Edificio Goya Calle Nuñez de Balboa 35, Madrid, tel: 914 23 32 50.
UK: Calle de Fernando el Santo 16, Madrid 4, tel: 917 00 82 00.
US: Serrano 75, 28006 Madrid, tel: 915 87 22 00.

Emergency Telephone Numbers
General Emergencies 112
Policia Nacional 091
These 24-hour numbers may not connect you with the nearest station but will get your message relayed. Describe the nature of the emergency (*urgencia*), your location and the services required.
Fire *(Bomberos)* 080
Medical Emergencies 061
Ambulance Red Cross *(Cruz Roja)* 902 22 22 92

Entry Regulations
Visitors must have a valid passport to enter Spain. Nationals of EU countries, Norway, Iceland, Canada, the USA and Japan do not need a visa for stays of up to 90 days. Check with your local embassy.

Health
Residents of EU countries are entitled to some free medical treatment on production of a European Health Insurance Card (EHIC) obtained before departure. However, it is wise to take out a comprehensive travel insurance policy which provides full health cover.

Passengers on all flights to and from Spain must supply advance passenger information to the Spanish authorities – full given names, surname, nationality, date of birth and travel document details, namely a passport number. Some airports may have a self-service kiosk for this, or staff at check-in desks may be able to collect the information.

Motoring
For information on motoring in Spain, see pages 158 159.

Public Holidays
1 January – Año Nuevo
6 January – Día de los Reyes (Epiphany)
Good Friday – Viernes Santo
1 May – Día del Trabajo (May Day)
15 August – Asunción
12 October – Día de la Hispanidad
1 November – Todos los Santos (All Saints' Day)
6 December – Constitucíon
8 December – Immaculada Concepción
25 December – Navidad (Christmas Day)

Telephones
All telephone numbers in Spain have a nine-digit system, starting with 9 and incorporating the area code.
International access codes are as follows: to call Spain from Australia, dial 00 11; New Zealand 00; UK 00; US and Canada 011 (followed in each case by 34 for Spain, then the subscriber's number). Country codes are: Australia 61; Canada 1; New Zealand 64; UK 44; US 1.

Time
Spain is two hours ahead of GMT in the summer and one hour ahead in the winter.

Tourist Offices
Spanish National Tourist Offices.
UK: PO Box 4009, London W1A 6NB. Tel: 020 7486 8077.
US: 666 Fifth Avenue, New York, NY 1013. Tel: (212) 265-8822.

Useful Words
The following words and phrases may be helpful.
English *Spanish*
hello *hola*
goodbye *adiós*
good morning *buenos días*
good afternoon *buenas tardes*
good evening and goodnight *buenas noches*
do you speak English? *¿habla usted inglés?*
yes/no *sí/no*
please *por favor*
excuse me, I don't understand *perdón, no entiendo*
thank you *gracias*
I am/my name is... *soy/me llamo*
how are you? *¿como está?*
very well *muy bien*
where is ... ? *¿dónde está ...?*
open/closed *abierto/cerrado*
I would like ... *me gustaría ...*
do you have ... ? *¿tiene ... ?*
how much is ... ? *¿cuánto es/vale/cuesta ...?*
1 to 10 *uno, dos, tres, cuatro, cinco, seis, siete, ocho, nueve, diez*

CATALUNYA, THE LEVANT & THE BALEARICS

This region offers a variety of panoramas, bound together by its long sweep of Mediterranean coastline and a common language. It includes three of Spain's best-known tourist areas – the Costa Brava, the Costa Blanca and Mallorca.

The capital of Catalunya is Barcelona, a thriving commercial centre. To the north are the eastern Pyrenees, which separate the Iberian peninsula from the rest of Europe. This is a sparsely populated area dominated by rugged mountains and green valleys irrigated by the rivers Ter, Llobregat and Segre, together with tributaries of the Ebro. To the east, the rugged coastline of the Costa Brava features high cliffs, rocky coves and sandy beaches.

The Levant, including the Valencia region, famous for rice-growing, extends to the palm groves south of Alicante. The coast flattens out into long stretches of sandy beaches broken up by rocky promontories. This is the region of the *huertas*, fertile cultivated lands, irrigated by water from the Turia and Jacar rivers, that produce a rich harvest of oranges, lemons, olives, vegetables and flowers. Inland, in the south, lie desolate areas, reminiscent of lunar landscapes.

Opposite the Levant lies Mallorca, the largest of the Balearic Islands. Between the Sierra de Tramuntana in the west and the gentler slopes of the Sierra de Levante in the east is a plain of orchards, fields and windmills. Known for the beauty of its coast, pinewoods and olive groves, the island is at its best in spring when the almond blossom is in bloom.

Numerous invasions and occupations have shaped the culture. Phoenicians, Greeks, Carthaginians, Romans and Moors have all played their part and left testimonies to their presence.

The official language is Catalan. Following periods of suppression it is again widely spoken in Catalunya and street names and place names are written in Catalan. A variant of the language is spoken in Valencia as a result of its conquest in the 13th century by King Jaime I of Aragón. Mallorca has its own version, known as Mallorquín.

Sunflowers throw back the light of the sun all over Spain

Tour 1

Scenery is the emphasis of this itinerary, which takes you into the heartland of the eastern Pyrenees. This provides wonderfully varied landscapes, from mighty mountain ranges to green valleys, rivers and lakes. Along the route are little Pyrenean towns and castles dating back to medieval or even Roman times, along with churches built in the typical Catalan Romanesque style. A highlight is undoubtedly the visit to Spain's most sacred sanctuary in the spectacular setting of the great Montserrat massif.

Tour 2

The once desolate Costa Brava ('wild coast') has long since become one of Spain's most popular holiday areas. Parts are still very attractive, however, with picturesque little fishing villages set in sandy coves surrounded by pine-clad hills. The drive offers stretches of stunning beauty, as steep cliffs drop sharply into the sea. The vivid blues and greens of the Mediterranean and purple shades of the mountains,

coupled with the fragrance of the pines, are a part of its attraction. Visits to ancient Greek and Roman ruins, inland towns and a beautiful old monastery provide cultural interest.

Tour 3

The first part of the journey takes you down the Costa Dorada (golden coast), named for its splendid sandy beaches. The route passes through attractive scenery, where stretches of twisting hair-pin bends give way to more relaxed driving through rolling hills and valleys. Along the way there are picturesque resorts, old towns and one of Spain's greatest Roman cities. Travelling inland along part of the old Cistercian Route, the tour visits three beautiful monasteries in lovely surroundings.

Tour 4

The route begins with Valencia and continues along part of the Costa Blanca ('white coast'), known for its beaches of fine white sand, holiday resorts and mild winter climate. Dramatic rock formations provide impressive landscapes along the route.

The coast of Mallorca near the charming mountain village of Deià

Inland is a sharp contrast in scenery and interest, with several fascinating old towns.

Tour 5

A visit to a unique palm forest is followed by a drive down Spain's southeastern coast, where the Costa Blanca leads to the Costa Calida ('warm coast'). The tour combines wild, rugged mountain scenery inland with beautiful stretches of coastal road. The area of the Mar Menor, with its large saltwater lagoon and tourist development, is an interesting part of the country.

Tour 6

There are two Mallorcas: that of mass tourism, and the Mallorca of fine mountain scenery, almond trees and olive groves. This tour visits some of its best features: monasteries, Roman remains, spectacular caves and picturesque fishing villages. There are beautiful stretches of coastline, with rocky coves and sandy beaches, the essence of this very Mediterranean island.

The Catalan
Pyrenees

Barcelona is the capital of Catalunya, Spain's second city and its principal port. Its medieval past lives on in the old Barri Gòtic, while the elegance of the 19th century, shown in the Plaça Reial, contrasts with the unique flamboyance of Gaudí-designed buildings.

2/3 DAYS • 492KM • 305 MILES

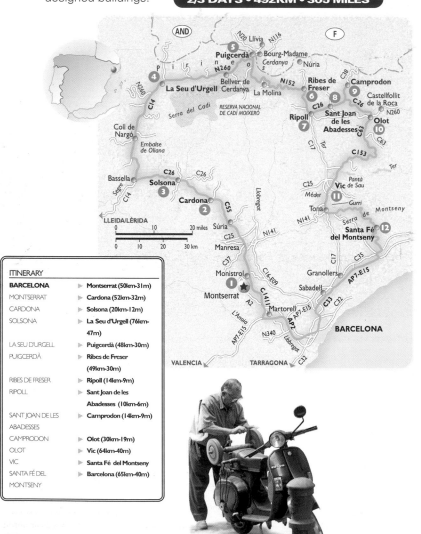

ITINERARY

BARCELONA	▶	**Montserrat (50km-31m)**
MONTSERRAT	▶	**Cardona (52km-32m)**
CARDONA	▶	**Solsona (20km-12m)**
SOLSONA	▶	**La Seu d'Urgell (76km-47m)**
LA SEU D'URGELL	▶	**Puigcerdà (48km-30m)**
PUIGCERDÀ	▶	**Ribes de Freser (49km-30m)**
RIBES DE FRESER	▶	**Ripoll (14km-9m)**
RIPOLL	▶	**Sant Joan de les Abadesses (10km-6m)**
SANT JOAN DE LES ABADESSES	▶	**Camprodon (14km-9m)**
CAMPRODON	▶	**Olot (30km-19m)**
OLOT	▶	**Vic (64km-40m)**
VIC	▶	**Santa Fé del Montseny**
SANTA FÉ DEL MONTSENY	▶	**Barcelona (65km-40m)**

ℹ️ *Plaça de Catalunya 17–S*

▶ *From Barcelona, take the* **AP2** *towards Lleida/Lérida. Leave at junction 22 near Martorell for the* **NII**, *going northwest, and after a few kilometres turn right on to the* **C1411** *towards Manresa. At Monistrol village follow the road up the mountain to the monastery car-park.*

❶ **Montserrat,** Barcelona
Set among wild rock formations and jagged peaks is the Monestir de Montserrat, which contains Catalunya's most sacred sanctuary. Vast numbers of pilgrims gather each year to venerate the Black Virgin, patron of Catalunya, who is kept here. The origins of the monastery, one of Spain's major

---

RECOMMENDED WALKS

Montserrat has several short walks in stunning scenery to places such as Sant Miquel and Sant Joan.

The monastery of Montserrat, spectacularly set high up in the Montserrat mountains

tourist attractions, centre on the legend of the miracle-working statue of the Virgin, supposedly found in a cave near by in 880. A chapel dedicated to her was erected, and in 976 monks of the Benedictine order founded a monastery that steadily grew in size and importance.

The church was rebuilt by Philip II, who greatly favoured the place. The monastery was fortified by the Catalans during

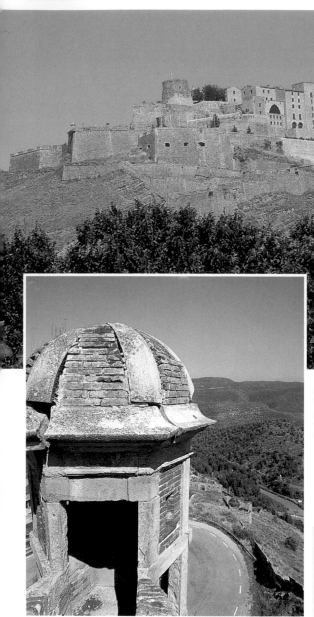

Above: the medieval castle of
Cardona on its hilltop is now a
parador (hotel). The view from the
fortifications, with their pepper-pot
turrets, is stunning (left)

altar is the polychrome statue of
the dark-faced Virgin. It can be
reached by a staircase and may
be touched through a circle cut
in the glass. The library

SPECIAL TO...

When you visit the Monestir
de Montserrat, it is worth
making the effort to hear the
Escolanía. This is one of the
oldest boys' choirs in Europe,
dating back to the 13th century. The boys are brought up in
the monastery and receive a
religious education. The singing
is dedicated to the Virgin of
Montserrat. The choir
performs Sun–Fri at 1pm
(except for July and Christmas
and some other festive
periods).

---

the Peninsular Wars, but in 1812
it was sacked by the French,
with the result that most of the
present structure is from the
19th century, with some parts
completed only after World
War II. Before entering the
monastery, stop for a moment
on the observation platform to
have a look at the dramatic
surroundings. The most important part of the building is the
Basilica, built between 1560 and
1592 in the Renaissance style,
and restored in the 19th century. The interior is a vast dark
area lit by a mass of tiny lights.
In a glass niche above the high

contains an impressive collection of books, and there are several museums.

A short ride by funicular takes you on an awe-inspiring journey to the Sant Joan ridge, where an observation terrace affords spectacular views of the great Montserrat massif.

> Rejoin **C1411** and continue north to Manresa. Turn left on to the **C55** and continue northwest to Cardona.

2 Cardona, Barcelona
A final turn in the road reveals the magnificent sight of the old medieval castle of Cardona. Rising from a great brown rock cone, it looms over the little village below, offering magnificent views. The castle is made up of a group of buildings that were constructed between the 10th and 19th centuries. It has now been converted into an attractive *parador*; however you can still visit its fine collegiate church, Colegiata de Sant Vicenç, and crypt below, which have been well preserved.

> Continue on the **C55** for 20km (12 miles) to Solsona.

3 Solsona, Lleida/Lérida
Solsona is a picturesque little town with quaint streets, old houses and the remnants of medieval ramparts. There are ruins of a 12th- to 13th-century castle at the top of the hill. Near the bridge is the cathedral. Erected in the 12th century and rebuilt between the 14th and 15th centuries, it shows a combination of Romanesque and Gothic styles. The Diocesan Museum in the Palau Episcopal has a good collection of paintings, frescos and fine altar fronts, while the exhibits in the salt museum are fashioned out of blocks of salt from Cardona.

> Take the **C26** west and turn on to the **C14** northeast to La Seu d'Urgell (Seo de Urgel).

4 La Seu d'Urgell, Lleida/Lérida
Serving as a natural gateway to the tiny republic of Andorra, La Seu d'Urgell lies in a typical Pyrenean valley, surrounded by high wooded mountains. It is the centre of a bishopric and has a fine Romanesque cathedral dating back to the 12th century, with later additions. The Diocesan Museum has an interesting display of religious art Other buildings of note are the 11th-century Romanesque Chapel of Sant Miguel and the 15th-century Casa de la Ciutat, built in Gothic style.

> Ⓘ Avenida Valls d'Andorra 33

> Continue east on the **N260** to Puigcerdà.

5 Puigcerdà, Girona/Gerona
Puigcerdà has a cosmopolitan atmosphere typical of border towns. It is attractively situated on a hilltop overlooking the Cerdanya, a district that is split between Spain and France. A bridge connects the town to Bourg-Madame in France. The main buildings of interest are the 15th-century Ajuntament, the 13th-century church of Sant

Domenéc and the church of Santa Maria, which is also 13th century. The town is a pleasant place to explore, with its lively main square, busy little streets and pretty houses with balconies. The boating lake to the north is a favourite resort both in summer and winter. You can take a short side trip to Llívia, about 5km (3 miles) northeast. This little medieval town is a Spanish enclave within France and has a small museum displaying items from its pharmacy, apparently one of the earliest in Europe.

> Ⓘ Querol 1

> Take the **N152** southeast for 49km (30 miles) to Ribes de Freser.

6 Ribes de Freser,
Girona/Gerona
This popular resort lies on the River Freser in an attractive setting of green forests. It is the starting point for a funicular ride up to Núria. The journey takes about 45 minutes and passes through mountains and pine forests. The Núria Sanctuary is a famous pilgrimage centre and the place is also a popular winter sports resort.

☐ *Plaça de l'Ajuntament 3*

▶ *Continue south for 14km (9 miles) on the C17 to Ripoll.*

7 Ripoll, Girona/Gerona
Although the town is essentially industrial, stop here to visit the Antiguo Monestir de Santa Maria which stands in the square. Founded in the 9th century, it was subsequently destroyed – first by an earthquake, then by fire – and later restored. It has a richly carved Romanesque door and a cloister with a fine collection of capitals depicting religious scenes.

☐ *Plaça de l'Abat Oliba s/n*

▶ *Take the C26 northeast to Sant Joan de les Abadesses (San Juan de las Abadesas).*

8 Sant Joan de les Abadesses, Girona/Gerona
As you arrive you will see the lovely 12th-century bridge over the River Ter. In the centre of the town stands the magnificent Abbey of Sant Joan. It was founded in the 9th century and belonged originally to the Benedictines. During the course of time it suffered severe damage and had to be rebuilt several times. The impressive Romanesque church and the magnificent Gothic cloister are fine examples of the architecture of these periods. In the central apse above the high altar is a beautiful 13th-century carving in wood of the 'Descent from the Cross'.

☐ *Palau de l'Abadia 9*

▶ *Take the C26/C38 northeast for 14km (9 miles) to Camprodon.*

9 Camprodon,
Girona/Gerona
Camprodon lies in the heart of the Pyrenees, surrounded by mountains and woods. Attractive houses with red-tiled roofs and balconies look down on narrow, winding streets and squares. A familiar sight is the lovely 16th-century arched bridge that spans the river. Buildings of special interest include the Romanesque Monestir de Sant Pere (St Peter's), the parish church and the Ajuntament (town hall). Many Spanish families come to Camprodon in the summer to enjoy the healthy mountain air and good walking in beautiful surroundings.

☐ *Plaça d'Espanya 1*

▶ *Return south on the C38 and take the C26 southeast to Olot.*

10 Olot, Girona/Gerona
Olot is famed for the painted and carved figures that are used for the Nativity performances. It is also known for its 'Olot School' of 19th-century Catalan painters. Many of these works, along with some fine sculptures and examples of modernistic art, can be seen in the Museu Comarcal de la Garrotxa, as well as exhibits which trace Olot's development as a textile centre.

The town is in a volcanic region and evidence of old craters still remain all around, although they are mostly covered by vegetation. The small museum, Casals dels Volcans, located within the botanical garden, Jardí Botànic, on the outskirts of town, has an interesting display of photographs, manuscripts and exhibits on the subject. A detour of some 7km (4 miles) east along the C150 will take you to the black basalt village of Castellfollit de la Roca, which is perched on a clifftop looking over the River Fluvià.

☐ *Hospici 8*

▶ *Take the C63, turning right on to the C153 south for 64km (40 miles) to Vic.*

RECOMMENDED WALKS

There is a lovely walk from Olot that takes you through the magnificent Fageda d'en Jordà beech forest to the large crater of the Volcà de Santa Margarida (Santa Margarita volcano). Another route from Olot follows the River Fluvià down the Vall d'En Bas, passing through several charming villages.

11 Vic, Girona/Gerona

The old episcopal town of Vic lies at the confluence of the rivers Méder and Gurri. Its two main attractions are the Plaça Major (main square) and the cathedral, which is situated on the edge of town. Founded in the 11th century and restored in the 18th, it features a handsome Romanesque bell tower. Inside, look out for the richly ornate 15th-century marble altar and the elegant cloister, which is graced by a splendid monument to Jaime Balmes, counsellor to Pope Pius IX. The adjoining Museu Episcopal has an impressive collection of Romanesque art, works from the Gothic period and Roman relics.

The heart of the old town is the large and lively Plaça Major,

Wall paintings by Sert of the Stations of the Cross in the 18th-century cathedral at Vic

which is lined with arcades and handsome buildings. This central square is surrounded by an area of narrow streets, winding alleys and little hidden squares. Among them you will find the Casa Consistorial (town hall), a fine building of Gothic origin, with more recent additions. Near by are the remains of a Roman temple dating back to the 2nd or 3rd century AD, and medieval walls.

[i] *Ciutat 4*

▶ *Take the C17 south. By Tona take unclassified roads southeast to Santa Fé del Montseny.*

12 Santa Fé del Montseny

The Sierra del Montseny is a magnificent range of mountains luxuriantly covered by green forests. There are several routes through the Sierra that you could take on your homeward journey, all passing through attractive country. The suggested drive takes you through some exceptionally beautiful scenery to the Ermita de Santa Fé del Montseny, which stands at an altitude of 1,100m (3,610 feet) and offers wonderful views of the area. The tiny village here provides an excellent base for mountaineering in the area, or for those who want to walk.

▶ *Continue southeast and then return to Barcelona on the AP7-E15.*

TOUR
2

The Costa
Brava

ITINERARY

BARCELONA	▶	**Arenys de Mar** (40km-25m)
ARENYS DE MAR	▶	**Blanes** (25km-16m)
BLANES	▶	**Tossa de Mar** (15km-9m)
TOSSA DE MAR	▶	**Sant Feliu de Guíxols** (23km-14m)
SANT FELIU DE GUÍXOLS	▶	**Palamós** (12km-7m)
PALAMÓS	▶	**Palafrugell** (9km-6m)
PALAFRUGELL	▶	**La Bisbal d'Empordà** (12km-7m)
LA BISBAL D'EMPORDÀ	▶	**Girona** (24km-15m)
GIRONA	▶	**Empúries** (37km-23m)
EMPÚRIES	▶	**Figueres** (25m-16m)
FIGUERES	▶	**Besalú** (24km-15m)
BESALÚ	▶	**Banyoles** (14km-9m)
BANYOLES	▶	**Barcelona** (118km-73m)

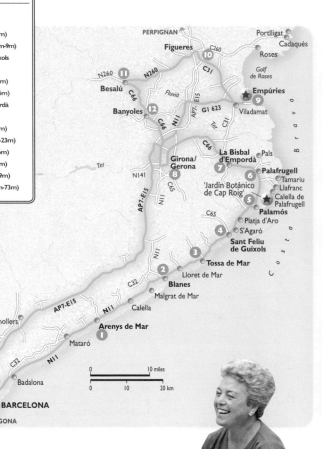

2/3 DAYS • 378KM • 235 MILES

Barcelona is a city for strolling. Take the elegant Passeig de Gràcia or follow the tree-lined Ramblas down to the Columbus Monument and the port area, redeveloped for the 1992 Olympics, and now opening the city to the sea.

Map labels: PERPIGNAN, Portlligat, Cadaqués, Figueres, C260, Roses, Golf de Roses, N260, C31, Empúries, N260, Besalú, Fluvià, C66, AP7-E15, GI 623, Viladamat, Banyoles, C66, NII, Ter, C31, La Bisbal d'Empordà, Pals, Ter, C66, Girona/Gerona, Palafrugell, Tamariu, N141, 'Jardín Botánico de Cap Roig', Llafranc, C65, Calella de Palafrugell, AP7-E15, NII, Palamós, C65, Platja d'Aro, S'Agaró, Sant Feliu de Guíxols, NII, Tossa de Mar, Lloret de Mar, C32, Blanes, Malgrat de Mar, AP7-E15, NII, Calella, Granollers, AP7-E15, Arenys de Mar, Mataró, C32, NII, 0 10 miles, 0 10 20 km, Badalona, BARCELONA, TARRAGONA

14

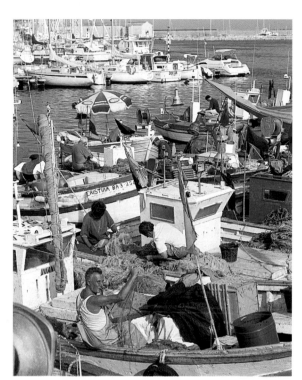

Despite the yachts and the holiday-makers, fishermen still ply their trade from Arenys de Mar

up, the Church of Santa Maria looks down on the roof-tops. A climb up to the top of the Sa Palomera, southwest of the harbour, provides a good view of the sandy bay of Blanes.

ⓘ *Plaça Catalunya 21*

▶ *Follow the road through Lloret de Mar to Tossa de Mar.*

🖪 Tossa de Mar
Girona/Gerona
Tossa de Mar was called 'The Blue Paradise' by the French artist, Marc Chagall, who produced many paintings of the town in the 1930s. Some of his works are exhibited in the Museu Municipal, along with other paintings and a mosaic from the Roman settlement here. The old town is picturesque, with its narrow streets and medieval houses contained within massive walls and turrets from the 12th century. There is also a splendid view from the lighthouse.

ⓘ *Avenida del Pelegrí 25, Edificio Terminal*

ⓘ *Passeig de Gracia 107*

▶ *Leave Barcelona from the Plaça Glòries Catalanes and take the A19 coast road east. Turn right at Badalona and join the NII through Mataró to Arenys de Mar.*

🯃 Arenys de Mar,
Girona/Gerona
The main attractions in Arenys are its pretty little port and its reputation for excellent seafood. The fishing harbour is fun to explore and is full of activity when the catch comes in. The large marina is now an international regatta centre.
The Church of Santa María (begun in 1584 by the French) is worth a visit to see the magnificent 18th-century retable (decorated panels above the altar) by the artist Pablo Costa. Arenys has a long tradition of white bobbin lace-making and you may still see some of the local women,

known as *puntaires*, sitting out on their doorsteps practising their ancient skills.

▶ *Continue on the NII coastal road. At Malgrat de Mar branch northeast to Blanes.*

🯄 Blanes, Girona/Gerona
Blanes, the start of the Costa Brava, is a popular resort in an attractive setting. After exploring the harbour you can stroll along the promenade to the old town which has a Gothic fountain in the main square. Further

---

BACK TO NATURE

Just beyond the harbour of Blanes is the Botanical Garden of Marimurtra (sea and myrtle), where you will find hundreds of species of plants, largely from the Mediterranean area. The garden is beautifully laid out on an original design by the German Karl Faust.

SCENIC ROUTES

The route between Tossa and Sant Feliu is particularly beautiful. Its tortuous bends take you high over mountain tops and down among the pine forests, with magnificent views of cliffs. The stretch between Besalú and Banyoles on the C66 also offers some splendid mountain scenery.

▶ *Continue northeast to Sant Feliu de Guíxols.*

🯅 Sant Feliu de Guíxols,
Girona/Gerona
This large, cheerful town is considered to be the capital of the Costa Brava. Its busy port and lack of a good, sandy beach

gives it a different ambience to some of its neighbours. The 11th-century Porta Ferrada (iron gate) and the adjoining church are the remains of a Benedictine monastery.

The Ermita de Sant Elm, on the outskirts of town, offers a splendid view of the coast.

i *Plaça Mercat 28*

▶ *Continue to Palamós.*

5 Palamós, Girona/Gerona
Palamós's main attractions are its beautiful setting in a wide

---

FOR CHILDREN

Children will enjoy a visit to Water World, a lively water park located near Lloret de Mar.

---

curved bay and its lively port and yacht harbour. A major fishing centre, it is one of the most important towns in the region. Colourful fish auctions take place in a hall called the Lonja.

In the old part of the town is the 14th-century Gothic Church of Santa Maria amid the original narrow streets.

i *Passeig del Mar, 22*

▶ *Take the **C66** inland for 9km (6 miles) to Palafrugell.*

6 Palafrugell, Girona/Gerona
Palafrugell is a busy commercial and shopping town, with a few remains of Moorish walls and the little Gothic Church of San Martí. This is a good spot for a detour to some of the Costa's most delightful resorts. A short drive through pine woods leads

---

to Tamariu and another road takes you to the attractive resorts of Calella de Palafrugell and Llafranc. There is a stunning view of the bays from the lighthouse below the Ermita de Sant Sebastià, poised on top of the hill.

i *Plaça de la Iglesia s/n*

▶ *Continue northwest for 12km (7 miles) to La Bisbal d'Empordà.*

BACK TO NATURE

In season a mini-train runs from the centres of Llafranc and Calella de Palafrugell to the attractive Botanical Garden (Jardín Botánic de Cap Roig), which features rare plants and Mediterranean shrubs.

The River Onar runs through the city of Girona

brown and yellow. While here, visit the large 14th-century Romanesque castle, once the seat of the ruling Bishops of La Bisbal d'Empordà, the parish church and the old bridge.

[i] *Plaça del Castell*

▶ *Continue west to Girona.*

8 Girona, Girona/Gerona
Founded by the Iberians, Girona was occupied by the Romans, the Moors, and retaken by Charlemagne in 785, later to form part of the kingdom of Catalunya and Aragón. The River Onar separates the new town from the old, which is located on the east bank and best explored on foot.

The old town is a step right back into the Middle Ages. You find yourself among dark, secretive streets, picturesque houses and hidden squares. The cathedral appears unexpectedly, rising majestically from a flight of steps. This impressive building, one of the finest cathedrals in Catalunya, dates back to the 14th century. The huge 12th-century embroidered 'Tapestry of the Creation' is a unique exhibit among many treasures in the museum. The adjoining 12th-century cloister is noted for its carved capitals. Other historic buildings are the former Iglesia Colegiata de Sant Feliu, with its tall tower, the old Episcopal Palace, which is now the Art Museum, and the 12th-century Banys Àrabs (Arab Baths). Interesting by day, the floodlit old town is magical by night.

Pleasant areas in the new town are the Plaça de la Independencia, surrounded by attractive arcades, and the Parque de la Dehesa.

[i] *Rambla de la Llibertat 1*

▶ *Take the NII north and make a right turn to Empúries on the GI 623.*

The remains of the Roman town at Empúries, overlooking Roses Bay

9 Empúries, Girona/Gerona
This impressive archaeological site is one of the most important in Spain and has both Greek and Roman ruins. It was originally founded by the Greeks in the 6th century BC and known as 'Emporion' which means market. The place flourished and produced coins which were used in the region. In the 2nd century BC the Romans arrived to fight the Carthaginians, and built on to the existing town. Some of the most valuable pieces that have been excavated from the site can be seen in the Archaeological Museum in Barcelona. Empúries (Ampurias) became a bishopric under the Visigoths, but was destroyed during the conflicts with the Moors. The museum

7 La Bisbal d'Empordà,
Girona/Gerona
La Bisbal d'Empordà is renowned for ceramics and has an Escola de Ceràmica (School of Ceramics). The tradition goes back to the Middle Ages, and contemporary work has been influenced by the designs of the Arabs, French and Italians. The pottery is to be seen all over the town and is recognisable by its dominant colours of green,

The fortifications on the medieval bridge, gateway to Besalú

has a collection of archaeological finds from the area, along with reconstructions of Greek and Roman life. A detour northeast to the coast takes you to the delightful whitewashed village of Cadaqués and nearby Port Lligat, where Salvador Dalí lived for many years.

▶ *Return to Viladamat and then take the **C31** northwest to Figueres (Figueras).*

10 Figueres, Girona/Gerona
Figueres is a major town of the Empurdà region. Buildings of historical interest include the 14th-century Church of Sant Pere, with a fine Romanesque tower, and the Castell de Sant Fernand, an impressive 18th-century fortress. The exhibits in the Museu de l'Empordà, on the town's tree-lined Rambla, include items from Empúries.

FOR CHILDREN

The Toy Museum in Figueres, Museu de Joguets, has a large collection of dolls from different countries and periods of history.

The real interest in Figueres, however, is the great Salvador Dalí, surrealist artist and eccentric, who was born here in 1904. The extraordinary Teatre-Museu Dalí (Dalí Museum), with its distinctive dome, topped by curious egg shapes, is not only a feature of the town, but a big attraction in Spain. Here, some of Dalí's works are presented in a most exciting and imaginative way.

[i] *Plaça del Sol*

▶ *Take the **N260** southwest for 24km (15 miles) to Besalú.*

11 Besalú, Girona/Gerona
A splendid old fortified bridge over the River Fluvià serves as the main entrance to the ancient town of Besalú. Once capital of the Garrotxa region, the town is a medieval treasure, with its narrow streets and old houses. Handsome buildings surround the Plaça Major, which is lined with attractive doorways. The massive Monestir de Sant Pere and the churches of Sant Vicenç and Santa Maria, are all from the 12th century.

[i] *Plaça de la Llibertat 1*

▶ *Take the **C66** southeast to Banyoles (Bañolas).*

12 Banyoles, Girona/Gerona
The popular lakeside town of Banyoles has a good beach, offering facilities for bathing and watersports. On the Plaça del Font (Fountain Square) is the Museu Arqueològic Comarcal which displays antiquities from the area. In the 10th-century Church of Sant Esteve (St Stephen), later rebuilt in the classical style, is a 15th-century retable, the work of the stone mason, Joan Antigo.

[i] *Passeig Industria 25*

▶ *Continue on the **C66**, then join the **AP7** southwards back to Barcelona.*

SPECIAL TO...

The *sardana* is an important part of Catalan folklore. The dance's origins are not clear, but it is thought to have roots in the Cerdanya region. It is danced all over Catalunya, at weekends or on festival days. Anyone may take part (but do try to learn some of the steps before joining in). The participants join hands and dance in a constantly moving circle to the accompaniment of the local *cobla* (band).

Roman Relics &
Golden Beaches

Barcelona's hills, Montjuïc and Tibidabo, are great places for entertainment. Museums, from modern to Romanesque art, and the Olympic Stadium are on Montjuïc, which rises above the city's brilliantly redeveloped seafront. Tibidabo has a funfair and stunning panoramic views. Below lies the amazing Gaudí creation of Parc Güell.

2/3 DAYS • 597KM • 373 MILES

ITINERARY

BARCELONA	▶ Sitges (40km-25m)
SITGES	▶ Vilanova i la Geltrú (6km-4m)
VILANOVA I LA GELTRÚ	▶ Calafell (11km-9m)
CALAFELL	▶ Tarragona (31km-19m)
TARRAGONA	▶ Cambrils de Mar (18km-11m)
CAMBRILS DE MAR	▶ Peñíscola (112km-70m)
PEÑISCOLA	▶ Tortosa (62km-39m)
TORTOSA	▶ Lleida (128km-80m)
LLEIDA	▶ Monestir de Poblet (53km-33m)
MONESTIR DE POBLET	▶ Montblanc (8km-5m)
MONTBLANC	▶ Monestir Santes Creus (35km-22m)
MONESTIR SANTES CREUS	▶ Barcelona (90km-56m)

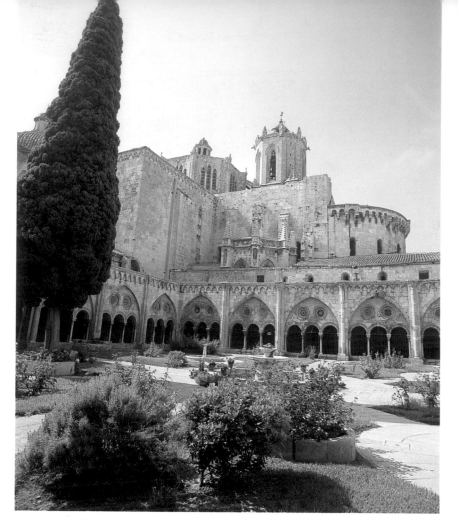

i Plaça de Catalunya 17–S

▶ *Leave Barcelona from the Plaça Espanya and take the C31 southwest to Sitges.*

❶ Sitges, Barcelona

Sitges is a traditional resort that lured Spanish families long before it became an international tourist centre. As well as its splendid sandy beach and shallow waters, Sitges is a picturesque little town with great charm. The local church, with its rose-coloured façade, adds to the picture. The Cau Ferrat Museum, once home of the painter Santiago Rusiñol (1861–1931), houses a collection of his paintings, together with works by El Greco, Picasso, Utrillo and others.

i Sínia Morera 1

▶ *Take a minor road southwest for 6km (4 miles) to Vilanova i la Geltrú (Vilanueva y Geltrú).*

The cathedral at Tarragona, built over a period of time in a mixture of Romanesque and Gothic styles.

❷ Vilanova i la Geltrú, Barcelona

This is an industrial town and a resort, with a fine sandy beach and picturesque fishing harbour. It has two museums of interest: the Museu Romàntic Casa Papiol, which is housed in an elegantly furnished town house and devoted to life in the early 1800s; and the Biblioteca Museu Balaguer, which is noted for its fine collection of antiquities and Catalan paintings.

[i] *Passeig del Carme (Parc de Ribes Roges)*

▶ *Continue down the C31 coast road to Calafell, 14km (9 miles).*

8 Calafell, Barcelona
The small fishing village of Calafell is another favourite summer resort with a long sandy beach, suitable for a quiet stop and a look at the Romanesque parish church and the ruins of the 12th-century castle.

▶ *Continue on the C31 to El Vendrell and join the N340 to Tarragona.*

4 Tarragona, Tarragona
The route passes through El Vendrell, the birthplace of the famous Spanish cellist, Pablo Casals (1876–1973).

The old Roman town of Tarragona was founded by Publius Cornelius Scipio during

The well-preserved Roman Aqueduct near Tarragona

the Second Punic War of 218 BC. A stroll along the attractive tree-lined Rambla Nova leads to the observation platform 'Balcó del Mediterrani', which offers a sweeping view of the coast. Below is the harbour and the Parc del Miracle, where you can see the remnants of a 2nd- or 3rd-century BC Roman amphitheatre, once the venue for combats between man and beast. The Museu Nacional Arqueològic has mosaics, ceramics and antiquities from the region. A climb from the centre of town takes you to the cathedral, which was built between the 12th and 14th centuries. It shows a harmonious blending of Romanesque and Gothic styles, with a fine façade and lovely rose window in the centre. The Passeig Arqueologic is a pleasant shaded walk along the foot of the massive city ramparts, which extend for some 1,000m (1,100 yards) and up to 10m (33 feet) in parts.

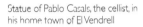

Statue of Pablo Casals, the cellist, in his home town of El Vendrell

The Museu y Necrópolis Paleocristina, on the outskirts of the town, has a fine display of tombs, mosaics and jewellery. Adjoining it is an old Christian cemetery dating back to the 3rd century.

[i] *Fortuny 4*

▶ *Continue on the N340 south to Cambrils de Mar.*

5 Cambrils de Mar, Tarragona
Cambrils de Mar is a picturesque little port with a maritime tradition. The

---

RECOMMENDED WALKS

Leave Tarragona from the Rambla Nova and drive 4km (2½ miles) north to the Roman aqueduct, the Acueducto de les Ferreres (El Pont del Dimoni or Devil's Bridge). A pleasant walk of about 30 minutes takes you through a lovely area of pines to the base. Part of the structure has long disappeared but two tiers of arches still stand and are an impressive sight.

harbour is dominated by an ancient church tower, originally a Roman defence fortification. The port becomes a hive of activity when the fishing fleet comes in, and has a reputation for good eating.

▶ *Continue south down the coastal road (N340) for 112km (70 miles) to Peñiscola.*

6 Peñiscola, Castellón
This is a veritable jewel of a place, rising like a fortress from a rocky peninsula that juts out to sea. The town was taken from the Moors in 1233 by King Jaime I. Its main feature is the castle, an impressive structure built by the Knights Templars. Later, the deposed antipope, Benedict XIII (Pope Luna), took refuge in the castle and spent his last years here until his death in 1422. The castle offers magnificent views of the coastline. Within the surrounding walls is the old town, a labyrinth of tiny winding streets – strictly for pedestrians only.

▶ *Drive inland to join the AP7 north, turning off after 46km (29 miles) on the C42 to Tortosa.*

7 Tortosa, Tarragona
The episcopal town of Tortosa holds a commanding position over the delta of the River

Ebre. The cathedral was begun in 1347 and built over a long period of time. The naves are 14th-century Gothic, while the façade and the chapel to the Mare de Deu de la Cinta (the Virgin), patron saint of the city, are baroque.

Other buildings of note are the 14th-century Palau Episcopal and the Colegio de Sant Lluis, which was founded in 1544 by Emperor Charles V for converts from the Moorish faith, and has an elegant courtyard with some fine decoration. Many splendid old palaces from the 15th and 16th centuries can be seen, as well as remains of the city walls.

ℹ️ *Plaça del Carrilet*

▶ *Take the C12 north to Maials, then on to Lleida (Lérida).*

8 Lleida, Lleida/Lérida
Originally an Iberian settlement, Lleida came under the Romans in the 2nd century BC and was the scene of numerous battles and sieges over the years. It was the birthplace of Enrique Granados (1867–1916), famed for his classical guitar compositions.

Enclosed within the city walls is the Seu Vella (old cathedral), which is dominated by a tall 14th-century octagonal

The ancient town of Tortosa is now a fascinating blend of old and new.

tower. Built between the 12th and 15th centuries, it shows the transition from Romanesque to Gothic. During the 18th century the cathedral was used as a garrison and has been undergoing restoration for some years. It has a fine Gothic cloister, noted for its tall, graceful arches.

Lleida also has a new cathedral. The Seu Nova was built in the 18th century in neo-classical style, and was the first of its kind in Catalunya. Other sights of interest include the 13th-century town hall; the Palau de la Paeria, which is noted for its fine

10 Montblanc, Tarragona

Montblanc is an impressive sight, with its massive medieval ramparts and towers and narrow entrance gates. Overlooking the town is the Church of Santa María begun in the 14th century and never fully completed.

▶ *Continue on the N240 southeast to Valls. Turn left on to the C51, then left again on a minor road, crossing the AP2 to Santes Creus.*

11 Monestir Santes Creus, Tarragona

The Santes Creus monastery rises grandly over the forest around it. It is a fine example of the Cistercian style and is, like Poblet, among Catalunya's most important monasteries.

Founded in 1157, the monastery was occupied by Cistercian monks from France. It long enjoyed the favour of the Kings of Aragón but, like Poblet, it suffered damage during the wars of the 19th century, and is also under restoration. The church is 12th-century Romanesque and contains the royal tombs of former kings of Catalunya including that of Pedro III.

▶ *Return south to the AP2 and join the AP7 back to Barcelona, 90km (56 miles).*

façade; and the churches of Sant Llorenç and Sant Martín. The 15th-century hospital of Santa María is one of the best preserved examples of Gothic architecture in Catalonia. Lleida is an excellent centre for excursions into the Pyrenees.

ℹ️ *Calle Mayor 31 bis*

▶ *Take the N240 southeast towards Tarragona. Shortly after going under the AP2 (motorway) turn right to the Monestir de Poblet.*

9 Monestir de Poblet, Tarragona

Tucked away on the lower slopes of the Prades Mountains, the Monastery of Santa María de Poblet was founded in 1149 by Ramón Berenguer IV as a token of thanks to God for the regaining of Catalunya from the Moors. The following year 12 Cistercian monks, sent from Fontfroide (near Narbonne in France), began building the monastery which is a fine example of Cistercian art. The monks benefited from the patronage of the Aragón kings, for whom the monastery became a favourite stopping place for royal journeys. The lovely Gothic cloister and adjoining chapter house contain a number of abbots' tombstones in the pavement.

▶ *Rejoin the N240 and continue for 8km (5 miles) to Montblanc.*

BACK TO NATURE

The delta of the River Ebre attracts huge numbers of birds, both migrants from northern areas and residents, so the Parc Natural del Delta de L'Ebre, west of Tortosa was created to protect them. Among the many species that can be seen are plovers, avocets, black-winged stilts and red-crested pochards. Flamingos gather on the Salinas marshes, although their presence and numbers are rather unpredictable. Other inhabitants include otters, the stripeless tree frog and terrapins.

The Costa
Blanca

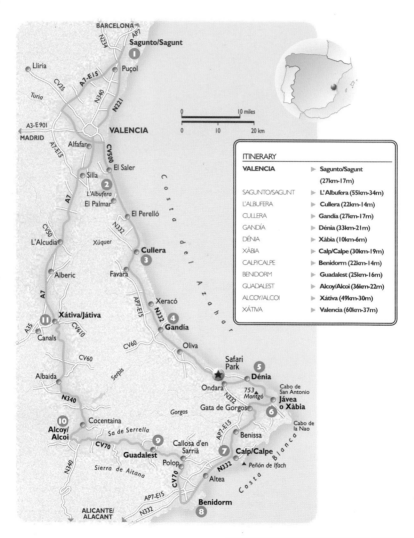

BARCELONA

Sagunto/Sagunt ①

Lliria · Puçol

Turia

A3-E901
MADRID

VALENCIA

Alfafar

Silla · El Saler ②

L'Albufera
El Palmar

El Perelló

L'Alcudia · Xúquer

Alberic · Favara

Cullera ③

Xeracó

Xàtiva/Játiva ⑪

Canals

Albaida

Oliva

Gandía ④

Safari Park

Dénia ⑤

Ondara · 753 Montgó

Cabo de San Antonio

Jávea o Xàbia ⑥

Gata de Gorgos

Gorgos

Cocentaina

Alcoy/Alcoi ⑩

Sa de Serrella

Callosa d'en Sarrià

Benissa

Cabo de la Nao

Guadalest ⑨

Polop

Calp/Calpe ⑦

Peñón de Ifach

Sierra de Aitana · Altea

Benidorm ⑧

ALICANTE/ALACANT

0   10 miles
0 10   20 km

ITINERARY

VALENCIA	▶	**Sagunto/Sagunt** (27km-17m)
SAGUNTO/SAGUNT	▶	**L'Albufera** (55km-34m)
L'ALBUFERA	▶	**Cullera** (22km-14m)
CULLERA	▶	**Gandía** (27km-17m)
GANDÍA	▶	**Dénia** (33km-21m)
DÉNIA	▶	**Xàbia** (10km-6m)
XÀBIA	▶	**Calp/Calpe** (30km-19m)
CALP/CALPE	▶	**Benidorm** (22km-14m)
BENIDORM	▶	**Guadalest** (25km-16m)
GUADALEST	▶	**Alcoy/Alcoi** (36km-22m)
ALCOY/ALCOI	▶	**Xàtiva** (49km-30m)
XÁTIVA	▶	**Valencia** (60km-37m)

Valencia is Spain's third city **2/3 DAYS • 396KM • 247 MILES** and a busy port. The cathedral (1262–1482) and La Lonja (Silk Exchange) are among its finest buildings, while the new City of Arts and Sciences stands out as an example of the new dynamic architecture to be seen in this fast-growing city.

► *Take the **N221/N340** north from Valencia to Sagunto.*

❶ **Sagunto/Sagunt,** Valencia
The original *Saguntum* was founded by the Iberians but was later allied to Rome. The town was attacked by the great Carthaginian general, Hannibal, in 218 BC. Abandoned by Rome, the citizens resisted for several months until the city finally fell to the enemy, sparking off the Second Punic War. Five years later the Romans recaptured the town and rebuilt it. Later, it was under Moorish occupation.

On one side of the Plaza Mayor (main square) stands the 14th-century Gothic Iglesia de Santa María, which has an 18th-century gilded altar with a fine cross in mother-of-pearl. From the road up the hillside, you can see stone arches over some of the streets, which once framed the old gates leading to various parts of the town. A highlight is the Teatro Romano (Roman Theatre). Dating back to the end of the 2nd century AD, it has a diameter of 50m (165 feet), with a capacity for some 6,000 spectators. There is a small museum alongside.

The road winds up to the Castillo de Sagunto, which has sweeping views over the coast and the town. The ruins of the fortress, spread over the hillside, show evidence of Iberian, Carthaginian and Roman occupation; the walls are mainly from the Moorish period.

i *Plaza Cronista Chabret*

► *Return southwest on the **A7-E15** for 6km (4 miles). Join the **A7** heading southwest around Valencia. After 20km (12 miles) turn left off the **A7**, travelling south of Valencia, and join the coastal road **CV500** south to El Saler and L'Albufera.*

The walls of the ruined old fortress of Sagunto, perched high on a rocky promontory, are nearly 1km (half a mile) long

BACK TO NATURE

The large freshwater lagoon of L'Albufera is a nature park of great ecological importance, and is a paradise for birdwatchers.
Among the species of birds that breed here are redcrested pochards, purple herons, black-winged stilts and numerous warblers. Little egrets are often seen feeding in the water and, in the autumn, thousands of wildfowl, lapwings and golden plover arrive to spend the winter. The arrival of these migratory birds can be watched from the village of El Palmar, on the lagoon. The flight of the ducks is a famous sight in L'Albufera.

2 L'Albufera, Valencia
A short drive south beyond Valencia's El Saler beach will bring you to L'Albufera, Spain's largest lagoon (the name derives from the Arabic for 'small sea'). The lagoon is surrounded by rice fields and separated from the sea by a sand bar known as La Dehesa. Three channels carry fresh water into the sea.

▶ *Continue south to Cullera.*

3 Cullera, Valencia
The effects of tourism have taken their toll on Cullera, like many other resorts, once a tiny fishing village and now characterised by high-rise blocks. The place still retains some of its old charm, however, and it is worth

going up the hill to the Ermita de Nuestra Señora del Castillo, which contains a venerated image of the Virgen del Castillo, patron saint of the town. Near by are the ruins of an old castle and a splendid view of the coast and surrounding rice fields.

ℹ *Carrer del Riu 38*

▶ *Join the N332 and travel south for 27km (17 miles) to Gandía.*

4 Gandía, Valencia
Gandía was formerly the seat of a dukedom given to the Borja family in 1485 by Ferdinand the Catholic. Of major interest is the Palacio Ducal (Ducal Palace), a handsome

Fishing boats gather in the harbour at Gandía, the town from where the Borjas set out for Italy

SCENIC ROUTES

The coastal road from Gandía to Dénia is very pleasant, with long sandy beaches broken up by dramatic rock formations. There are many areas of lush vegetation with palm forests, orange groves and beautiful oleander and cypress trees. The road south of Xàbia to Benidorm, the route to Guadalest, inland on the C3313, and the section from Alcoy to Xàtiva on the N340 are particularly scenic.

Renaissance building notable as the birthplace and residence of Francisco Borja (1510–72), who became the 4th Duke of Gandía. Borja was the superior of the Jesuit Order, and was canonised as Saint Francis Borja in 1671.

The building has seen considerable alterations since the 16th century and is now a Jesuit college. The state apartments are richly decorated and the patio is attractively adorned with coats of arms. The distinctive flooring is laid out to represent the four elements of the Creation and bordered by lovely ceramic tiles.

A few kilometres from the town is Gandía's lively coastal resort, which offers a long stretch of sandy beaches backed by modern blocks and good facilities for water sports.

[i] *Avenida Marqués del Campo s/n*

▶ *Continue on the N332 south. At Ondara turn left to Dénia.*

5 Dénia, Alicante
The original Dénia is thought to have been colonised by the Greeks before the 8th century BC and known as *Hemeroskopeion*. Under the Romans it became *Dianium*, after the temple of Diana. It flourished as a port during the time of the Moors (715–1253), and at one time it controlled the Island of Mallorca. Today it is principally a seaside resort and port.

The town is crowned by the remains of the old fortress, which provides a fine view of the surroundings. The area around the fishing port is fun to explore. Take a look at the small 18th-century Iglesia de Santa María and the 17th-century Ayuntamiento.

The Sierra del Montgo towers over the southern end of the town, rising to a height of 753m (2,470 feet). The climb to the top is arduous, but the views from the summit are superb. On a clear day you can see the outline of Ibiza, more than 100km (65 miles) away to the east.

[i] *Plaza del Oculista Buigues 9*

▶ *Take the regional road down the coast for 10km (6 miles) to Xàbia (Jávea).*

FOR CHILDREN

Between Ondara and Oliva, just off the N332, is the Safari Park Vergel, which features free roaming animals, a funfair and a dolphinarium, among other attractions for children.

6 Xàbia (Jávea), Alicante
The small fishing port of Xàbia spreads along a wide bay between two pine-covered rock masses, which descend sharply to the sea. The pretty setting, combined with a pleasant yacht marina and fine sandy beaches, makes it a popular resort with locals and foreigners. In the old port area look out for the small modern church, shaped like a ship's hull.

At one end of the resort is the great rock of Cabo de la Nao, with some caves in its steep cliff face. Opposite is the tiny island of Portichol. The lighthouses and Cabo de San Antonio Nature Reserve on the outskirts offer excellent excursions for nature lovers.

[i] *Plaza de la Iglesia 6*

▶ *Return westwards to the N332 and continue south for 30km (19 miles) to Calp.*

7 Calp/Calpe, Alicante
Your approach to Calp is heralded by the magnificent sight of the Peñón de Ifach – a famous landmark of the Costa Blanca – rising majestically from the sea. Nestling beneath this great volcanic mass is Calp, whose dramatic setting features among its main attractions.

It is another in the long line of popular resorts to be found down this coast, with a fine

RECOMMENDED WALKS

The fit and energetic should enjoy a walk up a good path to the summit of the Peñón de Ifach (about 1½ hours), from where there is a panoramic view of the Costa Blanca.

The Peñón de Ifach towers over the resort of Calp. This landmark rock is 332m (1,089 feet) high

sandy beach and busy fishing
harbour. In the old part of town
is a small Gothic-Mudéjar
church and a 16th-century
tower, all that remains of the
fortified walls.

[i] *Avenida Ejércitos Españoles 44*

▶ *Continue along the N332
for 22km (14 miles) to
Benidorm.*

8 Benidorm, Alicante
Benidorm is the Costa Blanca's
most famous resort, attracting
multitudes of visitors each year.
The place has changed beyond
recognition since the days when
it was a sleepy little fishing
village. It is now an international fun city, crammed with
bars, shops and nightspots that
provide non-stop entertainment, which holds particular
appeal for the younger set. Tall
hotels and apartment blocks
dominate the skyline all along
the bays.
   One of the resort's major
features is its dramatic setting,
with two splendid bays of
golden sands and high-rise
blocks silhouetted against the
high mountains. Steer clear of
the tourist area and explore the
old fishing quarters, which have
narrow streets and a pretty
church with a blue dome. A
rather elegant look-out terrace
near by offers a sweeping view
of the bay and the little island of
Plumbaria. If you have time,
take a boat trip to the island and
enjoy a swim.

[i] *Avenida Martínez Alejos 16*

▶ *Take the CV70 north
towards Polop and on to
Guadalest.*

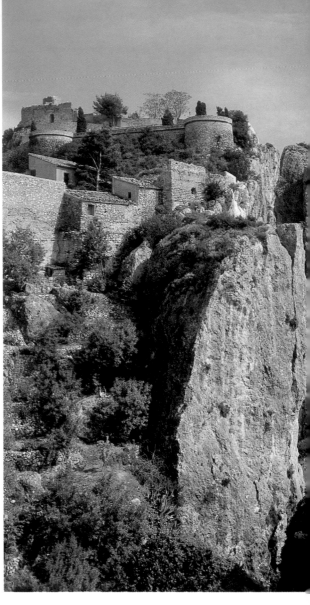

FOR CHILDREN

Terra Mítica is a spectacular
theme park where children
and families alike can have fun
in five different settings –
Egypt, Greece, Rome, Iberia
and the islands.

---

9 Guadalest, Alicante
A drive through some spectacular scenery will bring you to the
dramatic sight of Guadalest, a
tiny village with a Moorish
castle, perched on top of a lofty
mountain crag. Most of the
village was destroyed by an
earthquake, but you can clamber up to the fortress, known as
the Costa Blanca's 'eagle's nest'
for its impregnable position and
superb views over the surrounding landscapes.

▶ *Continue on the CV70
west for 36km (22 miles)
to Alcoy/Alcoi.*

10 Alcoy/Alcoi, Alicante
The town of Alcoy lies in a
setting of olive groves and vineyards against a backdrop of the
Sierra de Montcabre, presenting
an attractive picture as you
approach it. Alcoy is famous for
its *peladíllas*, a very popular
sweet in Spain, made of sugar-
coated almonds. The town has

The ruins of the Moorish castle at Guadalest in an impregnable position on a crag above the village

two fine churches, the Iglesia de Santa María and the Iglesia de Santo Sepulcro, which has attractive tile decorations.

The Casal de Sant Jordi, housed in an 18th-century mansion, has a display of the costumes used for Alcoy's famous festival.

i San Llorenc 2

► Take the **N340** north to Xátiva (Játiva).

11 Xátiva (Játiva), Valencia
The ramparts of Xátiva are apparent from some distance, rising from twin peaks. Set among olive groves and vineyards, Xátiva is an attractive little town of fountains and trim trees, with a number of interesting monuments. Some fine old palaces and fountains can be seen on and around Moncada Street, which is a very picturesque area. The Colegiata (Collegiate Church) is an excellent example of the 16th-century Renaissance style and the municipal hospital opposite has a fine 16th-century Plateresque façade. Allow time for a visit to the

Museo Municipal, which has an extensive collection of antiquities, including the Pila de los Moros, a Moorish basin dating from the 11th century with, unusually for a Muslim work of art, decorations that depict human figures.

There are good views from the cypress-planted Calvary and the Ermita de San Feliu (hermitage of St Felix). A further climb up the hill takes you to El Castillo, a 16th-century castle built on Iberian and Roman foundations, from which there is a magnificent view of the surrounding countryside.

i Calle Alameda Jaime I 50

► Return to Valencia on the **A7**.

Palm Forests &
Rugged Peaks

Alicante, or Alacant, main gateway to the Costa Blanca, is a pleasant southern city. Attractions include its palm-lined esplanade, busy marina and the picturesque old quarters of Barrio Santa Cruz. See also the Town Hall, the cathedral, Iglesia de Santa María, and the panoramic view from the Castillo de Santa Barbara.

2/3 DAYS • 396KM • 247 MILES

ALBACETE

'Fort West'

ALICANTE/ALACANT

Crevillente

Elche/Elx ❶

Santa Pola

Albatera

Orihuela ❷

Guardamar del Segura

Mula

Alcantarilla

Murcia ❸

Santuario de la Fuensanta

Torrevieja

RESERVA NACIONAL DE SIERRA DE ESPUÑA

Alhama de Murcia ❹

Aledo ❺

Totana ❻

Ermita de Sta Eulalia

San Javier

San Pedro del Pinatar

Mar Menor

Lorca ❼

La Manga del Mar Menor

Mazarrón ❾

Cartagena ❿

La Unión ⓫

Cabo Negrete

Puerto de Mazarrón

Golfo de Mazarrón

Águilas ❽

Cabo Cope

Costa Blanca

ALMERÍA

0		10		20 miles
0	10	20		30 km

The Explanada de España, with wavy multicoloured pavings, extends along the seafront at Alicante. *Left:* the harbour

i Rambla Méndez Núñez 23

▶ Take the **N332** south and turn on to the **N340** to Elche/Elx.

❶ Elche/Elx, Alicante

The main attraction of Elche is the unique palm forest which surrounds the town, adorning its parks and gardens and shading its streets. There is an excellent view over the town and palm grove from the tower of the 17th-century baroque Santa María Basílica. The Palacio de Altimira near by was built in the 1400s as lodgings for the kings of Spain. In the Museo Arqueológico there is a copy of the *Lady of Elche* sculpture, thought to be from the 4th or 3rd century BC, found in the vicinity and now in the Arch-aeological Museum of Madrid.

The Palmeral de Europe (Palm Forest of Europe), the largest date palm grove in Europe, lies to the east of the town and was originally planted by the Moors. Many of the palms reach a height of 25m (82 feet). In the Huerto del Cura (Priest's Orchard) you can see the impressive trees of the 'Palmera Imperial' species, which are thought to be at least 150 years old and have seven stems that grow out from the main trunk. The dates are cut in winter from the female palms, while some of the male trees are bound to bleach the fronds. These are then sold for Palm Sunday processions.

i Parque Municipal

The Renaissance belfry of the Cathedral at Murcia

▶ *Continue on the **N340** for 33km (21 miles) to Orihuela.*

2 **Orihuela,** Alicante
Orihuela lies on the banks of the River Segura, which provides irrigation for the surrounding orange and lemon groves. The Cerro de Oro (Hill of Gold) rises in the background. The name of the town is thought to be derived from the Roman *Aurariola*. The town suffered severe damage from an earthquake in 1829. Among the few old buildings to survive are the El Salvador cathedral, built in the 14th and 15th centuries, with fine Gothic vaulting; the late-Gothic Santiago Church,

and the Santo Domingo College, former home of the University of Orihuela, founded in the 16th century.

ⓘ *Francisco Díe 25*

▶ *Continue for 24km (15 miles) on the **N340** southwest to Murcia.*

3 **Murcia,** Murcia
Capital of its province, Murcia spreads along both sides of the Río Segura, in the heart of the *huerta* (a fertile, irrigated region). Murcia is the seat of a bishopric and a university town. The cathedral, built in the 14th century with later Renaissance and baroque additions, features an impressive façade and splendid 18th-century belfry. Inside are lavish Renaissance decorations in the Capilla de los Junterones and the rich late-Gothic of the Chapel of los Velez. One of several museums in Murcia, the Museo Salzillo displays a striking collection of figures carved by the 18th-century sculptor Francisco Salzillo that are carried in the Holy Week processions.

ⓘ *Plaza Julián Romea 4*

▶ *Take the **A7-E15** southwest to Alhama de Murcia.*

4 **Alhama de Murcia,** Murcia
On the way to Alhama de Murcia, stop at Alcantarilla, 9km (6 miles) out of Murcia, to visit the Museo de la Huerta. Outside is a giant old waterwheel called a *noria*, which the Moors used for irrigation purposes.

Continue through orange and lemon groves, then by cornfields to a large, craggy rock topped by the tower of an old Moorish fort. Below lies the ancient spa town of Alhama de Murcia, which is known for its warm, medicinal sulphur springs, and still has traces of Roman occupation.

▶ *Continue southwest to Totana and take a right turn and drive to Aledo.*

5 **Aledo,** Murcia
At the southern end of the Sierra de España is the small medieval town of Aledo, famous for its old castle, which was held for a long period by the Knights of the Calatrava (1085–1160) during the Moorish occupation.

▶ *Return on the same road to Totana, 9km (6 miles).*

6 **Totana,** Murcia
Totana was a town of some importance under the Romans. The 16th-century Iglesia de Santiago (St James) has a fine 17th-century baroque portal and Mudéjar coffered ceiling. Some 7km (4 miles) away is the Ermita de Santa Eulalia, the town's patron saint, famed for its Mudéjar roof and 16th-century murals.

▶ *Continue southwest to Lorca.*

7 **Lorca,** Murcia
At the entrance to the Valley of El Guadalentín lies the town of Lorca, an important agricultural centre. Lorca was a bishopric

under the Visigoths, called *Ilurco* by the Romans, and *Lurka* by the Moors. Above the town are the remains of the old Moorish castle, built between the 13th and 15th centuries, and the medieval churches of Santa María, San Juan and San Pedro.

Further down the hill is the Iglesia de San Patricio, with a Renaissance tower and baroque doorway, and the elegant Ayuntamiento.

▸ *i* Calle Lope Gisbert 12

▸ Take the **C3211** south to Águilas.

8 **Águilas,** Murcia

The seaside town of Águilas dates back to the 17th century and is comparatively unchanged. Its two most impressive buildings are the Mudéjar-style Ayuntamiento and the Iglesia de San José. A climb up to the Castillo de San Juan de las Aguilas on top of the hill provides a fine view of the bay and distant mountains.

▸ Take the **C3211** north, then turn on to the **N332** to Mazarrón.

9 **Mazarrón,** Murcia

The main features in this small inland town are the Castillo de los Vélez, with the remains of an old watch tower, and the Iglesia de San Andrés, which has a fine 16th-century Mudéjar coffered ceiling. A short drive leads to Puerto de Mazarrón, which lies in a splendid bay.

▸ *i* Plaza Toneleros, Puerto de Mazarrón

▸ Continue on the **N332** eastwards for 39km (24 miles) to Cartagena.

> **RECOMMENDED WALKS**
>
> The Sierra de Espuña offers many lovely walks in pine forests and mountain terrain.

10 **Cartagena,** Murcia

Cartagena is Spain's major naval base and a big commercial port. Founded by the Carthaginians in the 3rd century BC, it became the region's capital under the Romans. It declined under the Moors but rose to importance during the 16th century. Worth visiting are the Iglesia de Santa María la Vieja, the Roman Torre Ciega (literally, blind tower) and the Ayuntamiento. On the main quay of the port is the world's first submarine, launched by Isaac Peral in 1888

▸ *i* Plaza Almirante Bastarrache s/n

▸ Take the **N332** east to La Unión.

11 **La Unión,** Murcia

La Unión emerged as an important centre for lead mining a century ago. The Mercado (market) and the Casa del Piñon are two examples of early 20th-century architecture, making full use of wrought-iron. The August festival of the 'Cante de las Minas' (mining songs) is held in the market-place.

East is the modern resort of La Manga del Mar Menor with golf, tennis and watersports.

▸ Return to Alicante on the northeast coast road (**N332**).

The ornate doorway of the Church of San Patricio, Lorca, is a fine example of baroque carving

The Magic of
Mallorca

Although for many it is just a gateway to beach resorts, Palma has charm and it is well worth exploring its historic buildings – the impressive Gothic Cathedral (La Seu), the Palau de l'Almudaina and La Llotja, the former Exchange, as well as the lively Passeig de Borne, crammed with shops and bars. West of Palma, the 14th-century Castell de Bellver, built on a hill by Mallorcan kings and now a museum, has fine views of Palma Bay from its commanding postion.

3 DAYS • 358KM • 223 MILES

_i_ Plaça de la Reina 2

▶ From Palma take the **MA1/MA1C** southwest to Port d'Andratx.

❶ **Port d'Andratx,** Mallorca
From a tiny fishing village, Port d'Andratx has become one of Mallorca's most prominent yachting centres, with sailing vessels of all shapes and sizes moored in the harbour. The town is set in an attractive bay surrounded by hills and has a pleasant seafront promenade lined with bars and restaurants. The yachting set provides an international atmosphere during the season.

▶ Take the **MA10** and branch off right to Valldemossa.

❷ **Valldemossa,** Mallorca
To many, the name of Valldemossa conjures up visions of Chopin, music and romance. The Polish composer Frédéric Chopin spent the winter of 1838

Fishing boat with floats in the harbour at Port Andratx

to 1839 here with the French authoress George Sand. The Cartoixa Reial (Royal Carthusian Monastery), where they stayed, is the main feature of the village. After the monks were expelled in 1835 the place served as lodgings for travellers. The apartments, or rather cells, where the couple stayed are furnished in the style of the period, and include the piano on which the great master composed some of his best-known works. In the cloister is

Terrace at Valldemossa monastery where Chopin stayed

a very old pharmacy. First established by the monks as early as 1723, it looks much the same as it must have done then. Take a look, too, at the small museum in the monks' library.

▶ *Rejoin the MA10 for 10km (6 miles) to Deià (Deyà).*

3 Deià (Deyà), Mallorca
Deià has long been a favourite haunt for writers and artists, such as the poet and writer Robert Graves who spent some time here after World War II. The village is a delightful cluster of red houses on top of a hill, idyllically set among almond trees and groves of oranges, lemons and olives. Behind the parish church is the cemetery where Graves is buried. There is a wonderful view from here of the surrounding mountains and rocky coves below. A somewhat precipitous climb down the hill takes you to the sea.

▶ *Continue on the MA10. Take a left turn to Port de Sóller.*

RECOMMENDED WALKS

Mallorca has so many attractive areas for walking that you can more or less make a choice anywhere along the route. The Serra de Tramuntana in the northwest of the island offers countless hikes in magnificent scenery. Booklets can be obtained from the local tourist office.

4 Port de Sóller, Mallorca
The route from Deià passes through the small hamlet of Lluc Alcari, where Pablo Picasso lived for a time.
The picturesque old fishing port of Port de Sóller is now a popular tourist spot. It has an attractive harbour, framed by the pine-covered hills of the Serra de Tramuntana, and an excellent sandy beach. The Santuario de Santa Catalina, by the old fishing quarter, provides a fine view of the resort. Five

The mellow village houses of the mountain village of Deià set among olive groves and almonds

kilometres (3 miles) inland is Sóller town, linked to Port de Sóller by a tramway – known as the Orange Express, due to the fact that it meanders through orange groves – or by road, where the Convent de Sant Francesc is worth a visit.

[i] *Canonge Oliver 10*

▶ *Rejoin the MA10 and branch off left to the Monestir de Lluc.*

5 Monestir de Lluc, Mallorca
Situated on one of the highest points of the island is Mallorca's principal monastery and pilgrimage centre. The entrance is lined with houses and door-ways, which once provided shelter for pilgrims who arrived here to venerate the Virgin of Lluc, patron saint of the island. Inside the monastery is a

Back in the town, other places worth a visit are the Gothic chapel of Roser Vell, which has a fine altarpiece, the church of Montision (both 18th-century), and the baroque-style Convent de Sant Domènech. There is a Roman bridge just outside town.

Port de Pollença, some 6km (4 miles) away, is an attractive little fishing port set in a wide bay framed by the dramatic silhouette of the Sierra de Sant Vincenc (San Vincente mountains). It continues to grow as a popular beach resort and yachting centre.

If you have time, do not miss a side trip to the Formentor peninsula, one of the most scenic parts of the island. A drive to the lighthouse at the end of Cap de Formentor offers magnificent views of this superb coastline.

▶ From Port de Pollença take the coast road for 15km (9 miles) to Alcúdia.

RECOMMENDED WALKS

A pleasant stroll can be taken in Port de Pollença along the seafront promenade, which starts from the northern end of town and follows the sea, shaded by trees and lined with villas and open-air cafés and restaurants.

7 Alcúdia, Mallorca
The little medieval town of Alcúdia is encircled by some impressive old ramparts dating back to the 14th century. Inside are small narrow streets and handsome mansions, mainly from the 16th and 17th centuries. The town had quite a sizeable Roman population and the local museum has exhibits of Roman times as well as prehistoric artefacts. A colourful market takes place on Tuesdays and Sundays just outside the old city walls.

wooden statue of the Virgin encrusted with jewels. There is also a 17th-century church, and a small museum with a collection of paintings, ceramics and religious items. Mass is celebrated each day, when you can hear the stirring singing of the famous boys choir of Lluc.

▶ Continue on the **MA10** for 21km (13 miles) to Pollença (Pollensa).

6 Pollença, Mallorca
Pollença's crowning glory is the Calvari (Calvary), which stands at the top of an impressive flight of 365 steps. Those who make it to the top will find a little white 18th-century chapel with an old crucifix and a good view over the bays of Alcúdia, Pollença and even as far as Cap de Formentor. On Good Friday there is a service in the chapel followed by a torchlit procession down the steps.

Steps lead up through the village of Pollença to the Calvary standing some 35m (115 feet) high, overlooking the sea. They consist of a vast number of caverns and are noted for the extraordinary, sometimes grotesque shapes of the stalactites and stalagmites.

Artà itself features some attractive mansions, churches and the Almudain, a medieval fortress containing a sanctuary. Near by, the Ermita de Betlem (Sanctuary of Betlem) stands high on a hill with a fine view of the bay of Alcúdia.

▷ *Head southwest for 29km (18 miles) to Manacor.*

9 Manacor, Mallorca
Manacor has a long tradition of furniture-making dating back to the 17th century, when it became a centre for wood craftsmen. Its main claim to fame, however, lies in the production of pearls, an important industry in Mallorca and internationally known. You can visit the factory and see how the pearls are produced in a simulated process that resembles the natural one.

FOR HISTORY BUFFS

Petra (northwest of Manacor) is the birthplace of the Franciscan, Fray Junípero de la Serra (1713–84), famous for his mission work in California and Mexico. San Francisco, San Diego and Santa Barbara are three of his former missions that grew into large towns. Junípero's home is now the museum of the Casa Museu Fray Junípero de la Serra, and his statue stands in the town.

A Roman theatre about 1.5km (1 mile) south is situated in some fields. The theatre was carved from rock, and items uncovered here are to be seen in the museum in the Castell de Bellver, Palma.

▷ *Take the MA12 southeast to Artà. Continue southeast on a minor road to the Coves d'Artà (Caves of Artà), 45km (28 miles).*

8 Coves d'Artà, Mallorca
On the beach of Canyamel are the caves of Artà. The largest known caves on the island, they are said to have provided the inspiration for Jules Verne's famous story *Journey to the Centre of the Earth*. They are reached by a huge opening in the cliff,

Tourist development at Porto Cristo has changed the little port but not spoilt its character

---

BACK TO NATURE

Birdwatchers should stop at S'Albufera, a partly dried-up lagoon in swamp lands southwest of Alcúdia, where you can see many species of birds. Look for black-winged stilts, stone curlews and little egrets. In the south of the island Sa Marina de Llucmayor is an area of strange rock formations that are of geological interest, with extensive views from the top. The rocks and lagoons are also a natural habitat for sea birds and marine plants.

Other places of interest include the church of the Virgin of the Sorrows, noted for its large domed ceiling and unusual Christ figure, and the Museo Arqueológico, which is housed in the Torre dels Enegistes.

▷ *Take the MA4020 east to Porto Cristo, a distance of 13km (8 miles).*

10 Porto Cristo, Mallorca

The attractive little port of Porto Cristo is one of the oldest anchorages on the island, confirmed by the discovery of a sunken Roman ship in the area. In the Middle Ages the port flourished for it was the main entry point for the island's imports. As with so many other seaside villages and towns in mainland Spain and in the Balearics, it has developed over recent years into a popular holiday destination, which has inevitably changed its old character. Nevertheless it still remains a picturesque little resort with considerable charm.

▶ *Near by are the Coves del Drac.*

Giant saguaro cacti flourish in Mallorca's warm climate

Post boxes in Mallorca are easy to spot – their bright yellow paint enlivens the street scene

11 Coves del Drac, Mallorca

The caves of Drac are the best known in Mallorca, and no tourist trip is complete without a visit here. They stretch for some 2km (1½ miles) and visitors travel through a wonderland, over bridges and past a series of underground pools. Lago Martel (Lake Martell) is the largest underground lake in Europe and its transparent waters reflect the weird and wonderful shapes of the rock formations. In summer, concerts are held aboard a small vessel which floats on the lake. If you want to see more caves, the Coves dels Hams (Caves of Hams) near by are also magnificent, noted for the pure white of the stalactites, and lovely underground lakes.

▶ *Return to Manacor and take the MA14 south to Felanitx.*

12 Felanitx, Mallorca

The old town of Felanitx dates back to the 13th century. Visit the Convent de Sant Augustín and the parish church, which has a fine Gothic façade. Felanitx is the birthplace of the

artist Miguel Barceló who still keeps a studio here.

South of Felanitx is the old convent of Castillo de Santueri, perched on a huge rock mass.

▶ *Continue for 16km (10 miles) on the MA14 south to Santanyi (Santani).*

13 Santanyi, Mallorca

A massive gateway, known as Porta Murada, still remains from the town fortifications. These were built as a defence against piracy, which was once a recurrent problem in this part of the island. The parish church has an excellent rococo organ, and there is a fine Romanesque–Gothic oratory in the Roser's chapel. Near by are the remains of some interesting prehistoric sites and fortifications.

▶ *Head northeast to Llucmajor, then to Palma on the MA19.*

ANDALUCÍA

To many people the image of Spain is the reality of Andalucía: dazzling white villages perched on mountain tops silhouetted against brilliant blue skies. Forming a sharp contrast are the sun-soaked beaches and high-rise blocks lining its southern shores. Its past has included some 600 years of Roman domination and almost 800 years of Moorish occupation. This brought the region rich cultures and some unique monuments, of which the Alhambra in Granada, the Mosque of Córdoba and the Alcázar in Sevilla are the finest examples.

The region is renowned for its song and dance, from the gypsy lament of the flamenco to the twirling rhythms of the Andalucían dances known as *sevillanas*. It is also famed for its festivals. Sevilla's Holy Week Processions and Spring Fair are outstanding.

Andalucía is a vast region made up of the provinces of Huelva, Cádiz, Sevilla, Córdoba, Jaén, Almería, Granada and Málaga, with Sevilla as its capital. Its long coastline, which stretches from Portugal in the west to Almería in the east, is washed by both the Atlantic Ocean and the Mediterranean. These coasts are divided into sections knows as the Costa de Huelva, Costa de la Luz (Light), Costa del Sol (Sunshine), Costa Tropical and Costa de Almería.

In the north is the Sierra Morena, while the land further south is dominated by the Andalucían Mountains, incorporating the beautiful snowcapped peaks of the Sierra Nevada including the Mulhacén, Spain's highest peak at 3,482m (11,424 feet).

Around the basin of the River Guadalquivir olive groves and cereals create patterns of green and gold, and forests of cork-oaks flourish. Further south are sugar-cane and banana plantations and cotton fields, while important wine-growing regions lie around Jerez de la Frontera, Málaga and south of Córdoba. In the southwest is a great expanse of salt marshes and fenland, called the 'Marismas', which contains one of Spain's most important nature parks.

Take some carriage exercise from the Plaza de Espana, Sevilla; a pleasant way to sightsee

Tour 7

This tour of eastern Andalucía takes you off the beaten track through a sparsely populated area of rugged mountains, deep valleys and vast plains, a veritable journey into the unknown. Further north is one of Spain's best-known nature parks in a magnificent setting of high mountain peaks, fresh green forests and rivers. Dotted about the landscape are historically interesting little towns. Old cave dwellings also add interest to the journey through this unusual part of Spain.

Tour 8

On this tour you travel through some of the most impressive scenery to be found in southern Andalucía, combining beautiful mountain roads, woods and valleys, with a drive along one of the most attractive parts of the coast. The highlight of the trip is a visit to one of Spain's most important Moorish legacies. Added to this is the splendid setting with the snowcapped mountains of the Sierra Nevada in the background.

Tour 9

The sun soaked coastline of Spain's southern coast with its familiar skyline of modern highrise blocks contrasts sharply with the magnificent mountain landscapes and charming Andalucian villages of the hinterland. Two special features on this tour are the stunning view of the coast's famous landmark, the rock of Gibraltar, and one of Spain's best-known bridges.

Tour 10

This drive through the basin of the River Guadalquivir goes through cornfields and groves of old twisted olive trees, and past small farmhouses. There are wine-growing areas among the gentle hills, and views of distant mountains. The villages are Moorish in appearance – square white houses, red-tiled roofs and little old streets. The highpoint is Spain's Moorish Mosque, magnificent in its entirety.

Tour 11

The first part of the tour leads through the forested mountains of the Sierra Morena, and then down, passing through olive groves and fig plantations. These, in turn, lead to the shores of the Atlantic. In the southwest corner, close to the Portuguese border, is the area referred to as the 'cradle of new civilisations'. It was from here that many expeditions by Spanish explorers set sail across the Atlantic in the 15th and 16th centuries to the lands of golden promise.

Tour 12

Andalucía's 'white towns' are famous and several of these have been included on this

A cortijo or farm deep in the countryside near Cazorla

route. You will find that the names of many of these towns are followed by 'de la Frontera', an appellation dating from the 200 years of fighting between the Moors and Christians, when these towns determined changing frontiers, until Granada, last stronghold of the Moors, fell to the Christians. The tour also explores the coastline of sandy beaches and pine-woods, and several of Andalucía's ports and holiday resorts. A trip into Andalucía's foremost winegrowing region culminates in a visit to its renowned sherryproducing area.

Lunar
Landscapes
of the South

Almería was a flourishing Roman port; to the Moors it was Al-Mariyya – 'mirror of the sea'. The Alcazaba (fortress) overlooks the city, and the cathedral, rebuilt in the 16th century on the site of a former mosque, also resembles a fortress, to counter raids by Barbary pirates.

2/3 DAYS • 645KM • 402 MILES

*i Parque Nicolás Salmerón, Esq
Martínez Campos*

SCENIC ROUTES

Areas of outstanding scenery
include the stretch north of
Almería through the 'Wild
West' mountains around
Tabernas to Sorbas
(A370/N340); the area around
Mojácar; Mojácar north up to
Vélez Rubio (N340, C321 and
A327); the approach to the
Sierra de Cazorla; from Jódar
(south of Úbeda) down to
Moreda and beyond (C325 and
N401/N324); and Guadix
southeast on the A921/N324
nearly all the way to Almería.

▶ *Take the A92 north and join
the N340 northeast for
30km (19 miles) to Tabernas.*

❶ Tabernas, Almería
The little town of Tabernas has
a definite Moorish look, but has
Roman origins. Tucked away at
the foot of a hill, it lies on a vast
plain between the Sierra de los

Filabres and the Sierra de
Alhamilla. There are remains of
an old Moorish castle, and the
church has a fine Mudéjar
coffered ceiling. The area's wild,
barren landscapes were the
setting for many 'spaghetti
Westerns' during the 1960s and
'70s, and parts of *Lawrence of
Arabia* were shot in an area to
the northeast.

▶ *Continue northeast on the
N340 for 27km (17 miles)
to Sorbas.*

❷ Sorbas, Almería
Sorbas rates as one of the most
picturesque towns in the region.
A cluster of white houses is
perched on top of a high cliff
that descends sharply down to
the River Aguas and other small
streams. The remains of an old
Moorish castle form part of the
skyline. Sorbas is noted for
pottery and some of its work-
shops can be visited. There are
also cave dwellings in the area.

▶ *Continue east on the
N340. Branch off right to
Mojácar.*

Fortifications of the 16th-century
Moorish Alcazaba which still
dominates Almería

❸ Mojácar, Almería
A few kilometres from the sea
is the stunning little Moorish
town of Mojácar. Its flat white
buildings sprawl up a steep hill,
and it holds a commanding
position over the coast and
surrounding plains. Its former
name of Meschech-Masstia is

BACK TO NATURE

A road southeast of Sorbas
leads to the Cortijada de los
Molinos del Río Aguas, a good
point from which to explore
the River Aguas, where you
may find tortoises and a
wonderful range of colourful
flowers typical of this area.
Near by are some caves in
crystallised gypsum with an
inner lagoon. Further along is
the Parque Natural de Cabo
de Gata-Nijar, situated in the
volcanic mountain range of the
Sierra del Cabo de Gata.

The Sierra de Cazorla is part of Spain's largest natural reserve

one of the oldest known names in Spain. Of Carthaginian origin, the town was of some importance during Roman times, and strong influences remain from the Moorish occupation. Steep, narrow, winding streets lead to the top of the village, with fine views of the sea and countryside.

_i_ _Plaza Nueva s/n_

▶ _Return to the **N340** and continue north to Huércal-Overa, making a short detour to see the Cuevas de Almanzora cave dwellings just north of Vera._

4 **Huércal-Overa,** Almería
Huércal-Overa is an important agricultural centre. Formerly inhabited by the Moors, the

town became deserted when they were driven out of Spain. It was gradually repopulated during the 16th century. The most notable buildings in the town are the Iglesia de Nuestra Señora de la Asunción (Church of Our Lady of the Assumption) with a fine altar, the Ayuntamiento and the Plaza de Toros (bullring), which dates back to the beginning of this

century. Embroidery features among the traditional crafts practised here.

▶ _Take the **A327** north and join the **A92N** west to Vélez Rubio._

5 **Vélez Rubio,** Almería
Right in the middle of a wild, barren landscape lies Vélez Rubio, capital of the area since

8

Convento de San Luis, both showing Mudéjar and Renaissance styles. Its chief splendour, however, is the magnificent Renaissance castle on top of the hill overlooking the town and offering panoramic views of the surrounding landscape. The flamboyantly decorated 16th-century courtyard, however, is now in the Metropolitan Museum in New York.

On the outskirts of town is the Cueva de los Letreros, with neolithic cave paintings.

mountains. The discovery of an Iberian stone figure, the Dama de Baza (Lady of Baza), excavated here in 1971, was a find of some importance. Buildings of note include the 16th-century Iglesia Colegiata, built in the Renaissance style; the Iglesia de Santiago, also from the 16th century, with elegant Mudéjar coffered ceilings; and the Iglesia de San Juan y Los Dolores (Church of St John and the Sorrows). The Iglesia de Santo Domingo has fine cloisters. In the Iglesia de la Merced is the

Left: Vélez Blanco, with its dramatic mountain backdrop

▶ *Rejoin the **A92N** and continue on this road west to Baza.*

7 **Baza,** Almería
The old Iberian settlement of Baza lies in the valley of Baza, in the heart of a fertile plain surrounded by rather barren

The Santa María fountain in Baeza

image of Nuestra Señora de la Piedad, the town's patron saint. The Moorish Baths in the town centre have been preserved as a National Monument.

the beginning of the 18th century. The Convento de San Francisco, the parish church and the Iglesia de Nuestra Señora del Carmen (Church of Our Lady of Carmen) are all fine examples of baroque architecture. The old hospital and the Ayuntamiento are also notable buildings, and there are many elegant private mansions from earlier centuries.

▶ *Take the **A317** north for 6km (4 miles) to Vélez Blanco.*

6 **Vélez Blanco,** Almería
Built on the slopes of a mountain, Vélez Blanco has a rich heritage, with Roman origins. Buildings of special interest include the Iglesia de Santiago (Church of St James), with a fine Mudéjar ceiling, and the

---

SPECIAL TO...

An unusual celebration takes place between Guadix and Baza on 6 September in honour of Nuestra Señora de la Piedad, patron saint of Baza. A character from Guadix (known as 'El Cascamorras') has to travel to Baza to take possession of the statue of the Virgin, enduring insults and all sorts of abuses from the people of Baza during the course of the journey.

▶ *Continue on the **A92N** for a short distance before turning right on to the **A315** north. At Peal de Becerro take the **A319** east to Cazorla.*

8 **Cazorla,** Jaén
Capital of the area, Cazorla is dominated by the mighty mountain ranges of the Sierra de Cazorla and Sierra de Segura. Its two attractive main squares are surrounded by fine mansions. The ruins of the Iglesia de Santa María show the Plateresque style, and the two castles, Castillo de las Cinco Esquinas (Five Corners) and La Yedra, are both medieval. The

designated a nature park and provides excellent walks for serious hikers and a wonderful area for nature-lovers. There are good views of the area from here over the Valley of the Guadalquivir.

i St Martinez Falero 11

▶ *Return to Peal de Becerro and join the C328 to the A401 north to Úbeda.*

9 **Úbeda,** Jaén

Úbeda has some great palatial buildings and many fine churches. The Sacra Capilla del Salvador (Sacred Chapel of St Salvador) was built in an elaborate Renaissance style in the 16th century, and has a superb sculpture of the *Transfiguration* by Alonso Berruguete.

The Iglesia de Santa María was begun in the 13th century

town is particularly lovely in spring, when the purple blossoms of the many Judas trees are out.

Just north of Cazorla is the tiny village of La Iruela, perched on a high cliff, with a castle at the top. Just beyond this is the gateway to the Sierra de Cazorla and the Sierra de Segura. The area has been

and not completed until several centuries later. Of note inside are its lovely cloister and splendid grilles. The 13th-century Iglesia de San Pablo (Church of St Paul) boasts a fine portal.

From Úbeda the view is stunning, out over the ranks of olive groves to the distant hills

A few of the cave dwellings carved out of the soft tufa rock near Guadix are still inhabited

The heart of the old town is the Plaza Vazquez de Molina, an attractive square surrounded by elegant buildings. The Ayuntamiento is in the Palacio de las Cadenas (House of Chains), named after the iron chains that were once placed around the courtyard. It is a graceful building, flanked by arcades and with an unusual 16th-century fountain built into the wall.

Other buildings worth a mention are the Montiel Palace, Bishop Canastero's Mansion (note the coat-of-arms on the outside) and the Palacio de los Marqueses de Mancera, formerly the property of the Viceroy of Peru. In the centre of the old Plaza del Mercado is a monument to San Juan de la Cruz (St John of the Cross), famous poet and mystic. He died here in the Oratory, near the Plaza, in 1591.

🛈 *Plaza Baja del Marqués 4*

FOR CHILDREN

Children are sure to be thrilled by a visit to Mini Hollywood, one of three theme towns where some of the old Westerns were filmed. Typical cowboy-style entertainment includes mock gunfights, jail breaks and hangings. (Located off Carretera Nacional, some 10km/6 miles west of Tabernas.)

▷ *Take the **A401** south, then join the **A92** towards Guadix.*

🔟 **Guadix,** Jaén

The Renaissance cathedral is the most prominent building of the town and features a massive tower and a baroque portal. The churches of Santiago (St James) and Santa Ana (St Anne) have fine Mudéjar coffered ceilings.

In the upper part of the town is the Alcazába (Moorish palace), and other buildings of note are the Palacio Episcopal and the Palacio Peñaflor. The main square, Plaza Mayor, is a fine example of Renaissance architecture and from here there are attractive views over the rooftops.

Cave dwellings, hollowed out of the soft tufa rock, are one of Guadix's most interesting features. They are in the Barrio Santiago, beyond the Iglesia de Santiago, and some are quite spacious, with two storeys; many are comfortably fitted out with running water, electricity and television. The conical chimneys protrude from the pathways above, creating a strange spectacle.

🛈 *Avenida Mariana Pineda*

▷ *Return to Almería on the **A92/A324**, 120km (75 miles).*

Spain's
Moorish Legacy

Málaga is the 'capital' of the Costa del Sol, the main gateway to its famous resorts. Founded by the Phoenicians, it was held by the Moors from 711 until 1487, and the Alcazaba (Moorish palace), stands as a legacy of the past. An added attraction is the Picasso Museum, which houses a collection of works by the artist, a native of Málaga.

2/3 DAYS • 347KM • 217 MILES

ITINERARY

MÁLAGA	▶ Vélez-Málaga (37km-23m)
VÉLEZ-MÁLAGA	▶ Nerja (25km-16m)
NERJA	▶ Almuñécar (22km-14m)
ALMUÑÉCAR	▶ Motril (21km-13m)
MOTRIL	▶ Vélez de Benaudalla (14km-9m)
VÉLEZ DE BENAUDALLA	▶ Granada (54km-34m)
GRANADA	▶ Loja (52km-32m)
LOJA	▶ Antequera (43km-27m)
ANTEQUERA	▶ Álora (39km-24m)
ÁLORA	▶ Málaga (40km-25m)

Above: the Balcón de Europa at Nerja. *Left:* looking down from the Balcón, over the beach and the town to the mountains beyond

ⓘ *Pasaje de Chinitas 4*

▶ *From Málaga take the N340 east. At Torre del Mar turn north on to the A356 to Vélez-Málaga*

❶ Vélez-Málaga, Málaga
Lying towards the end of a valley among subtropical vegetation is the little white town of Vélez-Málaga. On top of the hill stands the old Moorish Alcázar, or castle. Take a look at the Iglesia de Santa María la Mayor (St Mary Major), the Iglesia de San Juan (St John) and the Ayuntamiento. Thursday is market day, always a busy, colourful event.

▶ *Return south and continue on the N340 to Nerja.*

FOR CHILDREN

Located in the residential area of El Tomillar, between Torre del Mar and Vélez-Málaga, is Aquavelis, a splendid aquapark for children, which offers 11 sorts of aquatic delights, including a large swimming-pool, water chutes and fast kamikaze slides. There is also a spiral slide and a children's playground.

❷ Nerja, Málaga
Its clifftop setting is one of Nerja's main attractions, with lovely views of the rocky coves below. Near the main square is a terrace with the famous Balcón de Europa (Balcony of Europe)

lookout point over the Mediterranean, so named by King Alfonso XII when he came here in 1885.

About 2km (1½ miles) away, near the village of Maro, are the impressive Cuevas de Nerja. They were discovered in 1959 and contain paintings from palaeolithic times.

ⓘ *Puerta del Mar 2*

▶ *Continue on the N340 for 22km (14 miles) to Almuñécar.*

❸ Almuñécar, Granada
This attractive little town is a cluster of whitewashed houses sprawling up a steep hill, crowned by the remains of an old Moorish castle. The ancient aqueduct and the Torre del Monje (Tower of the Monk) are Roman. Also of interest is the Cueva de los Siete Palacios (Cave of Seven Palaces, or

Vaults). The beaches of La Herradura and Punta del Mar have contributed to the growth in tourism. The nearby Punta de la Mona is a wonderful lookout point for views over the Mediterranean.

i *Avenida Europa (Palacete la Najarra)*

▶ *Continue east to Motril.*

4 Motril, Granada
Make a brief stop here before continuing on the next lap of your journey. Among the town's most important buildings are the Iglesia Colegiata de la

Encarnación (Collegiate Church of the Incarnation) and the Santuario de Nuestra Señora de la Cabeza, said to have been the home of the mother of Boabdil, the last of the Moorish kings of Granada.

▶ *Take the regional road north to Vélez de Benaudalla.*

5 Vélez de Benaudalla, Granada
Vélez de Benaudalla is a typical Andalucían village of white houses and red-tiled roofs clustering below a large hexagonal tower and with beautiful mountains around it. A good place for a break before you continue the next stage which is quite a drive.

Granada, the Alhambra. *Left:* intricate decoration in the Mexuar Court. *Inset: an* overall view

RECOMMENDED WALKS

A road branching off northeast from Vélez de Benaudalla leads to the region of Las Alpujarras (which stems from the Moorish 'Al-Busherat' meaning the grassland) and this offers some excellent walking in surroundings that are very agreeable without making too many demands on your stamina.

▶ *Continue north on the regional road for a short distance, and join the N323 north for 54km (34 miles) to Granada.*

6 Granada, Granada
The city of Granada is built on three hills: the Alhambra, the Albaicín and the Sacromonte, dominated by the beautiful snowcapped mountains of the Sierra Nevada. It is thought to have been founded by the Iberians. The Romans and the Visigoths were here later, and in 711 it was conquered by the Moors. The town was called Gharnatha and a fortress erected on the Alhambra Hill. During the Reconquest it became the last stronghold of

SCENIC ROUTES

Solynieve is a winter resort in the Sierra Nevada that offers excellent facilities for winter sports, normally under a brilliant blue sky. The area is reached by a very winding mountainous road southeast of Granada in beautiful scenery. A further drive takes you along one of the highest roads in Europe to the Pico de Veleta, second-highest peak in the Sierra Nevada. In spring the whole area is a fairyland of pink blossoms.

the Moors until 2 January, 1492, when the Moorish Caliph, Emir Abdallah Mohammad XI, known to the Spaniards as Boabdil, the Boy King, was deposed and Moorish domination of Spain came to an end.

You can either walk up the hill to the Alhambra or take the longer route by car. The entrance is through the Puerta de las Granadas (Gateway of the Pomegranates), built by the Habsburg Emperor Charles V. A short walk up a pathway lined by elm trees (planted by the Duke of Wellington) leads to the Puerta de la Justicia (Gate of Justice). On the west side of the square stands the oldest

structure of all, the Alcazaba. Dating back to the 9th century, only its outer walls remain.

To the east is the Palacio de Carlos V (Palace of Emperor Charles V). Begun in 1526 and never completed, it was built in classical Renaissance style, in sharp contrast to the style of architecture which characterises the Alhambra. Many beautiful treasures can be seen in the two museums here, the Museo Provincial de Bellas Artes (Museum of Fine Arts) and the Museo de la Alhambra (Museum of the Alhambra), noted for its priceless Alhambra Vase, which dates back to 1320.

To the north is the masterpiece itself, the Alcázar, or Casa Real (Royal Palace). Started in 1334 and completed in 1391, it is a remarkable architectural achievement, characterised by rich and elaborate decorations. Entrance is through the Patio del Mexuar (Mexuar Court), formerly the council chamber and later used as a chapel, which leads to the lovely Patio de los Arrayanes (Court of the Myrtle Trees). Adjoining this is the Sala de los Embajadores (Hall of the Ambassadors). Originally used as a throne room for the Moorish kings, it is noted for its rich decorations and magnificent domed ceiling.

The Italian style gardens, refreshed with fountains, at the Generalife Palace, once the summer residence of the Moorish kings

The Mozárabes Gallery leads to the splendid Patio de los Leones (Court of Lions), a main feature of the palace and the old heart of the harem. Chambers leading from here include the Sala de los Abencerrajes (Abencerrajes Gallery) to the south, with an impressive stalactite ceiling and a marble fountain; and the Sala de los Reyes (King's Chamber) to the east, noted for its alcove paintings of historical scenes. The Sala de

The white houses of Andalucía set off the flowers the Spanish love to tend; here, in Antequera

las dos Hermanas (Hall of the Two Sisters), on the north side, features an intricately decorated honeycomb dome. This leads, in turn, to the Sala de los Ajimeces (Ajimeces Gallery) and on to the Mirador de Daraxa, a charming little look-out balcony. The Patio de Daraxa (Daraxa Courtyard) is a lovely inner courtyard with cypresses and orange trees.

More galleries and patios may be visited before you make your way to the Generalife, on the Cerro del Sol (Hill of the Sun). The Palacio del Generalife was completed in 1319 and served as the summer residence of the Moorish kings. The Patio de la Acequia (Canal Court) is planted with roses, laurels and orange trees and the surrounding gardens are laid out in Italian style.

Allow time to explore the town itself. The heart of the city is the large square Plaza de Isabel la Católica, where a monument stands to commemorate the Santa Fé Agreement of 1492 made between Isabel la Católica and Columbus. The 19th-century Ayuntamiento stands in the smaller Plaza del Carmen. Near by is the 18th-century Palacio Arzobispal (Archbishop's Palace). A little further on is the Catedral de Santa María de la Encarnación (St Mary of the Incarnation). Begun in 1523 and consecrated in 1561, it stands as a memorial to the victory of Christianity in Spain. It has a richly decorated interior and a fine Capilla Real, which is noted for its high dome and beautiful stained-glass window. Other buildings of interest include the Carthusian Monastery, the Audiencia (Law Court), the 16th-century Iglesia de Santa Ana and the Casa de Castríl, which houses the Museo Arqueológico (Archaeological Museum). On the right bank of the Darro ravine is the Albaicín, the old

Moorish quarter, where a wander around its narrow, cobblestoned streets and hidden corners recaptures the past. Behind the Albaicín is the Sacromonte Hill, where the gypsies live in caves and put on flamenco shows.

Beware when the bullfight is on. All streets become one-way, leading right to the bull-ring, where you might find yourself inadvertently spending the rest of the day!

[i] *Corral del Carbón, Plaza Mariana Pineda 10 Bajo*

▶ *Take the A92 west to Loja.*

7 Loja, Granada
Located in the west of the province of Granada, Loja is dominated by the ruins of an old Moorish castle. Buildings of interest in the town include the 15th-century Iglesia de la Encarnación, the 16th-century Iglesia de San Gabriel and the Convento de Santa Clara (Convent and Church of Santa

Clara), which has a fine Mudéjar ceiling. Take a look also at the Ayuntamiento, the Granary, the Hospital de la Misericordia and the old Alcazaba (fortress) that overlooks the town.

In the vicinity are two lovely waterfalls, the Colas de Caballo (Horsetail Falls), and Los Infiernos (Hell), which cascade into the River Genil.

SPECIAL TO...

The Renaissance Palacio de Carlos V (Palace of Emperor Charles V) provides one of the beautiful settings for the Festival of Music and Dance, which is held here annually at the end of June/ beginning of July and is recognised as an important international event. The programme includes concerts, ballet, guitar recitals and other events, with performances by famous artists and orchestras.

▶ *Take the **A92** west and branch off left to Antequera, soon after passing Archidona.*

8 Antequera, Málaga

The presence of prehistoric dolmen caves in the area indicates this market town's ancient origins. The old castle on top of the hill was the first fortress to be taken by the Christians (in 1410) during the reconquest of the Province of Granada, although it was later recaptured by the Moors. There is a fine view across the plains from its well-preserved ramparts. Close to the castle is the 16th-century Colegiata de Santa María la Mayor, noted for its Mudéjar ceiling. The churches of San Sebastián and St Augustín feature Mudéjar belfries and the churches of El Carmen and los Remedios have fine baroque interiors. If you visit the Museo Municipal, look for the bronze statue of a Roman boy called Efebo.

BACK TO NATURE

Some 15km (9 miles) south of Antequera is El Torcal Antequera, an area of deep ravines, where great limestone boulders have formed bizarre shapes, suggesting a petrified forest. It is rich in plant life, including the Spanish bluebell, rare species of iris and a number of different types of orchid. Twenty-four kilometres (15 miles) northwest of Antequera, off the N334, is the Laguna de la Fuente de Piedra, Andalucia's largest lake and an important breeding ground for flamingos. Other species of birds seen here include black-headed gulls, mallards, red-crested pochards and even the occasional white stork.

The dolmen caves are to the left of the Granada road. These prehistoric caves served as burial places in neolithic times and are of great historical significance.

[i] *Plaza San Sebastian, 7*

▶ *Take the **A343** southwest for 39km (24 miles) to Álora, which lies slightly off the road.*

9 Álora, Málaga

Álora stands high above the River Guadalhorce in an area of olive and citrus groves. This charming town has a ruined castle, a 17th-century church with an unusual wooden roof and a few fine buildings.

▶ *Continue on the **A343** and join the **A7054** and **A357** back to Málaga.*

The dramatic tower of the cathedral at Málaga

FOR HISTORY BUFFS

Santa Fé, west of Granada, was the scene of two great historical events; the signing of the surrender of Granada in November 1491, and the signing, on 17 April, 1492, of the agreements with Christopher Columbus that paved the way for his first voyage of discovery across the ocean.
A few kilometres away is the village of Fuente Vaqueros, where the famous Spanish poet Federico García Lorca was born in 1899; his former home is now a museum. La Huerta de San Vicente (San Vicente Orchard), where he spent many summers writing, has also been converted into a museum and is a centre for studies on the poet. The Federico García Lorca Memorial Park, between Viznar and Alfacar (northeast of Granada), marks the place where he is believed to have been shot, in 1936.

The Sun Coast
& Medieval Villages

Pleasant features of Málaga are its lively harbour and the seafront promenade, or Paseo Marítimo. In the old part of town is the Market Hall (Mercado Atarazanas) which teems with life and, dotted around the narrow twisting streets, are plenty of old *bodegas* (wine vaults); Málaga is known for its production of sweetish wines from the muscatel grape.

3 DAYS • 403KM • 250 MILES

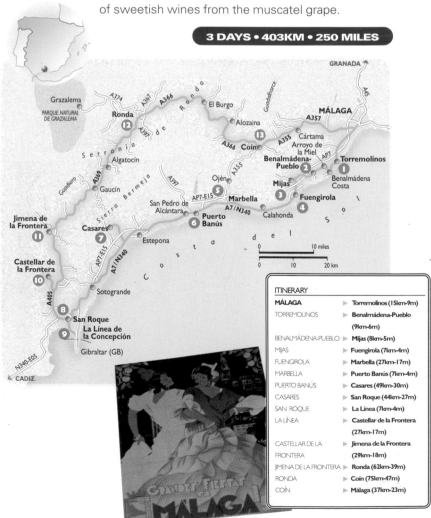

ITINERARY		
MÁLAGA	▶	**Torremolinos** (15km-9m)
TORREMOLINOS	▶	**Benalmádena-Pueblo** (9km-6m)
BENALMÁDENA-PUEBLO	▶	**Mijas** (8km-5m)
MIJAS	▶	**Fuengirola** (7km-4m)
FUENGIROLA	▶	**Marbella** (27km-17m)
MARBELLA	▶	**Puerto Banús** (7km-4m)
PUERTO BANÚS	▶	**Casares** (49km-30m)
CASARES	▶	**San Roque** (44km-27m)
SAN ROQUE	▶	**La Línea** (7km-4m)
LA LÍNEA	▶	**Castellar de la Frontera** (27km-17m)
CASTELLAR DE LA FRONTERA	▶	**Jimena de la Frontera** (29km-18m)
JIMENA DE LA FRONTERA	▶	**Ronda** (62km-39m)
RONDA	▶	**Coín** (75km-47m)
COÍN	▶	**Málaga** (37km-23m)

i *Pasaje de Chinitas 4*

▶ *Take the **N340** to Torremolinos. Follow signs into town.*

❶ Torremolinos, Málaga
This is the start of the most developed part of the Costa del Sol. One of the first resorts in the area to cater for mass tourism, it still retains a certain charm, with life centering around the pedestrianised Calle San Miguel. Steps lead down to the beaches and a seafront esplanade, which links the resort to the picturesque district of La Carihuela.

i *Plaza Blas Infante 1*

▶ *Continue along the coast road to Benalmádena Costa. Turn right for 4km (2½ miles) to Benalmádena-Pueblo.*

❷ Benalmádena-Pueblo, Málaga
Benalmádena Costa offers good beaches, a casino, golf club and the marina (Puerto Marina).

A short drive inland leads to Benalmádena-Pueblo, a delightful Andalucian village dating back to the time of the Phoenicians, with relics of the Romans and Moors. At Arroyo de la Miel, near by, there are ruins of a Roman arch, once the entrance to a building known as El Tribunal (Tribune).

i *Avenida Antonio Machado 10*

▶ *Continue on the regional road northwest for 8km (5 miles) to Mijas.*

❸ Mijas, Málaga
The little town of Mijas is so picturesque that it was quickly 'discovered' by tourists, with all the inevitable changes that result. It is still appealing, however, with pretty whitewashed houses, tiny winding streets and flowers everywhere. There are wonderful views down to the coast. Renowned as

The view from Mijas over the surrounding countryside

SCENIC ROUTES

Although parts of the coast road are dominated by high-rise blocks, the sea views and dramatic silhouette of the mountains in the hinterland make up for it. The drive to Mijas and back through the pine-clad mountains offers good views of the coast. The mountain road up to Casares is also very attractive. From San Roque the road winds up to Jimena de la Frontera (on the C3331), then goes through the dramatic landscapes of the Serranía de Ronda, with its wild, eroded rock formations.

a crafts centre, it specialises in ceramics and basket weaving.

i *Plaza de la Virgen*

▶ *Take the regional road south for 7km (4 miles) to Fuengirola.*

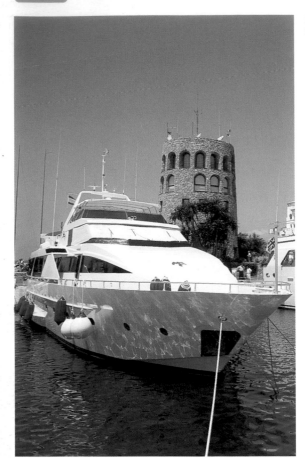

Boats of many nationalities crowd the marina at Puerto Banús

flower-decked balconies. These open out on to the Plaza de los Naranjos (Square of Oranges), an enchanting square edged with orange trees and surrounded by restaurants and boutiques. A walk along the old fortifications overlooks the area, with the old Moorish castle way above.

The town of Ojén, 8km (5 miles) inland, is reached by a winding road. It has a pleasant 16th- to 18th-century church, a beautifully laid-out Andalucían cemetery, and is well known for its pottery.

[i] *Glorieta de la Fontanilla*

▶ *Continue for a short distance along the coast road. Branch off to Puerto Banús, 7km (4 miles).*

6 Puerto Banús, Málaga
The short stretch between Marbella and Banús, known as the Golden Mile, is one of the most attractive parts of the Costa del Sol, with luxurious properties set in lovely gardens. The plush marina of Puerto Banús is seen as the coast's star attraction. The first of Andalucía's village-type harbour develoments, it has long served as a magnet for jet-setters, celebrities and tourists. With its abundance of fashionable bars and restaurants, boutiques and luxury yachts moored in the marina, it continues to draw in the crowds.

▶ *Continue along the A7-N340 coast road. Just past Estepona take a right turn to Casares, a distance of 20km (12 miles).*

7 Casares, Málaga
This part of the tour takes you inland to the Sierra Bermeja and, although it means returning to the coast by the same road, you will not regret it when you catch your first glimpse of Casares on the hill high above.

4 Fuengirola, Málaga
Fuengirola has also changed beyond recognition, from a sleepy fishing port to a resort of high-rise blocks. It has extensive beaches, bars, restaurants, lively evening entertainment, and attracts the crowds in the summer. It has also become a favoured winter retreat for retired people. Culture is minimal here, though there are the ruins of a 10th-century castle.

[i] *Avenida Jesús Santos Rein, 6*

▶ *Continue on the A7-N340 for 27km (17 miles) to Marbella.*

5 Marbella, Málaga
Marbella is the centre of the Costa del Sol. The description

'playground of the rich' refers to the international set who stay in luxurious surroundings and frequent the smart restaurants and nightspots to be found along this part of the coast. The appearance of tall, modern blocks over the years has inevitably changed Marbella's skyline and character. However, it has some attractive areas, including its busy harbour and a seafront promenade with bars and restaurants.

On a clear day Africa is faintly visible, while at the western end of the scene is the unmistakable outline of the Rock of Gibraltar. Marbella's hidden delight, however, is the old town behind the main street, with its narrow streets, whitewashed houses and

The medieval village of Casares overlooked by a Moorish castle

This medieval village is one of the most attractive in the area. A gentle stroll up the steep, winding streets leads to the ruins of its Moorish castle. There are two 18th-century churches, the parish church and the Iglesia de San Sebastián, and a beautifully laid-out cemetery adorned with flowers.

▶ Return to the **A7-N340** and continue to San Roque.

8 San Roque, Cádiz
San Roque was founded in the 18th century by the Spanish inhabitants of Gibraltar, who left after it was taken by the British in 1704. The town is on a low hill, with pleasant views. Places of interest include the Iglesia de Santa María and the Palacio de los Gobernadores.

▶ Take the **A383** for 7km (4 miles) to La Línea de la Concepción.

9 La Línea, Cádiz
La Línea de la Concepción stands at the foot of the Rock of Gibraltar and is the border town between Spain and the British colony of Gibraltar. Closed for many years, the frontier reopened in 1985 for travel between the two countries. Whether or not you decide to visit, it is worth making the drive to get a close look at this gigantic piece of rock silhouetted against the sky, an impressive sight and the landmark of the whole coast.

▶ Return to San Roque and take **A7-N340** west for 3km (2 miles); turn right on the **A405** to Castellar de la Frontera, 7km (4 miles) along an unclassified road.

FOR HISTORY BUFFS

The Cuevas de la Pileta, some 27km (17 miles) southwest of Ronda, shelter paintings of animals in shades of red and black and drawings of huge fish, believed to date back some 25,000 years. The paintings resemble those in the Altamira Caves in northern Spain.

Bridge over the gorge of the River Guadalevín which divides Ronda

⑩ Castellar de la Frontera, Cádiz

Your route now takes you into the hinterland of southern Spain, where you can enjoy superb mountain scenery and visits to some of Andalucía's famous white towns.

Castellar de la Frontera is one of these lovely old walled cities, crowned by a large Moorish castle. Its white houses, red tiled roofs and surrounding forests all add to its attractions. Ancient walls dating back to the 13th century enclose the old part of town, which has tiny streets and pretty squares.

▶ *Return to and continue north on the A405 for 29km (18 miles) to Jimena de la Frontera.*

⑪ Jimena de la Frontera, Cádiz

This little town is also an attractive cluster of whitewashed houses built up a hillside. It was under Moorish occupation for a considerable time and has a well-preserved castle from that period, reached through a triple-arched gateway.

▶ *Take the A369 northeast for 62km (39 miles) to Ronda.*

⑫ Ronda, Málaga

Ronda is well known for its spectacular setting, in particular the dramatic view of the bridge over the gorge of the River Guadalevín, which splits the town in two. It lies on the edge of the Serranía de Ronda, against a backdrop of sheer rock. Its unique situation, together with its attractive old quarter and historic interest, makes it a fascinating place to visit. It is one of the oldest towns in Spain and was for a long time capital of an independent Moorish kingdom, conquered by the Catholics in 1485. In the new part of town is one of the oldest bullrings in Spain.

There are magnificent views from here of the deep river valley and rugged splendours of the Serranía de Ronda. Across the famous Puente Nuevo bridge is La Ciudad, the old part. The bridge was built between 1775 and 1793 and is an outstanding architectural achievement. The old town is a maze of narrow, twisting streets and houses. Buildings of note include the Colegiata de Santa María la Mayor, built on the site of a former mosque, and the Palacio de Mondragón, which combines Mudéjar and Renaissance styles of architecture. Follow the nearby flight of steps down the hillside for a classic view of the bridge and the houses perched on the clifftop.

ℹ *Plaza de España 1*

▶ *Take the A366 to Coín.*

A typical Ronda house with doorway carvings and balcony

⑬ Coín, Málaga

Coín is a good place for a break on the last part of the return journey to Málaga. Set in the Valley of Orange Blossoms, this is a typical Andalucían market town of whitewashed houses and pretty squares, known for its colourful Saturday market.

▶ *Take the A366 eastwards and turn on to the A355 which leads to the A357 back to Málaga, a distance of 37km (23 miles).*

The Great
Mosque &
Moorish Towns

Sevilla lies on the River Guadalquivir, with the 13th-century Torre del Oro, built to guard the river, standing out as a landmark. The city was ruled by the Moors from 712 to 1248 and the minaret tower, known as La Giralda, rises above the city's great Gothic Cathedral, while the 14th-century Palacio Los Reales Alcázares is a masterpiece of Mudéjar art.

ITINERARY

SEVILLA	▶ **Carmona (32km-20m)**
CARMONA	▶ **Écija (55km-34m)**
ÉCIJA	▶ **Córdoba (54km-34m)**
CÓRDOBA	▶ **Baena (61km-38m)**
BAENA	▶ **Priego de Córdoba**
	(29km-18m)
PRIEGO DE CÓRDOBA	▶ **Cabra (27km-17m)**
CABRA	▶ **Lucena (11km-7m)**
LUCENA	▶ **Estepa (45km-28)**
ESTEPA	▷ **Osuna (24km-15m)**
OSUNA	▶ **Sevilla (90km-56m)**

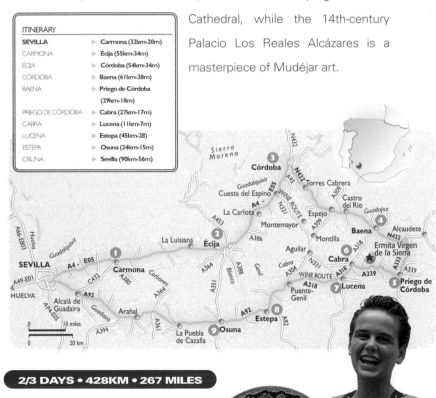

2/3 DAYS • 428KM • 267 MILES

ℹ️ *Avenida de la Constitución 21B, Sevilla*

▶ *From Sevilla take the **A4-E05** east for 32km (20 miles) to Carmona.*

1 Carmona, Sevilla

The town of Carmona stands on the highest point of a flat plain. It has a Moorish fortress, which holds a commanding position and offers good views of the countryside. This delightful little town has two old entrance gates, known as the Córdoba Gate and Sevilla Gate.

SCENIC ROUTES

The first part of the journey takes you through the fertile plains of the Guadalquivir valley, with patches of yellow and green fields relieved by olive groves and gently rolling hills, offering pleasant rather than remarkable scenery. There is a very scenic stretch between Priego de Córdoba and Cabra on the C336, and some attractive scenery round Lucena.

The Iglesia de Santa María de la Asunción is 15th-century late Gothic, and you can see the patio of the Great Mosque on whose foundations the church was erected. The Santuario (1525–51) has a notable retable while Roman mosaics decorate the Ayuntamiento.

West of the town is a Roman necropolis. This network of underground tombs was arranged in groups, with a crematorium at the front. Look out for the tomb known as El Elefante for its unusual carving of a young elephant.

▶ *Continue east on the **A4-E05** for 55km (35 miles) to Écija.*

2 Écija, Sevilla

The ancient town of Écija lies beside a small basin on the River Genil. Thought to date back to Greek times, it was known to the Romans as *Astigi*, and pottery, mosaics and other items found during excavations have given some insight into its early history. Its baroque belfries, decorated with colourful tiles, are an attractive feature of the town. The

Delicate stonework ornaments the Renaissance façade of Sevilla's splendid Ayuntamiento

Iglesia de Santiago, entered through an 18th-century patio, has Mudéjar windows from a previous building, and an elaborate Gothic retable. There are several handsome 18th-century palaces in the town including the Palacio Benamej, the Palacio Peñaflor, decorated with paintings on the outside, and the Palacio Valdehermoso, which has a fine Renaissance exterior.

▶ *Continue on the **A4-E05** northeast for 54km (34 miles) to Córdoba.*

RECOMMENDED WALKS

A detour north of Écija takes you to the village of Hornachuelos, which is on the edge of a large game-hunting area. This stretches away to the north of the region and offers some excellent walking.

---

3 Córdoba, Córdoba

Córdoba, a town of narrow streets and alleyways, is situated on a plain between the Sierra de Córdoba and the River Guadalquivir. Córdoba suffers from extremes of climate, with very hot summers and cold winters.

Already quite prominent when the Romans arrived, the town continued to flourish and

materials, designed to catch the light, forming a myriad colours. The columns are topped by capitals and crowned with striking red-and-white-striped arches, typical of Moorish art. An important feature of a mosque is the mihrab, a sacred niche hollowed out from the wall. They are always built to face Mecca in the east, although this one points more

Orange Trees) is particularly attractive in spring when it is filled with the scent of orange blossom. Through the Puerta del Perdón (Gate of Forgiveness) a flight of steps leads up to the baroque Campanario (bell tower). It provides a superb view of the rooftops of Córdoba and the sweep of the River Guadalquivir.

The Museo Arqueológico has interesting exhibits of sculptures and Roman antiquities, and the Museo de Bellas Artes has a fine collection of paintings. Those with an interest in bullfighting should visit the Museo Municipal Taurino (Museum of Bullfighting). A statue of the famous Spanish bullfighter, Manolete, stands in the Plaza San Marina de las Aguas.

The Zoco (from the old Arab souk) has displays of handicrafts and occasional flamenco performances.

in 152 BC became the capital of Hispana Ulterior.

It developed into a prosperous city under the Moors and was an important cultural and artistic centre. The town was conquered by the Catholic King Ferdinand in 1436, having long been used by Christian leaders as a centre for plotting the retaking of Granada from the Moors. It was in Córdoba that Christopher Columbus was granted the commission by Queen Isabella for his first exploratory expedition to the New World.

The great Mezquita (mosque) was constructed by the Moors between the 8th and 10th centuries. It is one of the largest mosques in the world and is a remarkable achievement of Moorish architecture. Its beauty lies in its interior. As you enter you are confronted by hundreds of columns made of onyx, marble and other

The red-and-white striped arches in the mosque at Córdoba

south than east, owing to a miscalculation. From 1436, when Córdoba was taken by the Christians, the mosque became the cathedral. The Patio de los Naranjos (Court of

FOR CHILDREN

Córdoba's zoo, located on Avenida Linneo (in front of the Jardín Botánico), has a wide variety of animals. Another treat for children could be a tour around town in an elegant horse-drawn carriage. Aquatic parks near Córdoba include the Aquopolis, at Sevilla-Este (open May to September) and Aquasierra (June to September) in Villafranca de Córdoba.

FOR HISTORY BUFFS

On the N432 between Córdoba and Baena is the small town of Castro del Río, where Spain's famous author, Miguel de Cervantes, was imprisoned for a time in 1592. You can take a look at his old prison, which is housed in the Ayuntamiento. The town also features the ruins of an ancient castle and a Roman bridge.

▶ Take the **N432** southeast for 61km (38 miles) to Baena.

4 Baena, Córdoba

The route continues through some of Andalucía's delightful *pueblos blancos*, or white towns. While sharing many common characteristics, each has its own style. Baena is an oil-producing town and is typically Andalucían. A cluster of whitewashed houses climbs up a slope, dominated by the remains of old Moorish battlements. The Iglesia de Santa María la

Mayor dates back to the 16th century. The Convento de la Madre de Dios was built in the Mudéjar style and has an interesting carved retable.

▶ Continue southeast on the **N432**. Close to the River Guadajoz turn south on the **A333** to Priego de Córdoba.

5 **Priego de Córdoba,** Córdoba

Priego de Córdoba is one of the region's little gems. Its dazzling white houses, flower-decked windows and tiny, winding streets give it a very Moorish look. Elegant 17th- and 18th-century mansions reflect prosperous times when Priego was the centre of the silk and textile industries. Several churches including La Asunción and La Aurora are masterpieces of fine baroque architecture. An abundance of springs here feed the splendid Fuente del Rey.

Alcalá Zamora, first president of the Second Republic of Spain (1931–6), was born here in 1877. His former home now contains the tourist information office and the museum Casa Natal de Niceto Alcalá Zamora.

ℹ️ *Calle del Río 33*

▶ Take the **A339** west, then right on to the **A318** for 2km (1 mile) to reach Cabra.

6 **Cabra,** Córdoba

The pleasant Parque del Fuente del Río (Park of the Source of the River) welcomes you to Cabra, a delightful town with white houses, red-tiled roofs and old narrow streets. The Iglesia de San Juan Bautista dates back to the time of the Visigoths.

▶ Take the **A318** southwest to Lucena, just off the road.

7 **Lucena,** Córdoba

At the foot of the Sierra de Arcos is the attractive little town of Lucena renowned for its bronze, furniture making and copperware. Fine churches are the 15th-century Renaissance Iglesia de San Matéo, the Iglesia de Santiago and the Convento de San Francisco. Lucena was the scene of the capture of the boy-king Boabdil, the last Moorish ruler, by the Count of Cabra in 1483, during an unsuccessful revolt against the Christians.

▶ Rejoin the **A318 west** to Estepa.

The main square at Lucena and the Iglesia de San Mateo. *Inset:* detail of the doorway of Iglesia de Santiago

Carriage rides are a restful way of
sightseeing in Sevilla, especially
through the Parque de Maria Luisa

8 Estepa, Córdoba
Estepa, lying among farmlands,
is known throughout Spain for
its confectionery, especially its
Christmas cakes known as
mantecados and *polvorones*. As
well as the churches of Santa
María la Mayor, La Asunción
and Los Remedios, the 18th-
century Palacio de los
Marqueses de Cerverales is

BACK TO NATURE

The Lagunas de Córdoba, a
series of salt-water lakes
around Aguilar de la Frontera
northwest of Cabra, are inhabited by many different species
of waterfowl in the winter. An
attractive and rare visitor is
the white-headed duck, with its
lovely blue bill. Some of the
lakes shrink or dry up during
summer, but fill again after the
rains. Flamingos and shelduck
inhabit the Laguna del Salobral,
the largest of the lakes.

worth a look, along with the
Gothic interior of the old castle
keep and the splendid Torre de
la Victoria (Tower of Victory), all
that remains of a former
convent. There are good views
from a nearby lookout point
called El Balcón de Andalucía.

▶ Take the **A92** west to Osuna.

9 Osuna, Córdoba
The history of Osuna dates
back to the time of the Iberians.
Like so many towns in southern
Spain, Osuna was taken by the
Romans and then ruled by the
Moors until 1239, when it was
captured by Ferdinand III. Of
the many fine monuments note
the Colegiata, a Renaissance
church that houses valuable
works of art.

La Universidad (University)
is another important building,
with its minaret-like towers.
The Casa de los Cepeda,
Palacio del Cabildo Colegial
and Palacio de la Antigua
Audiencia have elegant façades.
The Museo Arqueológico is
in the old Torre de Agua
(Water Tower).

▶ Return to Sevilla on the
A92.

SPECIAL TO...

A turn to the right just before
Cabra leads to El Picacho and
the Ermita Virgen de la Sierra
(Shrine of the Virgin of the
Mountains), which contains the
much-venerated image of the
patron saint of Cabra.
The province of Córdoba has
quite a reputation for wines
and enthusiasts can follow the
Ruta del Vino (Wine Route)
which leaves Córdoba on the
N331 and goes southwest to
Montemayor and Montilla. You
can visit many of the wine cellars, which offer a number of
different sherry-type wines.

Exquisitely carved detail defines
the little balcony of the church of
La Merced at Osuna

Trail of the
New World
Explorers

3 DAYS • 353KM • 218 MILES

The Museo de Bellas Artes, housed in the former Merced Monastery, and the Museo Arqueológico in the Palacio del Renacimiento are among Sevilla's finest museums, while the 16th-century mansion Casa Pilatos is a real gem. Added attractions are its parks and gardens, particularly those

of the Alcázar, in addition to the picturesque old district of the Barrio Santa Cruz.

i *Avenida de la Constitución 21B*

▶ *From Sevilla take the motorway west over the river. Turn right on to the N630 to Santiponce.*

1 Santiponce, Sevilla
The chief monument in Santiponce is the former Monasterio de San Isidro del Campo, which was founded in 1298 by Alfonso Guzmán as a Cistercian house. Guzmán, known as 'El Bueno' (The Good One) was renowned for the heroic role he played in defending Tarifa castle against the Moors. The church contains a remarkable 17th-century retable by the artist Martínez Montañés, noted for the figure of St Jerome. Montañés also carved the effigies on the tombs of Guzmán and his wife. A second church marks the first resting place of the body of Cortés, conqueror of Mexico, before it was taken to Mexico.

▶ *Take an unclassified road left to Itálica.*

2 Itálica, Sevilla
The Roman ruins of Itálica are considered of major significance. Originally founded in 206 BC by Scipio Africanus as a place of retirement for his veteran soldiers, the city flourished and by the 2nd century AD had become one of the most important Roman cities in Spain. Two great Roman emperors – Trajan (AD 52–117) and Hadrian (AD 76–138) – were born here.
The most important building is the Amphitheatre, which was one of the largest in the Roman Empire, with a capacity of up to 40,000 spectators. Faintly visible traces can still be seen of a forum, city streets, the foundations of villas and mosaic floors: evidence of the old city. Treasures found here are on display in Sevilla's Museum of Archaeology.

▶ *Keep on this unclassified road and join the A66-E803. Continue north and after 25km (15 miles) take the N433 northwest to Aracena.*

Imagine a spectacle in this Roman amphitheatre at Itálica with 40,000 spectators cramming the terraces

3 Aracena, Huelva
The Convento de Santa Catalina (Convent of St Catalina) has a notable doorway. On top of the Cerro del Castillo (Castle Hill) are the remains of a castle, which was built in the 13th century by the Knights Templar. Of mixed Gothic and Mudéjar styles, it features an old tower, originally a minaret

---

SCENIC ROUTES

This route becomes very scenic after you have joined the N435 from Cortegana through to Zalamea la Real and on to Valverde del Camino. There is also some appealing scenery around Moguer. The route from Huelva to Matalascañas, should you visit the Coto Doñana, offers a beautiful drive along miles of deserted beaches.

---

and decorated in similar style to the Giralda of Sevilla.

Near Aracena are the Grutas de las Maravillas (Grottos of Marvels). Over 1,000m (1,094 yards) in length, they are noted for the variety of shapes and colours in the stalactites and stalagmites which are reflected in underground pools and rivers.

▶ *Take **N433** west to Cortegana, just south of this road.*

RECOMMENDED WALKS

Aracena is a good base for walks in the Sierra de Aracena, where you will find orange and lemon groves, great oak forests and tiny isolated villages. There is a superb view of the area from the top of La Peña Arias Montano.

4 **Cortegana**, Huelva

The small town of Cortegana was originally a Roman settlement known as *Corticata*. Its main assets are its beautiful setting, an interesting little parish church and an old castle.

▶ *Take the regional road southeast. Turn right on the **N435** to Zalamea la Real.*

5 **Zalamea la Real,** Huelva

The town's most notable building is the Iglesia de la Asunción (Assumption), an elegant neoclassical monument from the 17th century. There are several interesting old hermitages.

The impressive Minas de Ríotinto (Rio Tinto Copper Mines) are about 6km (4½ miles) east of town. Already in use during Iberian and Roman times, the mines were abandoned when the Visigoths came, and only regenerated in the 19th century. For a long time they were a British concern, reverting to Spanish ownership in 1954. There are still English-style houses, and a small mining museum in Río Tinto village.

Kite-flying by Aracena's castle ruins
Left: the 13th-century church

▷ *Continue on the same road south towards Valverde del Camino. Turn left where signposted into the town.*

6 Valverde del Camino, Huelva

The town of Valverde del Camino is noted for its production of wood, metal and leather goods, including leather wine bottles. Buildings of note include the attractive Ermita de la Trinidad and the Iglesia de Nuestra Señora del Reposo (Church of Our Lady of Rest).

▷ *Rejoin and take the N435 south. At Trigueros turn right on an unclassified road to Gibraleón.*

7 Gibraleón, Huelva

Gibraleón is a town with ancient roots. Some of the people may be descendants of the slaves brought here by the Spaniards in the 15th century. Among the most interesting buildings in the town are the Iglesia de Santiago, the Iglesia de San Juan and the Chapel of El Carmen. The 16th-century Convento del Vado still preserves the remnants of its old walls.

▷ *Take the N431 south. Continue straight on to Huelva when the N431 branches off east.*

8 Huelva, Huelva

The region played an important role in the events leading to the Voyages of Discovery across the ocean. Christopher Columbus came to Huelva with his son in 1485 and stayed in the nearby Monasterio de la Rábida. The first expedition set sail from the area in 1492, to reach land two months later. At the end of the Paseo del Conquero is the modest white shrine of Nuestra Señora de la Cinta, with a Mudéjar roof and a wall painting of the Virgin, patron saint of the city. A tile painting by the artist Zuloaga commemorates a visit made here by Columbus on his return from one of his voyages.

Huelva was severely damaged by an earthquake in 1755 and only a handful of buildings remain from the past. The 17th-century Iglesia de la Merced (now the cathedral) has an elegant doorway of mixed styles and houses an image of the Virgen de la Cinta. The 16th-century Iglesia de San

Pastel-washed houses with graceful balconies beside the Church of Our Lady of Rest at Valverde

Pedro features a tower with attractive tile decorations. The Iglesia de la Concepción, also dating from the 16th century, is noted for its paintings by the Spanish artist Zurbarán.

BACK TO NATURE

The Coto Doñana is one of Spain's largest and most important nature parks. This vast expanse of flat salt marshes (*marismas*), dunes and pine forests lies in the delta of the River Guadalquivir, covering an area of some 50,625 hectares (125,000 acres). Thousands of migratory birds come here, and large colonies of birds nest in the cork-oak trees. It is also the home of a variety of other animals, and has many rare species of flower and plant life. Matalascañas, located down the coast southeast of Huelva, is the usual starting point for visiting the reserve. It can only be visited as part of a guided tour or with special permission.

The Museo Provincial has a collection of antiquities from the region, including an impressive Roman water wheel, some beautiful amphorae (vessels) and a reconstructed Celtic house, in addition to a fine arts section featuring paintings by local artists.

ⓘ *Avenida de Alemania 12*

▶ *Take the A494 and cross over the Río Tinto. Shortly after, take a left turn to the Monasterio de la Rábida.*

9 **Monasterio de la Rábida,** Huelva

This old Franciscan monastery lies in beautiful surroundings at the mouth of the Río Tinto. It was here that Christopher Columbus received the necessary stimulus to persevere with his plans to sail across the ocean in search of the Indies. When he came to the monastery in 1485, he was well received by the monks. It was Father Antonio Marchena, in particular, however, who was instrumental in bringing

---

FOR CHILDREN

Anchored at the Carabelas Quay, Huelva, are replicas of the sailing ships *Santa María*, *Niña* and *Pinta* which carried Christopher Columbus and his men on their first expedition across the seas. Children are invited to clamber aboard and get a feel of the past.

---

influence to bear with Queen Isabella. After lengthy negotiations, the agreement was finally signed and Columbus was able to fulfil his dreams. The Lecture Cell is where Columbus held many meetings with the monks, the Chapter House displays relics of the explorer, and the Gallery has models of the three caravels that undertook the first voyage. The church

and courtyard date back to the early 15th century and are very attractive. Note the 14th-century statue of the Virgen de los Milagros, to whom Columbus offered his prayers before setting sail. In the beautifully laid-out garden is the Latin-American University, a centre for American studies, and a fine monument to the Discoverers of America.

▶ *Continue on the same road northeast to Moguer.*

10 **Moguer,** Huelva

Moguer is renowned as the birthplace and home of the great Spanish poet, Juan Ramón Jiménez (1881–1958), Nobel prize-winner for literature in 1956 and author of the delightful Spanish classic *Platero y Yo*, about a boy and his donkey. His former home is now a museum with relics from the poet.

The 14th-century Gothic-Mudéjar Convento de Santa Clara contains the tombs of the convent's founders and has been declared a National Monument. The parish church is noted for its tall, impressive tower.

▶ *Take the A494 north and join the A472 northeast to Niebla.*

FOR HISTORY BUFFS

Palos de la Frontera, 13km (8 miles) southeast of Huelva, is the place from which Christopher Columbus set sail on 3 August, 1492 in the *Santa María* on his first voyage of discovery. Columbus sighted land on 12 October and set foot on Cuba and Haiti, where he left some of his men to establish a colony before returning to Palos on 15 March, 1493.
In May 1528, Hernán Cortés landed in the port after he had overthrown the mighty Aztec Empire and conquered Mexico.

The Monasterio de la Rábida, where Columbus prepared for his voyage west, now has a centre for American studies in the garden

11 **Niebla,** Huelva

The ancient town of Niebla (its name means mist) lies on the bank of the Río Tinto. It was the last town in the Guadalquivir valley to fall to

---

SPECIAL TO...

South of Almonte in the village church of El Rocío is the Shrine of El Rocío, scene of Spain's most famous *romería* (pilgrimage to a church or shrine). This takes place at Whitsun. People from all over the region process to El Rocío on foot, horseback or in gaily decorated horse-drawn wagons, dressed in traditional costumes. Upon arrival in the village they celebrate with music, dancing and drinking until the climax of the festival, when the statue of the Virgin is brought from the church at dawn and paraded among the crowds by members of the Brotherhoods. Bells peal, fireworks explode and there is much celebration.

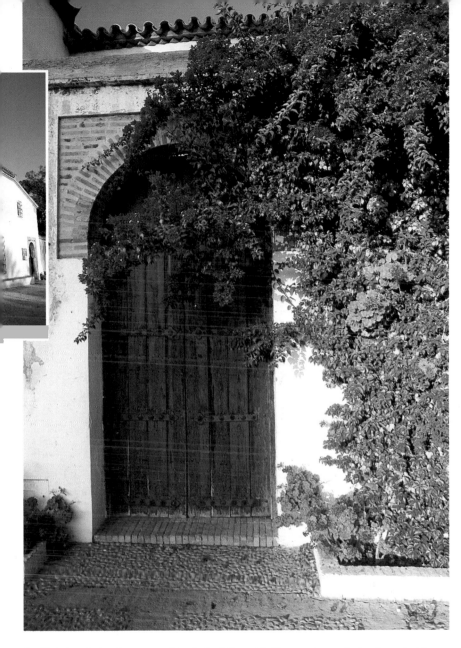

the Christians during the Reconquest of Spain, and is noted as being the first place in Spain where gunpowder was used in battle. Its main historical monuments are the Roman bridge over the river and four splendid Moorish entrance gates, known as the Puertas de Sevilla, Socorro, del Buey and del Agua. Of particular charm is the little chuch of Nuestra Señora de Granada (Our Lady of Granada). The Iglesia de San Martín and the 12th-century Castillo de Los Guzmanes also warrant a visit.

▶ Continue on the **A472** to La Palma del Condado.

⓬ La Palma del Condado,
Huelva

La Palma del Condado has long been the centre of a wine-producing area and is known for its pleasant white table wine. One of its main attractions is the 16th-century Iglesia de San Juan Bautista, a beautiful white monument with an attractively decorated steeple. The 15th-century Ermita del Valle (Hermitage of the Valley), is a fine example of the Mudéjar style.

▶ Return to Sevilla east on the **A472**.

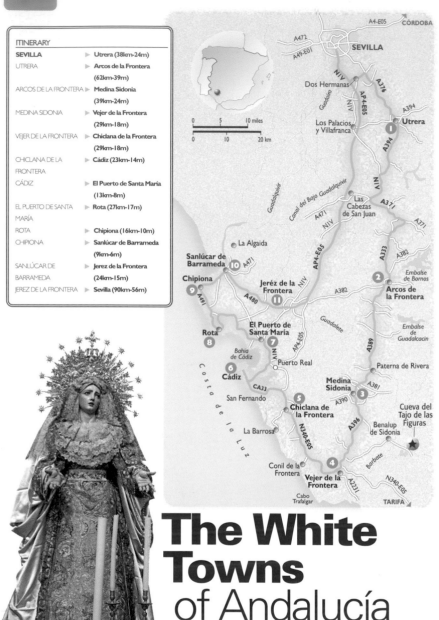

ITINERARY

SEVILLA	▶ **Utrera (38km-24m)**
UTRERA	▶ **Arcos de la Frontera (62km-39m)**
ARCOS DE LA FRONTERA	▶ **Medina Sidonia (39km-24m)**
MEDINA SIDONIA	▶ **Vejer de la Frontera (29km-18m)**
VEJER DE LA FRONTERA	▶ **Chiclana de la Frontera (29km-18m)**
CHICLANA DE LA FRONTERA	▶ **Cádiz (23km-14m)**
CÁDIZ	▶ **El Puerto de Santa María (13km-8m)**
EL PUERTO DE SANTA MARÍA	▶ **Rota (27km-17m)**
ROTA	▶ **Chipiona (16km-10m)**
CHIPIONA	▶ **Sanlúcar de Barrameda (9km-6m)**
SANLÚCAR DE BARRAMEDA	▶ **Jerez de la Frontera (24km-15m)**
JEREZ DE LA FRONTERA	▶ **Sevilla (90km-56m)**

The White Towns
of Andalucía

3 DAYS • 399 KM • 249 MILES   Sevilla's festivals are world-famous. During Holy Week there are processions every day and one at dawn on Good Friday. *Pasos* (platforms), carried by Penitents, show scenes of the Passion of Christ. The Feria de Sevilla takes place for six days in April, with horseback parades.

ⓘ Avenida de la
Constitución
21B

▶ From
Sevilla take the
A376 southeast to
Utrera.

❶ Utrera, Sevilla
The old town of Utrera
features an impressive
Alcázar with a square
tower, some fine Gothic
churches and an
attractive little main
square. The
Convento de
Nuestra Señora de
la Consolación on
the edge of the town
has a much venerated image of
the Virgin, which is believed to
work miracles. An annual
pilgrimage to the convent
takes place in September.

▶ Take the A394 south. Join
the NIV and turn left
on to the A371. Turn south on
to the A333 down to Arcos
de la Frontera, a distance of
38km (24 miles).

**❷ Arcos
de la
Frontera,**
Cádiz
The first stop
in the province
of Cádiz is Arcos de
la Frontera, one of the
most attractive towns in
the region. It is perched
on top of a high rock,
surrounded by steep
ravines that descend to
the River Guadalete.
The mass of white
and stone-coloured
houses is domi-
nated by a castle
and two churches.
Tiny narrow streets
and alleys wind their
way up the steep slopes, offering splendid views. The
Hospital de San Juan de Dios
has a white baroque façade and
a 16th-century crucifix in the
temple. Other outstanding
churches are those of Santa
María, with a Plateresque west
façade, and San Pedro, a
massive Gothic structure which
has a baroque bell tower, a
landmark for miles around.

San Pedro church in Arcos de la
Frontera stands high on a rock
above the River Guadalete.
Left: church clocks were timepieces
for everyone in the town

▶ Take the A389 south to
Medina Sidonia.

❸ Medina Sidonia, Cádiz
This is an historic little town
whose origins can be traced
back over 1,000 years. It was
once the seat of the dukes of
Medina Sidonia – the seventh
duke was the Commander in-
Chief of the Armada. The

SCENIC ROUTES

Some of the most attractive
scenery along this route is to
be found around Arcos de la
Frontera, which lies amid
rugged mountains and green
woods. The drive from Vejer de
la Frontera through to Cádiz
and on to El Puerto de Santa
María has long stretches of
white beaches and pinewoods,
indented at times by tall cliffs.

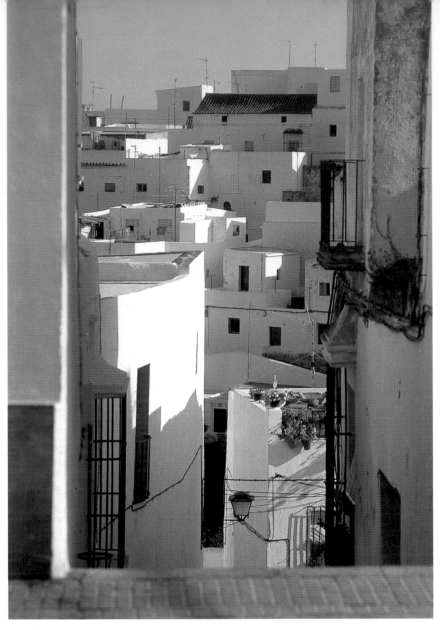

Iglesia de Santa María Coronada was built in the Gothic style at the time of Granada's recapture by the Christians. Some important religious paintings may be seen in the church. The Arch of 'La Pastora' (the Shepherdess) is set in the old Moorish walls in a horseshoe shape. Built in the 18th-century, the Ayuntamiento features an elegant, tiled staircase and the churches of San Agustín and Santiago are also worth a visit.

Some 7km (4½ miles) away are caves known as the Tajo de las Figuras.

▶ Continue south on the **A396** to *Vejer de la Frontera*.

4 Vejer de la Frontera,
Cádiz

The medieval town of Vejer de la Frontera is situated on the banks of the River Barbate high above Cabo de Trafalgar (Cape Trafalgar). The place is Moorish

The Moorish look of the White Town of Vejer de la Frontera

in appearance – in the dazzling white houses and tiny twisting streets, and also in its womenfolk, some of whom dress in black from head to toe, Arabstyle, and are known as *Las Cobijadas* (the covered ones). The town features little hidden squares and flower-filled patios, with streets so precipitous that handrails have been added for safety. Its most important building is the 13th-century Iglesia de El Divino Salvador. Built soon after the town was taken from the Moors, it reflects Romanesque, Gothic and Mudéjar styles and contains some fine 17th-century paintings.

From here you can make a detour to Tarifa southeast on the N340. When you stand on the Punta Marroquí, also called Punta de Tarifa, you are on the southernmost tip of Europe, with the African continent only 14km (8 miles) away. This is where the Mediterranean and the Atlantic meet. Tarifa has a Moorish look and some Roman remains.

▶ *Take the* **N340-E05** *northwest for 29km (18 miles) to Chiclana de la Frontera.*

5 Chiclana de la Frontera, Cádiz

Chiclana has neat white houses rising up the hillside and a Mosque-like parish church. A few kilometres away to the west is the splendid sandy beach of La Barrosa, a popular summer resort bordered by pinewoods.

▶ *Continue on* **N340** *northwest, then join the* **CA33** *for 23km (14 miles) to Cádiz.*

6 Cádiz, Cádiz

The old port of Cádiz is noted for its lovely setting. It is built on a rock platform jutting out into the Atlantic Ocean and is connected to the mainland by a bridge. The town's massive ramparts protect it against the force of the waves. It has tall white houses, many of which have *miradors* (lookout towers) and *azoteas* (roof terraces).

Cádiz is thought to be one of the oldest towns on the Iberian peninsula. It was founded by the Phoenicians in

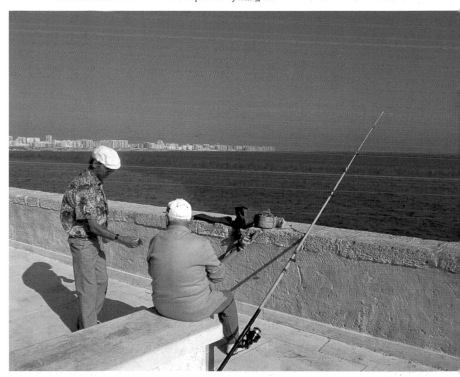

Cádiz juts out into the Atlantic and men still fish from the seafront

BACK TO NATURE

On this tour, look out for bee-eaters perched on wires beside the road – one of Spain's most colourful birds. Bee-eaters are summer visitors and excavate nest burrows in soft, sandy banks.
La Algaida, northeast of Sanlúcar de Barrameda, is a continuation of the Coto Doñana on the eastern side of the River Guadalquivir.
This area of dunes is used by migratory birds in the winter and is also home to the chameleon.

1100 BC under the name of Gadir and was a trading port. Later it came under the control of the Carthaginians, then the Romans.

Cádiz was used as a base for Spanish treasure fleets. In 1587 ships of the Spanish Armada, gathered in Cádiz harbour before setting sail for England. In 1805 the French fleet left from Cádiz before the Battle of Trafalgar. And, here, in 1812, the Spanish Parliament met to establish the first liberal constitution.

One of the town's most pleasing aspects is its lovely parks, among which those of Genovés, Alameda Marqués de Comillas and Alameda de Apodaca are the most attractive. The cathedral features a golden dome and a baroque façade. It was built in the 18th and 19th centuries and hoards of gold and silver treasures and gems may be seen in the museum. Its most precious piece is a processional cross by Enrique de Arfe, which is brought out for the Corpus Christi processions. In the crypt is the tomb of the Spanish composer, Manuel de Falla (1876–1946), who was born in Cádiz and drew inspiration from Andalucian folklore.

Since 2003, the cathedral's Torre de Poniente has added a new attraction to the city. Using a ramp, you can gain access to the bell tower from where there are some marvellous views of the city below.

The Museo de Cádiz features some great canvases by Zurbarán and works by Murillo.

Spain's first constitution was declared in 1812 in the Oratorio de San Felipe de Neri. Over the altar hangs a painting of the Immaculate Conception by the great Sevillian artist, Murillo.

The old town is a labyrinth of narrow streets opening out on to pleasant squares. Its central point is the attractive Plaza de Miña, shaded by palms and lined by elegant buildings.

⌐ *Paseo de Canalejas*

▷ *Take the N443 to join the NIV north to El Puerto de Santa María, 13km (8 miles).*

7 El Puerto de Santa María, Cádiz
The small fishing port of El Puerto de Santa María is noted for its sherry and brandy *bodegas* (cellars) and a tour of one is recommended. The town lies at the mouth of the Guadalete River and features a busy port, lively streets and miles of sandy beaches. The Moorish Castillo de San Marcos (St Mark's Castle) is a watch-tower over the river, where you can enjoy a lovely view of the coast.

⌐ *Calle Luna, 22*

▷ *Take the A491 for 27km (17 miles) northwest to Rota.*

8 Rota, Cádiz
The Spanish-American naval base is the major feature of Rota and has brought a cosmopolitan atmosphere to the town, with lively bars, shops and evening entertainment. The town has several pleasant beaches, some old walls and the Luna Castle by the fishermen's quarters. Rota is also an agricultural centre, noted for its tomatoes and watermelons.

▷ *Continue north on a minor road, then join the A491 to Chipiona.*

9 Chipiona, Cádiz
The lighthouse of Chipiona, visible from a great distance, is a famous landmark for navigators. This is a popular holiday resort with beaches of fine white sand and good fishing in some areas. The little town has white-washed houses, quaint streets and a profusion of flowers. The Iglesia de Santa María de la Regla contains a shrine to the Virgin, venerated by seamen.

▷ *Continue east to Sanlúcar de Barrameda.*

10 Sanlúcar de Barrameda, Cádiz
Lying at the mouth of the River Guadalquivir, the little port of Sanlúcar de Barrameda was the departure point for Columbus's third voyage to the New World in 1498, and the Portuguese Magellan also sailed from here in 1519 on his first voyage around the world.

Sanlúcar has a lively afternoon fish auction and is also the home of Manzanilla wine, a fine accompaniment to seafood.

▷ *Take the A480 southeast to Jerez de la Frontera.*

SPECIAL TO...

Jerez de la Frontera is famous the world over for its fortified wine, known to the English as sherry. Every visitor to Jerez will undoubtedly want to do the rounds of the *bodegas* or cellars. Visits to the large ones can be made by prior arrangement or on an organised tour. These usually take place in the mornings with a guide and a tasting at the end. September is the month for the Vintage Festival.
A ceremony for the blessing of the grapes is held on the cathedral steps with music, flamenco and much festivity.

1 Jerez de la Frontera,
Cádiz

Set among vineyards, the town of Jerez is the home of sherry, to which it has given its name. The *bodegas*, some of which are very grand, are the great attraction and tours can be made.

The town has a somewhat aristocratic air, with broad avenues and large squares. The Colegiata, built in the 17th and

The Plaza de Progresso in central Jerez de la Frontera

18th centuries in Gothic style, contains paintings by Zurbarán. The Alcázar is an impressive 11th-century building with a Gothic church and Arab baths.

ⓘ *Alameda Cristina*

▶ *Return on the **AP4-E05**.*

ARAGÓN, NAVARRA & LA RIOJA

Aragón, Navarra and La Rioja lie to the north and south of the basin of the River Ebro, which runs from the Cantabrian Mountains in the northwest through the Catalonian Mountains and down to the Mediterranean. Along the banks of the Ebro are the green irrigated lands known in Spain as *huertas*. The capital of Aragón, Zaragoza (Saragossa), lies in the Ebro depression on the right bank of the river and is a major agricultural centre. Southern Aragón is an area of arid plains and the bleak windswept plateaux that form part of the Montes Universales mountain range. Temperatures here are extreme.

To the northwest is the small province of La Rioja, one of Spain's most important wine-growing regions, known particularly for its red wines, which have an unmistakable flavour. The Upper Rioja is mountainous and humid, while the Lower Rioja consists of irrigated flatlands and enjoys a mild climate.

Upper Aragón and the northern part of Navarra lie within the great Pyrenees chain. Mountain peaks, lush green valleys and waterfalls, and rough stone houses with steep slate roofs are typical. To the west, the countryside changes and is divided into small, neat fields.

Navarra has links with the Basque country and was once the home of the 'Vascons', the Basque ancestors. Late in the 8th century Charlemagne wrested it from the Moors. During the 11th century Navarra was annexed for some time by the kingdom of Aragón. It was ruled by the kings of France between 1234 and 1512, when it was gained for King Ferdinand by the Duke of Alba and integrated with Castile. The pilgrim route to the shrine at Santiago de Compostela went through Navarra and as a result there was a great flowering of Romanesque art all along the 'Way of St James'.

The little village of Aguero set amongst lush fields under the harsh rocks of the Pyrenees

Many traditions in Navarra are rooted in Basque culture. The lively *jota* is danced in Navarra and Aragón, and one of Spain's most famous celebrations is Pamplona's riotous festival of 'Sanfermines'.

Tour 13

Southern Aragón is an area of arid plains, windswept plateaux and wild rugged mountains. While it may not appear to be the most hospitable of regions at first glance, there is some magnificent scenery. A visit to an oasis surrounding an old monastery, however, does provide a respite. Stops are included at several interesting little towns and villages, built from the stone of the region and barely distinguishable from the surrounding landscape. The area is rich in Mudéjar art (work of the Moorish people under Christian rule), and many fine examples of this intricate style of decoration can be seen along the route. South of Zaragoza is the most important wine-growing region of the province, labelled the 'wine route'.

Tour 14

Leaving the plains of Huesca, the route turns north and follows the course of the rivers to one of the important staging points of the Pilgrim's Way to Santiago. The landscapes change continuously with great panoramas of mountain peaks, eroded gorges and wooded valleys, fresh green forests and clear sparkling streams. All along the route are delightful Pyrenean villages, walled towns and castles, which bear traces of their medieval past. Many consist of a cluster of semi-detached houses rising up a steep hill to form a protective enclave. Here you will find evidence of the Mozarabic-Romanesque style that is characteristic of the region. A visit to an old fortress – ancient stronghold of King Sancho Ramírez of Aragón – is also included. Another attraction is a visit to one of Spain's most impressive national parks.

Tour 15

On this tour you will see a variety of landscapes, from the plains of the south, characterised by the rich reddish-brown colour of the terrain, to the fertile regions and mountains of La Rioja. This little piece of land lying on the western side of the Ebro Valley is one of Spain's important wine regions. The route passes through medieval walled towns and castles, a number of which were built in strategic positions on hilltops overlooking the neighbouring provinces of Aragón and Castile, separate kingdoms at the time.

You will find fine examples of Moorish, Romanesque and Gothic art in the churches and buildings, with some special historic interest provided by one of the staging points along the 'Way to Santiago'.

Pilgrims passing through the Puerta de Revellín (Revellin Gate) in the old town wall of Logroño

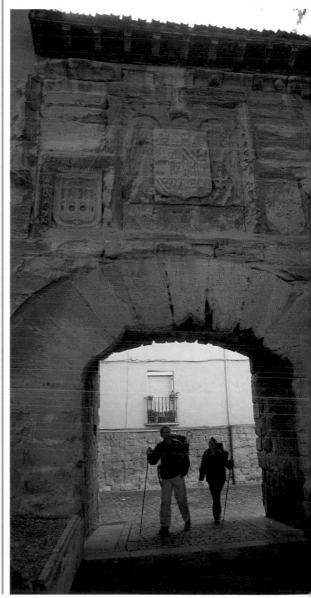

TOUR 13

The Ancient
Kingdom of Aragón

2/3 DAYS • 642KM • 398 MILES

Zaragoza is a busy commercial town, midway between Madrid and Barcelona. The Old Cathedral with Gothic and Mudéjar influences, the Renaissance-inspired La Lonja and the 11th-century Aljafería, built by the Moors, are prominent buildings.

ITINERARY

ZARAGOZA	▶	**Calatayud** (87km–54m)
CALATAYUD	▶	**Monasterio de Piedra** (28km–17m)
MONASTERIO DE PIEDRA	▶	**Daroca** (68km–42m)
DAROCA	▶	**Calamocha** (26km–16m)
CALAMOCHA	▶	**Orihuela del Tremedal** (80km–50m)
ORIHUELA DEL TREMEDAL	▶	**Albarracín** (47km–29m)
ALBARRACÍN	▶	**Teruel** (47km–29m)
TERUEL	▶	**Alcañiz** (158km–98m)
ALCAÑIZ	▶	**Zaragoza** (101km–63m)

[i] *Plaza del Pilar s/n*

▶ *Take the **A2-E90** southwest for 87km (54 miles) to Calatayud.*

1 Calatayud, Zaragoza

The history of Calatayud goes back to the time of the Moors and its name is derived from Kalat-Ayub, who founded the old castle, now in ruins, in the 8th century.

The town is on a hillside, merging with its surroundings. The Iglesia de Santa María la Mayor has an elegant Renaissance doorway and the Iglesia de San Sepulcro (12th to 17th century) was once the centre of the Knights Templars of Spain. A number of other churches in the town show attractive examples of the Mudéjar style of art.

[i] *Plaza del Fuerte*

▶ *Take the **A202** southwest for 28km (17 miles) to the Monasterio de Piedra (Monastery of Stone).*

2 Monasterio de Piedra, Zaragoza

The beautiful oasis that surrounds the Monasterio de Piedra makes a welcome change from the surrounding arid land, and a tour of the gardens will probably be as much of an attraction as a visit to the monastery itself. They have been turned into a lovely parkland of grottoes, pools and cascades sloping down to the banks of the River Piedra. Look out for the Cola de Caballo waterfall, which tumbles down from a considerable height and is most impressive. You can look

SCENIC ROUTES

The route runs through areas of rugged mountains, barren land and forests, and some spectacular scenery, especially around La Muela between Zaragoza and Calatayud (A2-E90); and past La Almunia de Doña Godina to Calatayud (A2-E90). The area around the Monastery of Piedra is lush with forests and waterfalls. The N234 from Calatayud to Daroca offers dramatic scenery. The road from Calamocha to Orihuela del Tremedal and on to Albarracín through the mountains of the Montes Universales is very attractive.

One of the waterfalls near the Monasterio de Piedra

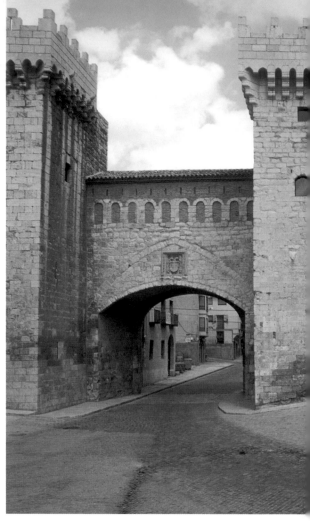

TOUR 13

FOR HISTORY BUFFS

The village of Fuendetodos is the birthplace of the great Spanish painter, Francisco Goya. It lies about 24km (15 miles) east of Cariñena, which is on the N330 between Zaragoza and Daroca. You can see the modest house where he was born in 1746 and visit the small museum which contains relics and a collection of transparencies of his works.

down on it from a lookout point, while a splendid view can be had from the Iris Grotto. On the way to the monastery you will see two beautiful little lakes known as the Baño de Diana and the Lago del Espejo lying between two tall rocks.

The monastery was founded as a Cistercian house in 1194 and the oldest parts are the keep, chapter house and refectory. The attractive cloister was built in the 13th-century, and the elegant staircase with an impressive vault dates from the 14th and 15th centuries.

▶ Take the **A202** back to Calatayud and join the **N234** (direction Teruel) to Daroca.

3 Daroca, Zaragoza

Daroca is a medieval delight. It lies tucked away in a gorge on the River Jiloca, surrounded by hills. The walls date back to the 13th century and extend for some 3km (2 miles), with over 100 towers still remaining from the past. The Colegiata de Santa María was built between the 13th and 15th centuries, and in the Chapel of the Holy Relics a shrine holds holy altar-cloths said to have been used to wrap the consecrated hosts during an attack by the Moors in the course of morning mass in 1239. The cloths were later found stained with blood and proclaimed sacred relics.

▶ Continue on the **N234** to Calamocha.

4 Calamocha, Zaragoza

Calamocha is a pretty little village with narrow streets and some fine, well-preserved mansions. It has an old Moorish bridge and tower, and a baroque-style parish church.

▶ Continue south on the **N234**. Turn right, taking the **A1511** through Santa Eulalia and on to Orihuela del Tremedal.

5 Orihuela del Tremedal, Teruel

The tour goes through some lovely mountain scenery to Orihuela del Tremedal, set among the pine-clad slopes of the Sierra de Albarracín. The parish church is an impressive baroque building and there is a fine 16th-century Ayuntamiento.

▶ Take the **TE903/A1512** southeast to Albarracín.

BACK TO NATURE

Bird-watchers will be in their element at the Laguna de Gallocanta, southwest of Daroca, Spain's largest inland lake. Among its inhabitants are red-crested pochards, larks and harriers. Little and great bustards can be found in the surrounding countryside and cranes are winter visitors.

82

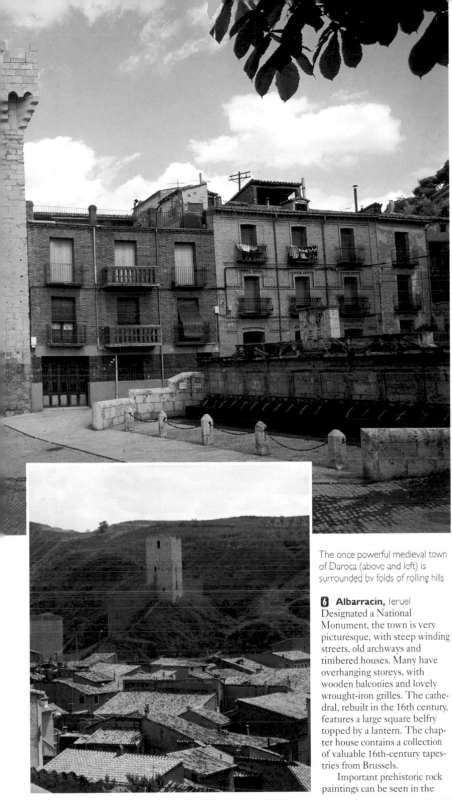

The once powerful medieval town of Daroca (above and left) is surrounded by folds of rolling hills

6 **Albarracin,** Teruel
Designated a National Monument, the town is very picturesque, with steep winding streets, old archways and timbered houses. Many have overhanging storeys, with wooden balconies and lovely wrought-iron grilles. The cathedral, rebuilt in the 16th century, features a large square belfry topped by a lantern. The chapter house contains a collection of valuable 16th-century tapestries from Brussels.

Important prehistoric rock paintings can be seen in the

RECOMMENDED
WALKS

The Montes Universales to the
south of Albarracín has a
National Game Reserve and
offers splendid walks among its
wild landscapes of barren
rocks and mountains with their
strange rock formations.

BACK TO NATURE

Northwest of Albarracín is the
Sierra de Albarracín. If you are
lucky you might spot a red
deer, while birds of prey
such as griffon vultures,
goshawks and red kites soar
overhead. Botanists will be
intrigued by the plant life, with
birthwort, dense-flowered
orchids and gromwells being
among the species to look for.
Butterflies include the
Camberwell Beauty.

The Old Cathedral at Zaragoza
with its 17th-century belfry. Above:
detail from the Moorish Aljafera

caves of El Callejón de Plou and
El Navazco, located a short
distance to the south.

i *Calle Catedral 5*

▶ *Continue on the A1512 and
join the N234 to Teruel.*

7 Teruel, Teruel
Teruel, capital of its own
province, stands high on a
plateau surrounded by a deep
moat, through which the River
Turia flows. The original town
of Turba was Iberian. Sacked
by the Romans in 218 BC, it
then came under Moorish
domination for several
centuries before being retaken
by the Christians. A large
number of Moors, known as
Moriscos, remained here,
however, and were renowned
for their skills in masonry and
ceramics.
    The town has five Torres
Mudejares (Mudéjar towers)
built between the 12th and
16th centuries. These have
square belfries on top adorned
with ceramic tiles. The base of
each structure has an arched
opening, which gives access to
the street, and the façade is
richly decorated with brick-
work and tiles. The ornate
towers of the churches of San
Martín and El Salvador are
considered among the finest
examples of their kind. Built in
the 12th century, almost side
by side, the 'twin towers' are a
handsome landmark of Teruel.
    The original stucture of
the cathedral dates back to the
12th century and was recognised as a cathedral only in the
16th century. It is noted for its

tall, slender tower and cupola,
which was built in 1538 and is
covered with colourful tile
decorations. The 13th-century
Iglesia de San Pedro shows
Mudéjar influence.
    Remains of the fortifications
include the solid tower, Torre
Lombardara, and the gates of La
Traición and La Andaquilla also
belonged to the old battlements.

SPECIAL TO...

The legend of the Lovers of
Teruel dates back to the early
13th century and tells of a love
affair between Diego de
Marcilla and Isabel de Segura,
two young people from Teruel.
An enforced separation ended
tragically in Romeo-and-Juliet
style. The bodies of the couple
lie in a mausoleum adjoining
the church of San Pedro. This
romantic story is popular all
over Spain, and has been told
in many poems and dramas.

A prominent feature of Teruel is
the Acueducto de los Arcos
(Aqueduct of the Arches), which
was constructed in 1558 by the
French architect Pierre Vedel
along Roman lines.

i *Glorieta Pio XII, Torreón de
la Zuda*

▶ *Take the N420 north, then
turn onto the N211 east to
Alcañiz, 158km (98 miles).*

8 Alcañiz, Teruel
The ancient town of Alcañiz is
built up a hillside, surrounded
by orchards and olive groves.
This fertile area is noted for the
production of high-quality olive
oil, and for *almendrados*, a sweet
paste made from almonds.
    The town is crowned by
the 12th-century Castillo de los
Calatravos, once the seat of the
military Order of Calatrava in
Aragón. Parts are Romanesque
in style, from the 12th century,
others are in Gothic style. The
castle is now a parador.
    One of Alcañiz's most
impressive buildings is the
Colegiata de Santa María la
Mayor. Built in 1736, it is very
tall with a magnificent portico.
Among the town's most delightful features is the Plaza de
España, a large square with the
attractive La Lonja, whose tall,
elegant portals were once the
meeting place of the market.
Adjoining is the handsome
Renaissance Ayuntamiento.
    At Valdealgorfa, 12km (7½
miles) away, is the Cueva del
Charco del Agua, where there
are prehistoric rock paintings.

i *Calle Mayor 1*

▶ *Return to Zaragoza on N232.*

Pyrenean Landscapes
of Upper Aragón

Huesca is a typical Pyrenean town. Its Gothic cathedral, Renaissance Ayuntamiento (town hall) and Romanesque former monastery, San Pedro el Viejo, are among the most interesting places to visit.

2/3 DAYS • 408KM • 253 MILES

The fortress-monastery looking
out from the hilltop at Loarre

i Plaza de la Catedral 1

▶ Take the **A132** northwest. At
Esquedas turn right and take
the **A1206** to Castillo de
Loarre.

❶ Castillo de Loarre,
Huesca

The last part of this journey
takes you through some stunning scenery to the impressive
Castillo de Loarre, which
towers majestically over the
Ebro Valley beneath the Sierra
de Loarre.

Originally built as a
fortress, it was actually in use
as a monastery in the 12th
century, even though the area
was under Moorish domination
at that time. The church building is encircled by massive
walls with cylindrical towers
and two entrance gates, from
which there are magnificent
views of the surrounding
landscape. The church was
completed in the 12th century
and features a tall nave and a
cupola in Romanesque style.

▶ Return to the **A1026** and
turn right through the village
of Loarre to Ayerbe, 8km
(5 miles).

❷ Ayerbe, Huesca
Stop here briefly to visit two
buildings. The Ayuntamiento,
housed in the Palacio del
Marqués de Ayerbe is a fine old
building from the 15th century.
The Torre de San Pedro dates
back to the 12th century.

▶ Take the **A132** north to join
the **N240** to Berdún.

❸ Berdún, Huesca
Berdún is a cluster of houses
huddled together up the hillside. This village forms an
excellent base for excursions
north into the Valle de Ansó,
which offers some spectacular
scenery of deep gorges and
green valleys, together with
some charming little villages.

▶ Return to and continue
along the **N240**. Turn right
on to the **A1603** to San Juan
de la Peña.

❹ San Juan de la Peña,
Huesca

Tucked away under a great
rock is the ancient
Monasterio de San Juan
de la Peña (St John of the
Crag). It has a magnifi-
cent setting overlooking
a Pyrenean valley with a

SPECIAL TO...

Aragón has a traditional dance
known as the jota, which dates
back to the 18th century. It is a
lively affair involving great
bounding steps and is accompanied by guitars or a small
version of the guitar known as
the bandurrias. The dance is
performed at festival times,
when the men wear the traditional costume of black velvet
jacket over a blouse with
slashed sleeves, black knee
breeches, a colourful cummer-
bund and a bright handkerchief
on the head.

beautiful view of snow-capped mountains to the north.

The original monastery was founded in the 9th century by a monk called Juan, who is said to have decided to end his wanderings on this spot. Additions were made later to the original structure, which was built from the rock, and the Benedictine monastery of San Juan de la Peña was then formally founded by Sancho Ramírez, son of King Ramiro I. The monastery is associated with the legend of the elusive Holy Grail, claimed to have been passed on to the monks here for safekeeping by

King Ramiro. The cloister was built in the 12th century and is a superb example of Romanesque art, with beautiful carved capitals showing scenes from the Bible. The tombs of noblemen can be found in the Pantheon of Nobility and the Pantheon of the Kings. Don't miss the delightful Gothic-style Capilla de San Vicente.

▶ Rejoin **N240** and go east to Jaca, 21km (13 miles).

FOR CHILDREN

There are a number of festivals that would appeal to children. On the first Friday in May a pilgrimage takes place in Jaca to commemorate the Christian victory over the Moors. This is a colourful festival, with mock fights between the warring forces, music and dancing. On 25 June is the feast of Santa Oroisa, which is celebrated with processions and traditional dances performed by dancers from Yebra de Basa.

A Spanish version of bowls/boules under the trees at Jaca

5 Jaca, Huesca

Jaca is one of the major stages on the Way to Santiago, the pilgrimage route to Santiago de Compostela in Galicia that was established after the supposed tomb of the Apostle James the Great was discovered there in the 9th century. The great days of the pilgrimages were in the 11th and 12th centuries and pilgrims came from all over Europe.

The cathedral of Jaca is an outstanding example of the so-called Romanesque style of the Pilgrim's Way, developed between the Pyrenees and Galicia. Notable are the chapels of San Miguel, the 16th-century Trinidad (Trinity), with a Romanesque grille, and the Capillo de San Jerónimo, a fine example of baroque art.

Housed in the cathedral's cloisters is the Museo Diocesano, which contains a fine collection of 12th to 15th century Romanesque and Gothic frescoes, collected from churches in the region.

BACK TO NATURE

The solitude of San Juan de la Peña and its surroundings provides ideal conditions for bird-watching. Look out for such species as griffon vultures who come to roost in the high cliffs that surround the monastery. Kestrels, golden eagles and rock thrushes may also be spotted here.

Below the 16th-century Ciudadela (Citadel) is the impressive medieval bridge, Puente San Miguel, which was much used in former times by pilgrims on the Way to Santiago. In contrast, take a look at the modern style of architecture of the Palacio de Congresos (Congress Palace) and the Palacio de Hielo (Ice Palace).

[i] *Avenida Regimiento de Galicia 2–local 1*

▶ *Continue southeast on the N330-E07 to Sabiñanigo.*

6 Sabiñanigo, Huesca
This small mountain town in beautiful surroundings has an interesting Museo Etnológico de Artes Populares, featuring regional art. Near by are several

At Jaca, the Ciudadela's moat must have been a formidable defence

churches of Moorish-Romanesque style, such as those in Larrede, Oros Bajo, Satue and San Juan de Busa.

▶ *Take N260 north to Biescas.*

7 Biescas, Huesca
Biescas is a pretty little summer resort with neat white houses and red-tiled roofs. The parish

church was erected by the Knights Templar. Look out for the Ermita de Santa Elena on the outskirts of town, perched on top of a steep rock.

If you have time, visit the picturesque little villages of Panticosa (with a spa and lake) and Sallent de Gallego, a good fishing and mountaineering centre (north on the C136).

▶ *Take N260 east to Torla.*

8 Torla, Huesca
The drive continues through typical Pyrenean scenery to the little mountain village of Torla, with its narrow, winding streets and hidden corners. Torla serves as the entrance to the Parque Nacional de Ordesa.

▶ *Take the road for a short distance into the Parque Nacional de Ordesa y Monte Perdido.*

9 Parque Nacional de Ordesa, Huesca
This is an area of exceptional beauty and great geological interest, covering a vast expanse of mountains, valleys and forests. It was designated a National Park in 1918 to protect the rich flora and fauna and the natural surroundings and has been increased in size over the years. A deep canyon through ridges of limestone has created gigantic rock formations in magnificent shades of grey, red and ochre. Weather conditions normally allow access by car between May and September. The park has marked pathways, which take you to caves, pools

11 Barbastro, Huesca

Barbastro is a city with ancient roots. The original town was devastated by Pompey and received the name of *Brutina*, after Decius Brutus. Occupied by the Moors, it was retaken by the Christians in 1064. The cathedral is a fine building in the late Gothic style. It has an elegant interior, with lovely stellar vaults and altarpieces by Damian Forment and his pupils. The Palacio de los Argensolas, built in the late 15th century, is now the Ayuntamiento.

▶ *Take the A1232 northwest for 23km (14 miles) to Alquézar.*

12 Alquézar, Huesca

A drive through rugged terrain takes you to this fascinating little village straggling up the slopes of a rock, overshadowed by a large castle. The town has a Moorish appearance, with reddish-brown buildings that merge in with the natural colours of the surroundings. Leave your car in a parking area at the entrance to the village and proceed on foot, through narrow streets lined with large arcades and galleries. Up the hill is the castle, built in the 12th century. The Colegiata, housed inside the castle, has the remains of an elegant Romanesque cloister and a small museum, which contains a beautiful Gothic statue of Christ.

▶ *Rejoin the N240 and return to Huesca, 61km (38 miles).*

and waterfalls, and a number of lookout points offering great views. Among the numerous beauty spots don't miss the Tamborrotera Waterfall, which can be viewed from a lookout point near the park's entrance.

▶ *Return to Torla and take the N260 south to Aínsa.*

Torla, a typical mountain village, overpowered by the dramatic cliffs of the Pyrenees

10 Aínsa, Huesca

The old walled town of Aínsa is built on a promontory overlooking the junction of the rivers Cinca and Ara. In the 11th century it was the capital of a small kingdom formed by García Jiménez after his victories against the Moors. The town has old stone houses and a pretty main square, the Plaza Mayor, bordered by attractive arcades. The Romanesque church features an interesting bell-tower and elegant cloister.

▶ *Take the A138 south and join the N123 west to Barbastro.*

BACK TO NATURE

The Ordesa National Park is home to mammals such as ibex, chamois, mountain goat, polecat, badger and wild boar and a great number of different species of birds, including some rare ones such as the golden eagle and bearded vulture.

RECOMMENDED WALKS

From Alquézar there is an interesting walk to the Grotto of Villacantal which is believed to date back to prehistoric times. Near by is another cave where animal paintings, thought to be some 4,000 years old, can be seen from the outside.

Navarra &
Wine Country

2 DAYS • 425KM • 263 MILES Pamplona (Iruña), the
Roman city of Pompey, is famous for the festival of
Sanfermines, the running of the bulls, held in July. Once capital
of the kingdom of Navarra, today it has to be content with a
province. A maze of narrow streets surrounds the massive
cathedral with its 14th-century cloister, an architectural gem.
The town's focal point is the Plaza del Castillo, partly encircled
by old ramparts.

The glassed-in balcony, offering protection from inclement weather, is found in many parts of Northern Spain; here in Pamplona

ℹ️ *Calle Eslava 1*

▶ *Take the N121 south. Branch off right and take the regional road southwest to Artajona.*

➊ Artajona, Navarra

From quite a distance you can spot the fortifications that surround the medieval town of Artajona. Known as El Cerco de Artajona, this conclave of solid ramparts and square towers is a very impressive sight. On the summit stands the fortified Iglesia de San Saturnino. Dating back to the 13th century, it is noted for its finely sculpted façade and 15th-century retable.

▶ *Take the regional road south-east for 11km (7 miles) to Tafalla.*

► *Take the* **NA132** *east and
branch off southeast to Ujué,
just after San Martín de Unx.*

3 Ujué, Navarra
The last bend in the road
reveals the sight of this quaint
hilltop village, dominated by a
huge fortified church. A walk
through its tiny winding streets
and alleys and up narrow steps
is a journey back into the
Middle Ages. The Iglesia de
Santa María dates back mostly
to the late 11th century, with
14th-century additions. In the
central chapel is a statue of
Santa María la Blanca. The
church is surrounded by the
massive towers of the old
fortifications with fine views of
the Pyrenees.

► *Return to San Martín de Unx
and take the regional road
southwest to Olite, 19km
(12 miles).*

4 Olite, Navarra
The medieval castle of Olite
gives the appearance of a whole
city in itself. It was once the
seat of the Court of Navarra and
has been excellently preserved.
The castle was built in the 13th
and 15th centuries and restored
in 1940. It is an imposing structure of massive walls and tall
square towers, part of which has
now been turned into a parador.
Below lies the little town of

Olite. The Iglesia de Santa
María la Real is noted for its
14th-century Gothic portal. The
Iglesia de San Pedro and the
convents of San Francisco and
Santa Clara all date from the
Middle Ages.

ℹ️ *Rua Mayor 1*

► *Take the* **N121** *south
towards Tudela, then turn left
for the* **NA134** *to Tudela.*

5 Tudela, Navarra
Tudela is an old episcopal town
as well as the second city of
Navarra. It lies on the banks of
the River Ebro, and is the centre

*The tower and turret, with arrow-
slit windows, add a fortress-like
element to this church at Olite*

2 Tafalla, Navarra
The ancient town of Tafalla lies
on the banks of the River
Cidacos, overlooked by the
11th-century fortress of Santa
Lucia. The old part of town is
around the main church and
here you will find the attractive
Plaza de los Fueros, together
with a network of little streets
and handsome mansions with
elegant façades. The Romanesque Iglesia de Santa María is
noted for the large 16th-century
Renaissance altarpiece by the
Basque sculptor, Juan de
Ancheta. Of interest, too, is the
16th-century retable from La
Oliva by the Flemish artist,
Roland de Moys, in the
Convento de la Concepción.

of a rich agricultural area. It was taken from the Moors in 1119, but retained Moorish influences for centuries.This is clear in the old Moorish quarter and the Mudéjar-style architecture of many of the brick-built houses.

The cathedral is an imposing monument, built between the 12th and 13th centuries. An outstanding feature is the Gothic entrance, known as the Puerta del Judicio (Doorway of the Last Judgement). A wide archway over the door is decorated with sculpted figures portraying the *Last Judgement*. Inside, the church has many notable works of art from the Gothic period. The 18th-century Capilla de Santa Ana is noted for its rich interior and fine baroque altarpiece. The Romanesque cloister, with finely carved capitals, contains the tomb of Don Fernando, son of King Sancho El Fuerte (The Strong One) whose tomb is in the nearby Iglesia de San Nicolás. He died in 1234 and lay here in Tudela until he was reburied in Roncesvalles.

Other buildings of interest include the Ayuntamiento, with notable archives, the Renaissance Palace of the Marquis San Adrián and the Iglesia de la Magdalena, which has a Romanesque tower and finely sculpted door. The Plaza Nueva was 'New' in the 18th century.

[i] Juicio 4

▶ Continue on the **N121** southwest to Tarazona.

6 **Tarazona,** Zaragoza
The present town of Tarazona was built on the site of the Celtiberian city of Turiaso. It was occupied first by the Romans, then by the Moors, and was recaptured in 1118 by the Christian King Alfonso I of Aragón. It continued as a royal residence until the 15th century. The town is noted for

the number of Mudéjar-style buildings and is often referred to as the 'Aragonese Toledo'.

The cathedral, begun in the 12th century, shows a combination of styles, mainly Mudéjar and Gothic, with influences of baroque and Plateresque art. The Iglesia de la Magdalena has an impressive Mudéjar tower, and the Guildhall façade has reliefs of the legends of Hercules. The 14th- and 15th-century Palacio Episcopal was once the residence of the Kings of Aragón. The 16th-century Ayuntamiento has a frieze around the building depicting the capture of Granada.

[i] Plaza de San Francisco 1

▶ Take the **N122** southwest for 20km (12 miles) to Agreda.

7 **Agreda,** Soria
Perched high on a rock is Agreda, once an important frontier town overlooking the kingdoms of Aragón and Castile. Dominating the town is the Castillo de la Muela, which still shows traces of old Moorish ramparts. Buildings of interest

include the Iglesia de San Miguel; the Iglesia de Nuestra Señora de la Peña, with panel paintings from the Gothic period; and the Convento de la Concepción, which contains the tomb of Sister María de Agreda (1602–65), mystic and religious advisor to Philip IV of Spain.

Agreda is a good base for trips into the Sierra del Moncayo, which can be explored by car or on horseback.

▶ Continue southwest on the **N122** to Soria.

8 **Soria,** Soria
Soria has inspired many Spanish poets. One of the most famous was the Sevillian poet, Antonio Machado (1875–1939), who lived here for a time. Outstanding among its many fine edifices is San Juan de Duero, a 12th-century monastery just outside the centre. At one time it belonged to the Knights Templars and features a beautiful cloister. The Palacio de los Condes de Gómara is a majestic building, built in the 16th century and dominated by an impressive

Terraced gardens at Agreda, once a stronghold on the frontier between Castile and Aragón tower. The Catedral de San Pedro (12th–16th centuries) is noted for its elegant doorway and Romanesque cloister. The 12th-century Iglesia de Santo Domingo has a richly decorated Romanesque façade, and the colonnades of the Iglesia de San Juan de Rabanera, preserved from the original cloister, have an unusual Romanesque-Oriental design.

About 8km (5 miles) north of the town are the remains of Numancia, an old Celtiberian fort renowned for its resistance to a siege by the Romans, until it fell in 133 BC. The Romans built over the old city and many objects of significance were discovered during 20th-century excavations; some are in the Museo Numantino in Soria.

[i] *Medinaceli 2*

▶ *Take NIII north to Logrono.*

9 Logroño, La Rioja
Logroño, capital of the region of La Rioja, stands on the banks of the Ebro. Its tower and the town's outline form a graceful silhouette, centred around the Iglesia de Santa María de la Redonda with its impressive baroque towers. The Imperial Church of Santa María de Palacio was founded in the 11th century and has a lofty pyramid-shaped tower built in the 13th century. The 15th-century cathedral has a baroque façade from the 18th century, and the 13th-century Iglesia de San Bartolmé is noted for its

Watching the world go by in the quiet town of Soria

Romanesque-Gothic doorway. An historic stone bridge used by the pilgrims on their journey to Santiago de Compostela spans the River Ebre.

[i] *Paseo del Espolón s/n*

▶ *Take NIII northeast to Estella.*

10 Estella, Navarra
The old town of Estella lies on the banks of the River Ega. During the Middle Ages it was the residence of the Kings of Navarra and a staging point for pilgrims. The Iglesia de Santo Sepulcro stands on the pilgrim route and has three palaces among its old mansions. The 12th-century Iglesia de San Pedro de la Rua has a fine façade and Romanesque cloister.

[i] *San Nicolás 1*

▶ *Return to Pamplona on NIII.*

SPECIAL TO...

La Rioja is famous for its wines. The best-known is the full-bodied *tinto*, a high-quality red wine. It also produces the *claretes*, which are light red wines and the golden *blancos* which are dry and aromatic. In late September there is a Wine Festival in Logroño, with bullfights, parades and poetry competitions.

FOR CHILDREN

Children should enjoy a festival that takes place in Anguiano (southwest of Logroño) on 21 and 22 July in honour of Mary Magdalene. The celebrations centre around the Danza de los Zancos, or Stilt Dance, when a troupe of dancers, wearing colourful traditional costumes, descend the steps of the church on stilts and then proceed down the hill at great speed.
Get the kids to keep an eye open for some spectacular birds of prey. The Parque Natural de Urbasa y Andía running alongside the NIII has eagles, vultures, owls and falcons.

CENTRAL SPAIN & THE WEST

A vast part of Spain is the great central plain known as the Meseta, or tableland, ringed by hills and bordering Portugal. In the centre lies Madrid, capital of Spain and the highest capital in Europe, at an altitude of 646m (2,120 feet). To the north is Castile-León, while the south contains Castilla-La Mancha. In the southwestern section is Extremadura, which is also part of the Meseta.

The main central Cordillera sweeps down the Castilian plain from northeast to southwest, and is divided into the Sierra de Guadarrama, Sierra de Gredos and the Peña de Francia. The dry, barren Toledo mountains dominate the landscape south of Madrid, while to the east is the wild Serranía de Cuenca. The Duero, Tajo, Guadiana and Guadalimar are four important rivers that rise in the heartlands of the region and flow down to the Atlantic. Dramatic changes of scenery and climatic differences are contained within the region, where wild eroded landscapes contrast with green forests and the dry flatlands of the south.

A profusion of pinnacles decorates Segovia's late-Gothic cathedral

Castile is derived from the word *castillo*, meaning castle. This was a land of castles built to defend its borders during the conflicts between the Moors and Christians. Later, further fortifications were erected between the kingdoms of Castile and Aragón. The marriage of Isabella of Castile and Ferdinand II of Aragón in 1469 joined these two kingdoms and unified Spain.

La Mancha is a vast plain, where windmills and castles serve as a reminder that this is Don Quixote land. Extremadura has played an important role in history as the birthplace of many of the great explorers. It presents a panorama of dry, rocky moorlands, with irrigated areas around the Alagón and Tajo.

Among the crafts still practised in Castile are the traditional blue-and-yellow ceramics from Talavera and pottery in La Mancha.

Tour 16

Art is the essence of this tour. Admirers of El Greco can see his greatest masterpieces in the best possible setting – Toledo. This jewel of a town is one of Spain's major attractions, renowned for its spectacular setting as well as for the treasures to be seen here. Another highlight is a visit to one of the famous Royal Palaces, with their lavishly decorated rooms and elegant gardens. A drive south through the plains of south Meseta is rewarded by a glimpse of La Mancha country.

Tour 17

This eastern section of Castilla-La Mancha offers an unusual itinerary with terrific scenery. The route takes in some of the splendid old fortified towns that once protected the borders between warring kingdoms. A total contrast is provided by a visit to the fascinating 'hanging houses', and a drive through some spectacular scenery to an

Plaza Mayor, the centre of old Madrid, is a great place to relax

area of extraordinary rock formations. The journey picks up the trail of Don Quixote, which leads down to the great plains and windmills of La Mancha.

Tour 18

The first part of this tour travels west through the Central Cordillera, with the magnificent scenery of the Guadarrama Mountains to the north and the southern peaks of the Sierra de Gredos. In the mountains are two special monuments: a great monastery and a memorial to the fallen of the Civil War, close in geography but centuries apart. A walled city in a dramatic setting and an ancient monastery are combined with visits to some fine churches and a crafts centre.

Tour 19

Royal palaces and ancient castles form the basis of this tour, with the focus on a beautiful golden city, where the famous Alcázar and Aqueduct rate high among Spain's many attractions. A number of palaces in this area were originally built

as Royal hunting lodges. The circular tour to the northwest of Madrid passes through the magnificent forests and lush green valleys found around the Guadarrama Mountains.

Tour 20

This tour explores a lesser known area of Spain. Extremadura is a sparsely populated region in the extreme west of the country, sharing an extensive border with Portugal. The fascination of the area lies in its very remoteness and the desolation of its landscapes, some of which are magnificent. Cortés and Pizarro were born here, as were many other great explorers.

Tour 21

This tour covers an area north west of Madrid. The region has close associations with Spain's great hero, El Cid, the valiant conqueror of the Moors. A dominant feature of the tour is one of the country's most famous cathedrals, which is known for its impressive interior, where you can see the tomb of El Cid.

Art Treasures of
Castilla-La Mancha

2 DAYS • 293KM • 181 MILES

Busy, modern Madrid, capital of Spain, still embraces the medieval city's narrow streets crowding the Calle Mayor which runs from Puerta del Sol, Madrid's focal point.

The richly carved alterpiece in Toledo Cathedral, one of the finest Gothic cathedrals in Spain

i **Plaza Mayor 3**

FOR CHILDREN

From mid-May to the end of September children can enjoy a ride on the 'Trena de la Fresa' (Strawberry Train), which runs from Madrid to Aranjuez at weekends. Wooden carriages are drawn by a steam engine and the name stems from when the service was used to transport strawberries during the last century. Today, strawberries are distributed among the passengers by hostesses in period costumes. The journey takes about an hour.

▶ *From Madrid take the* **N401** *southwest to Illescas.*

❶ Illescas, Toledo
Those with a special interest in art will want to stop here to look at paintings by El Greco. A collection of five works by the great master himself are to be seen in the church of the Hospital de la Caridad, among

them paintings from 1600 to 1604. While here, take a look at the 13th-century parish church of Santa María, which dates back to the 16th century and has a fine Mudéjar tower.

▶ *Continue on the* **N401** *to Toledo.*

❷ Toledo, Toledo
Toledo is indisputedly one of Spain's finest jewels. It is rich in art and treasures, combined with a great deal of historical interest. Once the capital of an Iberian tribe, it was taken over by the Romans in 192 BC and called *Toletum*. In 1085 the city was captured from the occupying Moors by King Alfonso VI of Castile and it became the residence of the kings of Castile, continuing to flourish as a centre of art and learning. It reached the height of its splendour at the end of the 15th and first half of the 16th centuries. When King Philip II transferred the capital to Madrid in 1561, however, Toledo lost its status.

The cathedral stands majestically on the Plaza Mayor (main

square). Built between 1227 and 1493 on the site of the Great Mosque, it is widely regarded as the finest Gothic cathedral in Spain after Burgos, with influences of the Mudéjar style to be seen in some parts. Its elegant tower looks over the city. The sanctuary is the most richly decorated area of the interior. Expanded in the 16th century, it is noted for the retable depicting the *Life of*

FOR HISTORY BUFFS

Eight kilometres (5 miles) east of Illescas is the small town of Esquivias, where Cervantes set up house after his marriage in 1548 to Catalina de Salazar y Palacios, who is said to have been the inspiration behind his poem *Galatea*. The records of his marriage can be seen in the registry of the church of Santa María.

Christ. The Chapter House is distinguished by its fine Mudéjar ceiling and ornate stucco doorways.

The Sacristy has an excellent collection of paintings by El Greco, Goya, Van Dyck and other famous artists. The Treasury Room boasts an elegant Plateresque door by Covarrubias and a fine Mudéjar ceiling. Of particular interest, however, is the splendid 16th-century gold- and silver-gilt monstrance by Enrique de Arfe. It stands 3m (10 feet) high and weighs about 200kg (440 pounds) and is carried through the streets during the Corpus Christi processions.

Toledo has been an inspiration for many writers and poets, but mention Toledo and most people think of El Greco, the name Domenikos Theotoko-poulos is usually known by, who came from Crete to Toledo around 1577. Here he remained and painted, producing many masterpieces. The Iglesia de Santo Tomé contains *The Burial of the Count of Orgaz*, one of his most famous paintings. The museum in the former hospital of La Santa Cruz has a collection of his work, including the notable *Assumption of Our Lady*. Other valuable works of art may also be seen in the Hospital de Tavera, a private collection which contains several paintings by El Greco.

Enthusiasts will want to visit the Casa y Museo de El Greco, which stands very close to the place where he lived from 1585 until his death in 1614. The famous *View of Toledo*

The spectacular setting of Toledo, overlooking the River Tajo

features among the superb collection of his work to be seen in the museum.

The Alcázar (Citadel) stands in a prominent position on the highest point of the town. It was

BACK TO NATURE

Situated in the wooded Montes de Toledo (Toledo mountains), in the southern part of the region, is the Coto Nacional de los Quintos de Mora (Quintos de Mora game reserve), which is the natural habitat of a wide variety of wildlife. Here you may spot any number of different animals, such as red deer, roe deer, boars, rabbits and hares. Birdlife includes partridges, wood pigeons, turtle doves, bee-eaters and quail. Also look for eyed and wall lizards among the rocks.

3 Consuegra, Toledo

This part of the itinerary takes you south to the flat desolate heartlands of La Mancha, immortalised by the pen of Miguel de Cervantes in his classic tale of the adventures of Don Quixote and his faithful servant Sancho Panza. The very essence of La Mancha is conjured up here by the silhouette of an old ruined castle and 12 white windmills, many of which have been rebuilt and some of which are museums for pottery and wine. The village of Consuegra has a charming main square overlooked by a large tower. It was here that Don Diego died, the only son of Spain's great hero, El Cid.

SCENIC ROUTES

This route travels south to La Mancha through vast flat expanses of fields that stretch away to invisible horizons. Occasional trees, hills and hamlets relieve the landscape. Its very remoteness and the subtle colours have a definite appeal, a sentiment shared by Cervantes, who chose this setting for the travels of Don Quixote. No visit to La Mancha is complete without a glimpse of the famous windmills in the southern part of the region. You will see them around Consuegra, but for a good 'windmill run' take the C400 southeast from Consuegra to Campo de Criptana (southeast on the C400, then left on to the N420).

At Consuegra, one of the famous windmills on the La Mancha plain immortalised by Cervantes

destroyed and rebuilt many times during the course of its history. In the 16th century Charles V had the fortress converted into a royal residence. It was damaged during the wars of the 18th and 19th centuries, and devastated by the siege in 1936 during the Civil War. The garrison, then a cadet school, was besieged by Republican forces. The inmates of the garrison, which included many women and children, held out heroically for some eight weeks until relief came. The reconstructed building is now a national monument.

i Puerta de Bisagra s/n

▶ Leave by the **N401** and branch on to the **CM400** southeast to Consuegra.

▶ Take the **CM400** east to Madridejos and join the **A4-E05** north. Continue for 78km (48 miles) to Aranjuez, 5km (3 miles) off this road.

4 Aranjuez, Madrid
The town is dominated by the famous Palacio Real (Royal Palace). Grand entrance gates lead to a large courtyard where you can admire the palace's lovely façade. It was built in the classical style, showing harmony and symmetry in its proportions. The central staircase is Italian in design, and the walls on either side are hung with tapestries from Belgium. The elegant salons include the Sala de la China, the Salon del Trono and el Arabe, which was built for Queen Isabella II and whose sumptuous decorations bear a resemblance to those of the Alhambra at Granada.

Close by is the Casa del Principe (Prince's House). This small palace was built in the neo-classical style by Charles IV for his son and is noted for the Pompeiian Gallery, which is filled with magnificent marbles and statues. Another important building is the Casa del Labrador (Labourer's House), which resembles the Petit Trianon at Versailles. Also neo-classical in style, it has an ornate interior decorated with silk hangings. Its collection of treasures includes Roman mosaics, porcelain clocks and a magnificent gallery of Greek statues.

Several gardens surround the palace and are beautifully

Fountains refresh the gardens of the Palacio Real, Aranjuez

laid out with waterfalls and pools, graceful statues and attractive little pavilions. The gardens bear different names, including the Jardín del Rey (King's Garden), Jardín de la Reina (Queen's Garden), Jardín de la Isla (Island Garden), on a tiny man-made island between two sections of the river, with its avenue of plane trees, and the Jardín del Principe (Prince's Garden), which contains many exotic species of trees.

i *Plaza San Antonio 9*

▶ *Take the regional road (**M305**) northeast to Chinchón.*

5 Chinchón, Madrid
One of the most attractive features of this charming little village is the Plaza Mayor. The square is surrounded by three- and four-storey houses with wooden balconies, from which spectators used to watch the famous bullfights here in the old days. The parish church overlooking the square contains a painting of the Assumption, which has been attributed to Goya (whose brother was once the town's parish priest).

▶ *Take the **M404** west to Ciempozuelos.*

6 Ciempozuelos, Madrid
A brief stop here is suggested for those with a special interest in art and architecture. Two monuments are of note. The Sanatorium is a magnificent example of the neo-Mudéjar

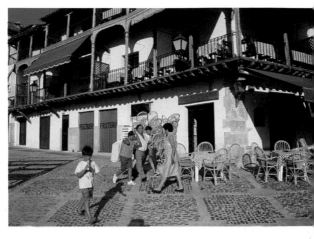

Houses in Chinchón's Plaza Mayor have balconies, once grandstands for bullfights in the square below

style of architecture, and the small parish church contains the fine painting, *The Head of Mary Magdalena*, by Claudio Coello.

▶ *Carry on along this road, then turn right on meeting the **A4-E05**. Drive north and turn left to Valdemoro.*

7 Valdemoro, Madrid
More works by the artist Claudio Coello can be seen in the little 16th-century parish church, along with paintings by Goya and by his brother-in-law, Francisco Bayeu.

▶ *Rejoin the **A4-E05** and continue north, turn left to Pinto after a short distance.*

8 Pinto, Madrid
The major attraction of Pinto is the Castillo de los Duques de Frías, an imposing structure dating back to the 15th century, where the Princess of Eboli, notorious for her intrigues at the court of Philip II, was confined from 1578 to 1581. The parish church was built in the Gothic-Plateresque style and has some finely carved decorations.

▶ *Take the **A4-E05** north again and turn left on to the **M406** to Getafe, 10km (6 miles).*

9 Getafe, Madrid
Getafe's most notable building is the Renaissance-style Iglesia de la Magdalena, with huge columns and a splendid retable. Inside there are paintings by two baroque artists, Claudio Coello and Alonso Cano.

Just beyond the junction of the M406 and the NIV, a turning to the right takes you to the Cerro de los Angeles (Hill of Angels). This conical hill is considered the geographical centre of Spain and is marked by the 'Corazón de Jesús' (Heart of Jesus) monument, which is topped by a figure of Christ and a church. There are superb views from here over the plains of Castile, the Guadarrama mountains and Madrid.

▶ *Take the road east to the **A4-E05** back to Madrid.*

FOR CHILDREN

Warner Bros Movie World in San Martín de la Vega, northeast of Ciempozuelos, has five themed areas based on sets and characters from Warner Bros films and cartoons. Attractions include a 100m (330-foot) free-fall tower, street pageantry and cinematic shows.

RECOMMENDED WALKS

The hot, dry plains of La Mancha may not be conducive to much walking, but the fresh green gardens of the Palace of Aranjuez are most agreeable for a quiet stroll. Among the several gardens in the palace grounds, the Jardín del Principe has inspired many artists with its shady trees and graceful monuments.

Traces of
Don Quixote

3 DAYS • 668KM • 416 MILES

The Madrid of the Habsburgs is best seen in the magnificent Plaza Mayor, the Casa del Ayuntamiento and the Convento de las Descalzas Reales. The Palacio Real, with superb painted ceilings and many treasures, exemplifies the neo-classical architecture in favour under Spain's Bourbon kings.

| i | *Plaza Mayor 69*

▶ *From Madrid take the A2, which becomes the A2-E90, east to Alcalá de Henares, a distance of 33km (21 miles).*

❶ **Alcalá de Henares,** Madrid
In 1998 the University and historic centre of Alcalá de Henares were named a World Heritage Site by Unesco. The University, founded in 1499 by Cardinal Cisneros, became an important centre for learning. In 1837 it was moved to Madrid, but re-established in Alcalá in 1977. Its central building, the Colegio de San Ildefonso, is noted for its elegant Plateresque façade. A guided tour will show you the Capilla de San Ildefonso, which houses the tomb of the cardinal, and

the Paraninfo (Assembly Hall), both richly decorated, with superb Mudéjar ceilings.
Alcalá de Henares is also known as the birthplace of Miguel de Cervantes, author of *Don Quixote de la Mancha*, and a small museum, the Museo Casa Natal de Cervantes, contains items relating to his life. The main square is called Plaza de Cervantes, and Calle Mayor, where Cervantes was born in 1547, leads off the square. Take a glimpse at the spectacular baroque dome in the Monasterio de las Bernardas and drop by the fine Palacio Laredo.

| i | *Plaza de los Santos Niños*

▶ *Continue on the A2-E90 to Guadalajara.*

Alcalá de Henares is renowned for its wide variety of sweets and delicious cakes. It is known especially for its *almendras garrapinadas* (caramelised almonds), which are produced by the nuns of the Convento de San Diego and can be bought at the door of the convent. Many different types of cakes, special to Alcalá, can also be found here, such as *rosquillas de Alcalá* (cakes in the form of a ring), *pestiños* (honey cakes) and *canutillos rellenos* (filled cakes in a tubular shape).

The 16th century buildings of the College of St Ildefonso, originally the University, at Alcalá de Henares

2 Guadalajara, Guadalajara

The finest feature of Guadalajara is the Palacio del Infantado. Built between 1461 and 1492 by Mendoza, second Duke of Infantado, the palace was severely damaged by bombs in 1936 during the Spanish Civil War, but has been restored. The pale façade has diamond stonework decorations and an intricately carved gallery on top. Inside is a lovely two-storey patio with notable Isabelline arching (a type of ornate decoration used in the 15th century during the reign of Queen Isabella the Catholic). Take a look, also, at the Roman bridge over the River Henares.

[i] *Plaza de los Caídos 6*

▶ *Take the **A2-E90** northeast, then branch left on to the **CM1101** to Sigüenza.*

3 Sigüenza, Guadalajara

The castle was founded by the Romans and rebuilt between

Erosion has sculpted the limestone rocks at La Cuidad Encantada

SCENIC ROUTES

The most spectacular part of the journey is between Cuenca and La Ciudad Encantada. The route follows a winding road through firs and pines up to the Serranía de Cuenca, with superb views of the surrounding mountains, gorges and plains. From a look-out point called El Ventano del Diablo (Devil's Window) you can see for miles over the mountains and plains. The route continues through great eroded landscapes to La Ciudad Encantada.

the 12th and 15th centuries, to become the residence of the bishops until the middle of the 19th century. It has a formidable fortress-like appearance, and has now been converted into a *parador* with magnificent views of the surrounding landscapes. The Plaza Mayor is overlooked by the cathedral, a solid structure of great towers and buttresses, built between the 12th and 14th centuries. It has a very significant art collection, including a fine painting of the Annunciation by El Greco.

▶ *Return to the **A2-E90**, turn right, then left to take the **N204** to Cifuentes.*

4 Cifuentes, Guadalajara

The name of Cifuentes means 'a hundred fountains', and indeed there are springs all over the area. In La Provincia square is the 12th- to 13th-century Iglesia de El Salvador, with a late Romanesque portal and a Gothic rose window, as well as the Convento de Santo Domingo. The ruins of a large 14th-century castle sit on top of the hill.

▶ *Continue south on the **N204** and just before Sacedon turn left on the **N320**, southeast to Cuenca.*

5 Cuenca, Cuenca

The little main square is dominated by the cathedral, an imposing structure with an attractive pale-coloured façade. Built between the 12th and 13th centuries, it shows a mixture of Gothic and Renaissance styles. Features of special note are the 18th-century high altar and elaborate 16th-century grille before the choir. Around the corner is the Museo Diocesano, which contains two fine El Greco paintings, some beautiful tapestries and a collection of rich gold religious crosses.

A path along the southern wall of the cathedral leads down to the spectacular 'Casas Colgadas', or Hanging Houses, for which Cuenca is famous. The buildings cling to the side of the cliff with balconies that protrude over the precipice. Originally built in the 14th century as a palace, they were

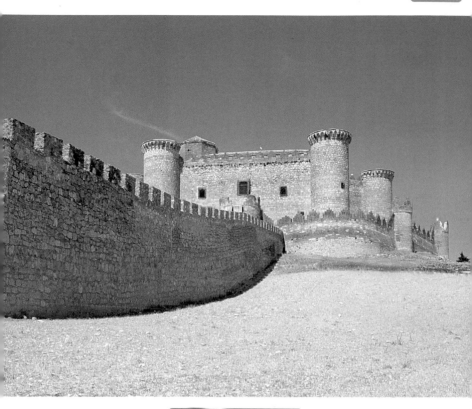

later used as a town hall. By the 19th century they had fallen into decay but were restored in the early part of the 20th century. One of the houses has been converted into the Museum of Abstract Art displaying large, mainly abstract canvases against pure white walls.

i Gonzalez Palencia 2–bajo

▶ *Take the regional road north. Soon after El Ventana del Diablo lookout point, turn right on to the minor road to La Ciudad Encantada (the Enchanted City).*

6 La Ciudad Encantada,
Cuenca
This is an extraordinary fantasy world of gigantic rock formations, the result of thousands of years of erosion. Nature really has had a go here, and the imagination runs riot with the sheer size and incredible shapes of

---

RECOMMENDED WALKS

Serious walkers will be in their element among the wild rocky landscapes of the Serranía de Cuenca. Northeast of La Ciudad Encantada is a lovely area of rich vegetation and pine forests, offering some gentle walks. A major attraction here is the sight of the source of the River Cuervo (Nacimiento del Cuervo), which emerges partly out of a cave in a series of rippling cascades.

---

the rocks, which resemble a Roman bridge, a giant mushroom, a human profile and even the 'lovers of Teruel' – Diego and Isabel (see page 84, Special To…). The route is indicated by arrows marked high up on the stones.

The walls and round towers of the 15th-century castle at Belmonte

▶ *Return to Cuenca by the alternative route, taking the regional road south, through Valdecabras. At Cuenca, take the **N420** south to Belmonte (via La Almarcha).*

7 Belmonte, Cuenca
Make a brief stop here to see the old castle on top of the hill. It has circular towers and was built by Juan Fernández Pacheco, Marquis of Villena, in the 15th century as a means of defending his extensive territories. It was later abandoned, but was restored and rebuilt in the 19th century. The old Colegiata church has an impressive collection of altarpieces from the 15th to 17th centuries and some fine choir-stalls.

▶ *Continue on **N420** southwest to Mota del Cuervo.*

The dramatic cliffs of Cuenca above the valley gardens

10 Uclés, Cuenca

The massive monastery, whose solemn appearance indicates a certain past importance, once belonged to the knightly Order of Santiago (St James). They were lords of the village from the 12th century, and the castle is sometimes referred to as the 'Escorial of La Mancha'. It has a magnificent Plateresque façade and an elegant 16th-century cloister. The two towers are impressive and parts of the old fortification walls still remain.

▶ Return to the **A3-E901** and head northwest to Tarancón.

11 Tarancón, Cuenca

The church here has a fine Gothic façade and a notable retable. Another building of interest is the handsome mansion built by Queen María Christina after she married a guardsman, who she made the Duque de Riansares.

▶ Continue on the **A3-E901** northwest to Arganda.

12 Arganda, Madrid

The splendid Renaissance Iglesia de San Juan Bautista, was built in 1525 and has notable altars in the Churrigueresque style. The Casa del Rey, a former country house in gardens, once belonged to the Spanish royal family, and there is a castle dating from 1400.

▶ Return to Madrid on the **A3-E901**.

8 Mota del Cuervo, Cuenca

Located right in the heartland of La Mancha country, the small village of Mota del Cuervo represents a typical image of Don Quixote's Mancha – the familiar sight of windmills silhouetted against clear blue skies, with parched plains stretching endlessly away. Take some time to explore the centre of the village, where many of the well preserved old townhouses, adorned with various coats of arms, represent a style that you will notice throughout this region.

▶ Take the **N301** to Quintanar de la Orden. Turn right on to the **CM310** and go northeast to the Parque Arqueológico de Segóbriga, just before the **NIII**, on the right.

SPECIAL TO...

Mota del Cuervo produces some interesting pottery and is the only place in the region where 'turntable moulding' is done exclusively by women. It is known for its small polished jugs, called *tinajas*, which have a slim shape and flat handle.

9 Parque Arqueológico de Segóbriga, Cuenca

Once the capital of Celtic Iberia, the ruins of Segóbriga include an amphitheatre, thermal baths and traces of an old wall. The Centro de Interpretación y Museo gives an insight into the town, with local finds.

▶ Take the regional road to join the **A3-E901**. Turn left after 2km (1 mile) then right to Uclés.

FOR HISTORY BUFFS

A short distance south of Quintanar de la Orden is the small village of El Toboso, which is claimed as the home of Dulcinea, legendary heroine of Cervantes' *Don Quixote*. The so-called Casa de Dulcinea contains a library relating to Cervantes. The village itself has one windmill and is charming, with little streets and patios, evoking scenes in the book.

Monuments &
Mountains

Madrid's Museo del Prado is a world-class museum, with paintings by El Greco, Velázquez, Goya, Murillo and Zurbarán, among the Spanish greats, and outstanding works from other nationalities. The Museo Nacional Centro de Arte Reina Sofia, home to Picasso's *Guernica,* and the Museo Thyssen–Bornemisza are are also top attractions.

2/3 DAYS • 585KM • 364 MILES

ITINERARY		
MADRID	▶	**Valle de los Caídos** (52km-32m)
VALLE DE LOS CAÍDOS	▶	**El Escorial (14km-9m)**
EL ESCORIAL	▶	**Ávila (63km-39m)**
ÁVILA	▶	**Piedrahíta (56km-35m)**
PIEDRAHÍTA	▶	**El Barco de Ávila** (21km-13m)
EL BARCO DE ÁVILA	▶	**Béjar (30km-19m)**
BÉJAR	▶	**Plasencia (59km-37m)**
PLASENCIA	▶	**Monasterio de Yuste** (47km-29m)
MONASTERIO DE YUSTE	▶	**Talavera de la Reina** (124km-77m)
TALAVERA DE LA REINA	▶	**Navalcarnero (86km-53m)**
NAVALCARNERO	▶	**Madrid (33km-21m)**

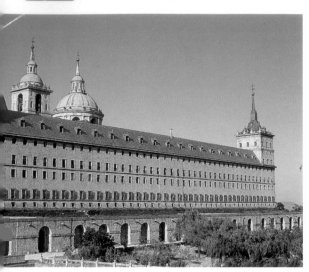

El Escorial, both monastery and palace, built for King Philip II

whose full title in Spanish is the Monasterio de San Lorenzo de El Escorial, stands as a testimony to King Philip II. He had it built to commemorate his victory over the French at the battle of San Quentin on 10 August (St Lawrence's Day), 1557, and also as a burial place for his father, the great Charles V. It was started in 1567 by Juan Bautista de Toledo, who had trained in Italy, and was completed by his assistant, Juan de Herrera, in 1584.

The building centres around the church, which has two tall towers and a dome. The main entrance is through a large courtyard known as La Lonja. This leads to the vestibule and follows through to the Patio de los Reyes (Courtyard of the Kings). A few steps take you to the entrance to the church, which marks the building's geometric centre.

i *Plaza Mayor 3*

▷ *From Madrid take NVI then A6. At exit 2 turn off to the southwest on M600, then almost at once turn right to the Valle de los Caídos.*

❶ **Valle de los Caídos,** Madrid

A tall cross rising in the distance from a rock mass marks the monument of the Valle de los Caídos, dedicated to all those who died in the Civil War (1936–9). At its base is the entrance to the basilica, cut out from the granite of the mountain. A flight of steps leads to the church. More steps lead to the crypt, covered by a huge underground dome, made up of several million mosaic pieces depicting saints, personalities and symbols of the Civil War. On opposite sides of the altar are the tombs of General Franco, who died in 1975, and José Antonio Primo de Rivera, founder of the Spanish Falange Party, who was killed in 1936. Behind the altar is the choir, with stalls for the Benedictine monks from the adjoining monastery.

You can also take a funicular up to the Cross from where there is a magnificent view of the surrounding landscape.

▷ *Rejoin the M600, turn right and continue to El Escorial.*

❷ **El Escorial,** Madrid

The Monasterio de El Escorial is one of the wonders of Spain. This great granite building,

---

FOR HISTORY BUFFS

A short drive south of El Escorial brings you to a spot known as the Silla de Felipe II (Philip II's seat). On the summit of a small hill among some boulders you will see what appear to be four seats carved from the rock. It is said that the king used to come here and meditate, while keeping a watchful eye on the progress of the construction of the monastery. There is a magnificent view from here of the monastery and the whole panorama.

The Panteón de los Reyes (Royal Pantheon) contains the sarcophagi of most of the Spanish kings since Charles I. A few still remain unoccupied. King Philip and his successors lived in the richly decorated Palacio Real. The Biblioteca de Impresos is sumptuously decorated with tapestries and frescoes by many painters. It contains some 40,000 volumes and hundreds of ancient manuscripts, codices and bibles. Two priceless items are the illuminated *Codex Aureus* made for the German Emperor Conrad II (completed in 1039) and the diary of St Theresa of Ávila.

The Arts Museum has a superb collection of paintings by famous masters. One of these is *The Martyrdom of St Maurice and the Theban Legionary* by El Greco. The Architectural Museum has a fascinating display of documents and plans relating to the construction of the monastery.

Of great interest, too, is the Habitación de Felipe II (Philip II's cell), where he spent the last years of his life in spartan conditions and troubled by pain. He died in an adjoining alcove in 1598. The Casita del Príncipe lies in lovely gardens to the east of the monastery. It was built by Charles IV, and contains elegant furniture and fine paintings.

i *Grimaldi 4*

▶ *Take the **M505** and **C505** northwest for 63km (39 miles) to Ávila.*

❸ Ávila, Ávila

The medieval walls of Ávila are a familiar landmark in the area and can be seen for miles around. With 88 round towers and nine gates, they encircle the town. The Catedral de San Salvador forms part of the wall and has a rather fortress-like appearance. It was built between the 11th and 13th centuries and combines Romanesque and baroque styles. Of special note inside are the 16th-century stained-glass windows, the painted altarpiece and the alabaster tomb of Cardinal Alonso de Madrigal, who was Bishop of Ávila and died in 1455. The Basílica de San Vicente is noted for its 14th-century façade and portal.

Ávila within its medieval walls

The Romanesque Iglesia de San Pedro (12th–13th century) has a lovely rose window and fine high altar. The 15th-century Convento de Santo Tomás features beautifully carved choirstalls and a fine retable by Pedro Berruguete. In the mausoleum is the tomb of Prince Juan, only son of the Catholic monarchs Ferdinand and Isabella, who died in 1497 when only 19. When you leave the cathedral by the other door you will find yourself within the walls of the old town. On this square stands the former Convento de Santa Teresa, which contains a chapel built in 1638 on the site of her birthplace. Inside you can see writings of the saint and relics – including her well-preserved ring finger. Facing the convent is the old palace of the former Viceroy of Peru. For more insight into St Teresa's life, look out for the Convento de la Encarnación, where she first took orders and spent some 30 years of her life, latterly as prioress. St Teresa was an exceptional person, remembered for her mystical writing and autobiography. Founder of a number of convents, she was canonised in 1622.

SCENIC ROUTES

West of Madrid the impressive mountain panoramas of the Sierra de Guadarrama give way to the brown windswept plateau and strange boulders to be found around Ávila. Beyond Ávila the route enters the Sierra de Gredos, an area of dramatic mountain ranges and high peaks. The stretch between El Barco de Ávila and Plasencia on the N110 passes through some spectacular scenery of mountains, valleys and pine forests. The drive from Plasencia to the Monasterio de Yuste and beyond Arenas de San Pedro (C501) also offers some outstanding scenery of heavily forested mountains.

BACK TO NATURE

The great mountain range of the Sierra de Gredos, which dominates the region to the west of Madrid, is an important habitat for birds of prey, and among the species that can be seen here are short-toed and booted eagles, red kites and goshawks, as well as the occasional black stork. Among the many flowers, you can find lupins, peonies and lilies-of-the-valley. The Spanish argus butterfly is special to the area. In the centre of this region is a national park, Coto Nacional de Gredos, where ibex live high up among the crags.

i *Plaza de Pedro Dávila 4*

▶ *Take the N110 southwest to Piedrahíta.*

4 Piedrahíta, Ávila
The summer resort of Piedrahíta was the birthplace of the Grand Duke of Alba, general of the army of King Philip II. Goya spent some time at the duke's palace here and it is said that there was a love affair between the painter and the Duchess of Alba, who was the model for his well known paintings of *La Maja.*

▶ *Continue on the N110 to El Barco de Ávila.*

5 El Barco de Ávila, Ávila
A drive through magnificent mountain scenery brings you to the town of El Barco de Ávila, where a brief stop will enable you to visit the 14th-century Castillo de Valdecorneja and the Gothic parish church, which contains some fine paintings. Spare a glance, too, for the old bridge over the River Tormes.

▶ *Take the C500 west to Béjar.*

6 Béjar, Salamanca
The Palacio Ducal, an elegant 16th-century palace with a Renaissance courtyard, is a school, but you can visit it in the mornings. The Ayuntamiento is noted for its attractive arcades. In the Iglesia de San Gil is a museum housing the works of the great sculptor Mateo Hernández, renowned for his animal figures sculpted from hard stone.

i *Carretera de Salamanca*

▶ *Take the N630 to Plasencia.*

7 Plasencia, Cáceres
The cathedral, started in the 13th century and never completely finished, is a splendid structure with an attractive Plateresque north doorway. Inside, notice the finely sculpted statues by Gregorio Hernández (17th century) on the altarpiece, a 15th-century retable by Hernández in the Capilla Mayor and a graceful 15th-century cloister. The old quarters around the cathedral contain narrow streets, fine façades and houses with attractive wrought-iron balconies. Stepped streets lead up to the old ramparts, where you can walk and enjoy the fine views.

▶ *Take the EX203 east, then turn off north to the Monasterio de Yuste.*

8 Monasterio de Yuste, Cáceres
Set deep in the woods is the old Monasterio de Yuste. It was founded by Hieronymite monks in 1404 and severely damaged by the French in 1809 during the Peninsular War. The monastery fell into decay for a long period until its recent restoration. This was where Emperor Charles V retired to in 1556 after his abdication, leaving the throne to his son Philip II. You can see the royal chambers where Charles lived until his death in 1558, including his bedroom from where he could hear mass. A path leads to a terrace from which there are good views of the surrounding plains.

Craftsmen took their skills to Mexico after the Conquest in 1521 and the traditional craft continued.

Places of interest in the town include the 13th-century Romanesque Iglesia de San Salvador, the Gothic Colegiata de Santa María la Mayor (13th–15th centuries), the Mudéjar-style parish church of Santiago, the Renaissance Church of San Prudencio and the Capilla de Nuestra Señora del Prado, which is adorned with beautiful glazed tiles dating back to the 16th and 18th centuries.

i Ronda Palenque, 2 Centro de Promoción de la Artesanía

▶ Return to and continue east on the **EX203**. Join the **N502** after Arenas de San Pedro and continue south to Talavera de la Reina.

9 Talavera de la Reina,
Toledo
Talavera de la Reina is famous for its attractive blue-and-yellow ceramic tiles, or *azulejos*, which have been produced since the 15th century. The tiles have been used over the centuries to adorn palaces, mansions, churches and other buildings.

▶ Join and take the **A5-E90** eastwards. Branch off left for a short distance to Navalcarnero.

10 Navalcarnero, Madrid
Make a brief stop here to take a look at the delightful little porticoed square and the parish church, which houses a notable retable and a fine work depicting the Apostles. Here, in 1649, Phillp IV was married to Anne of Austria.

▶ Join the **A5-E90** and return to Madrid.

The Route of
the Royal Palaces

The Puerta del Sol is the nerve centre of Madrid, an area for shopping enthusiasts with two large department stores, while the elegant part of town is to the north, around Serrano, Goya and Conde of Peñalver. On Sunday, visit El Rastro (the flea market), south of Calle Mayor, with its colourful stalls, stirring gypsy music and lively crowds.

2/3 DAYS • 364KM • 226 MILES

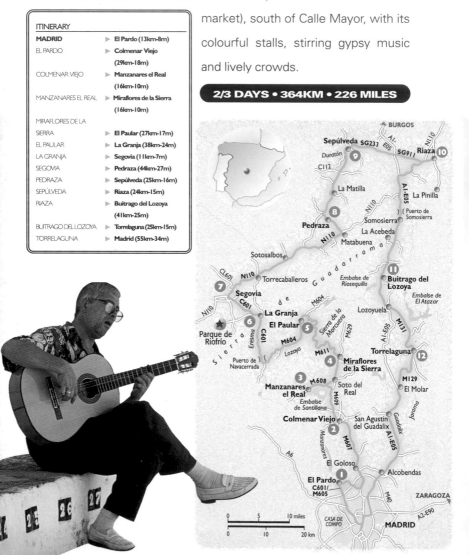

[i] *Plaza Mayor 69*

▶ *From Madrid take the NVI northwest. At Puerte de Hierro take the C601/M605 north to El Pardo.*

❶ El Pardo, Madrid
The way to El Pardo is through the Bosque del Pardo, delightful wooded parkland where you might glimpse deer, wild boar or an eagle soaring above. These were old royal hunting grounds dating back to the 14th century. In the middle of this lush greenery lies the little town of El Pardo and the Palacio Real El Pardo. The palace was built by Philip III over an earlier palace (built by Philip II and subsequently destroyed by fire), and was enlarged in the 18th century. General Franco resided

here for 35 years until his death in 1975.

Elegant reception rooms and private apartments are lavishly furnished with ornate clocks, mirrors, lamps and candelabra, as well as Sèvres' porcelain and a collection of 360 tapestries. Also on show are General Franco's Great Dining Room, where cabinet meetings took place, and his private office, which contains a notable portrait of Queen Isabella.

In the town across the river is the Convento de Capuchinos (Capuchin Convent), which contains a remarkable sculpture, the *Christ of El Pardo*, by Gregorio Fernández.

▶ *Head east to join the M607. Turn left and go north to Colmenar Viejo.*

SCENIC ROUTES

The most scenic parts of this route are to be found in the Sierra de Guadarrama, with its forested mountains and valleys. The road continues through hills and pine forest, and the land becomes lush and green near La Granja. From La Granja to Segovia it passes through rolling hills and plains, which become an ochre colour around Segovia. On the way back there are winding roads and sweeping views of the Sierras as you travel from Pedraza through Sepúlveda and Riaza to Buitrago.

King Phillip IV rides out in front of Madrid's neo-classical Royal Palace

2 Colmenar Viejo, Madrid
A drive past the old royal deer park takes you to the pleasant little town of Colmenar Viejo, where the main attraction is the Gothic parish church. It was built in the 14th century and has an impressive entrance door. Inside is a fine 16th-century Plateresque retable.

▶ *Continue north to rejoin the M607. Go straight across this road, however, and continue north on the M609. Take a left turn on to the M608 to Manzanares el Real.*

3 Manzanares el Real, Madrid
The 15th-century castle was once the property of the Marquis of Santillana, a famous poet at the court of King Juan II in the Middle Ages. It now belongs to the Dukes of El Infantada and has been passed to the state for restoration.

▶ *Turn northeast on the M608. Turn left at Soto de Real on to the M611 and continue north to Miraflores de la Sierra.*

RECOMMENDED WALKS

South of the castle at Manzanares el Real is the man-made lake, Embalse de Santillana, where you can stroll along the shores.

An 18th-century sphinx in the gardens at La Granja

FOR CHILDREN

Children will enjoy a visit to the Parque del Riofrío. Situated in the foothills of the Sierra de Guadarrama, 11km (7 miles) southwest of La Granja, these were old hunting grounds surrounding the Riofrío Palace, which stands in the middle of the park. Fallow deer and stags roam freely in this beautiful expanse of grasslands and oak woods.

---

4 Miraflores de la Sierra, Madrid
A lookout point on the outskirts of this picturesque town offers a magnificent view of the mighty mountains of the Sierra de Guadarrama. You can also see the source of the River Manzanares.

▶ *Continue northwest on the same road. Turn left on joining the M604 to El Paular.*

5 El Paular, Madrid
The old Carthusian Monasterio de Santa Maria de El Paular lies in the valley of the River Lozoya. It dates back to 1390 and was the first Carthusian monastery in Castile. It was

abandoned in the 19th century and fell into decay until 1954, when Benedictine monks began to restore the complex, which now comprises the monastery, church and a hotel. An impressive Gothic doorway leads to the interior of the church with an outstanding 15th-century alabaster altarpiece with rich sculptures and exquisite filigree work depicting scenes from the life of Christ.

▶ *Take the M604 southwest and join the C601 north to La Granja.*

6 La Granja, Segovia
La Granja de San Ildefonso, to give it its full name, is famous for its magnificent French-style palace. The present palace was commissioned by Philip V (grandson of Louis XIV) and was completed in 1723. A few years later it was remodelled and turned into a minature of Versailles. The main façade of the palace faces the gardens. Inside are a series of elegant rooms and galleries decorated in the rococo style. On the first floor are the sumptuous Throne Room and the Royal Bedroom. Outstanding is the magnificent collection of Spanish and Flemish tapestries.

Its extensive gardens feature terraces, sculptures, ponds and woodlands, centred around a series of baroque fountains, which are spectacular when operational.

▶ *Continue to Segovia.*

7 Segovia, Segovia
The aqueduct was built by the Romans in the 1st century AD, and is still used for conveying water from the neighbouring sierras to the town. It is considered one of the most impressive monuments of its kind and is a prominent landmark of Segovia. It consists of huge granite blocks held together by butterfly ties

formed by molten lead, and
features 118 arches, 43 of which
are double-tiered.

Segovia is also famous for
the view of its magnificent
Alcázar. This was first built in
the 12th century and remodelled later. A pathway leading
down to the aqueduct offers
wonderful views of the Alcázar
silhouetted against the sky, and
further views over the countryside. Within the Roman walls

are the old quarters, with a small
main square, picturesque streets
and elegant façades.

On the highest point of the
town is the cathedral, an elegant
structure built in the same
mellow-coloured stone, with a
tall square tower and pinnacles.
It was built between 1525 and
1593 and is a fine example of
late-Gothic art. Its large interior
is noted for its brilliant stained-
glass windows, impressive

Like something from a fairy-tale,
the Alcázar at Segovia stands
silhouetted above the town

sculptures and finely decorated
altars. The 15th-century cloister
was part of the original cathedral, which was destroyed in the
16th century but was reconstructed at a later date. A collection of 17th-century Flemish
tapestries is housed in the chapter house. Other places to visit

are the Capilla de Vera Cruz,
the Monasterio El Parral and
the 12th-century Iglesia de San
Martín, in the charming Plaza
San Martín.

[i] *Plaza Mayor 10*

▶ *Take the N110 northeast. At
Matabuena take the unclassified road left to Pedraza.*

Ordinary life continues beneath the
Roman aqueduct at Segovia

8 **Pedraza,** Segovia
Entry to this old walled village
is through the Puerta de la Villa
(town gate), which leads straight
to the delightful Plaza Major. A
stroll through its quaint narrow
streets and hidden corners will
take you past many fine build-

BACK TO NATURE

The Sierra de Guadarrama forms the northern part of the great Central Cordillera, which sweeps across the Castilean plains west of Madrid. This is a beautiful area of wooded mountains, valleys and rivers, with several tributaries of the Tajo and the Duero rising in the north-eastern peaks. The area serves as nesting grounds for a number of birds of prey, including imperial eagles, griffons and black vultures, goshawks, red kites and buzzards. Much of the region is covered with pine forests, among which you may find plants such as Pyrenean broom, bluebells and woodrushes.

9 Sepúlveda, Segovia
This attractive old town still has the remains of Roman fortifications. The focal point is the pleasant Plaza Major, which is overlooked by the old Ayuntamiento. Behind are the ruins of a castle. A walk around town reveals a number of interesting buildings in what is known as the Sepúlveda-Romanesque style. Up the hill is the ancient Iglesia del Salvador. Dating back to the 11th century, it features a galleried portico and separate belfry.

RECOMMENDED WALKS

You can do a lot of walking in the region of the Sierra de Guadarrama. The Valle de la Acebeda, in particular, offers a number of attractive walks.

▶ *Take the SG233 and SG911 east to join the N110. Turn left on this road to Riaza.*

10 Riaza, Segovia
Riaza is a picturesque little summer resort with ancient walls, old streets, arcades and

ings bearing coats of arms from bygone days. In the 16th century François I, King of France, and his son were imprisoned in the huge castle standing atop a massive rock.

▶ *Leave Pedraza to the north-west. At La Velilla turn right and take the regional road northeast to Sepúlveda.*

elegant mansions, which centre around its attractive main square. In the parish church is a notable pietà.

▶ *Take the N110 southwest to join the A1-E05. Turn left and continue south to Buitrago.*

11 Buitrago del Lozoya, Madrid
The small medieval town of Buitrago was once the domain of the noble Mendoza family, who wielded much power in Spain in former times. Access to the old town of narrow streets is through a gate in the ancient walls that surround it. To one side of the town is the castle.

▶ *Continue south on the A1-E05. At Lozoyuela turn left on to the M131 to Torrelaguna.*

FOR HISTORY BUFFS

Between Riaza and Buitrago the road climbs up to Puerto de Somosierra. Here in 1808, Spaniards defending the pass were defeated by a force of Polish lancers under Napoleon, thus clearing the way for his troops, who were able to advance to Madrid, which they entered five days later.

12 Torrelaguna, Madrid
Torrelaguna was the birthplace of the wife of San Isidro Labrador, patron saint of Madrid, and of Cardinal Cisneros, founder of the University of Alcalá de Henares, which was later moved to Madrid. Around the arcaded Plaza Mayor are the elegant Ayuntamiento and some fine palaces and mansions. An outstanding monument is the beautiful Gothic Iglesia de Santa María Magdalena.

▶ *Continue south on the M131. Turn right on to the M129, then rejoin the A1-E05 and return south to Madrid, 55km (34 miles).*

Remote Lands
of the West

Cáceres is one of Spain's hidden secrets, yet it has much to offer. The Celts, Romans and Visigoths have all been here and left their mark. The Plaza Santa María is a lovely square, lined with the golden façades of fine buildings, and the old quarters hold a wealth of treasures.

2/3 DAYS • 516KM • 321 MILES

ITINERARY

CÁCERES	►	Trujillo (47km-29m)
TRUJILLO	►	Guadalupe (83km-52m)
GUADALUPE	►	Mérida (132km-82m)
MÉRIDA	►	Badajoz (62km-39m)
BADAJOZ	►	Alburquerque (45km-28m)
ALBURQUERQUE	►	Valencia de Alcántara (35km-22m)
VALENCIA DE ALCÁNTARA	►	Arroyo de la Luz (92km-57m)
ARROYO DE LA LUZ	►	Cáceres (20km-12m)

⌐i⌐ *Plaza Mayor 3*

▶ Take the **N521** east to Trujillo.

❶ Trujillo, Cáceres

The old town of Trujillo is of great historical interest and has strong associations with the discoveries and conquests of the New World. It is sometimes referred to as the 'Cradle of the Conquistadores', as a number of leading explorers and conquistadores were born here. The most famous was Francisco Pizarro (1475–1541), who overthrew the mighty empire of the Incas and conquered Peru (1531–4), bringing untold wealth to Spain. He married an Inca princess, but was eventually killed in his own palace by compatriots.

Other natives of Trujillo who have their place in history include Alonso de Monroy, known for his exploits in Chile; Francisco de Orellana (who departed in 1542 to explore the jungles of the Amazon); Diego de Paredes (nicknamed the 'Samson of Extremadura' for his physique), whose involvement was with Venezuela; and Hernando de Alarcón, who explored California. The discovery of the Americas in 1492 and subsequent explorations put Trujillo on the map, and the town flourished during the Golden Age of Spain.

The main square, Plaza Mayor, is one of Trujillo's most attractive features. A splendid equestrian statue pays tribute to Pizarro. The monument in bronze (erected in 1927) is the work of the American sculptors Charles Runse and Mary

Southwestern Spain's hot climate makes eating at an outdoor café part of every holiday

Harriman. The square is built on different levels, connected by broad steps and lined with beautiful portals and façades. Of special interest is the Palacio de los Marqueses de la Conquista. This was built by Hernando Pizarro, brother of the Conquistador, who also went to seek his fortune in Peru, but later returned to his native lands. It is a magnificent palace built in the Plateresque style and noted for its elaborate window grilles and beautiful corner balcony.

Other buildings of special interest include the Palacio de los Duques de San Carlos, another palace built by the Pizarro family, and the Palacio de Orellana-Pizarro, which features an attractive courtyard adorned with the coats of arms of the Pizarros and the Orellanas.

The old part of town is a fascinating jumble of streets and alleyways, lined with many elegant mansions bearing coats of arms. A walk up narrow cobblestoned streets leads to the lovely 15th-century Gothic Iglesia de Santa María la Mayor. It features a Romanesque bell tower and has an attractive interior, which contains the tomb of Diego García de Paredes, born here in 1466. A Romanesque figure of the Virgin of La Coronada may be seen in the 13th-century Iglesia de

Santiago. At the top of the town is the old castle, which was built by the Moors on Roman foundations. A wall shrine with the figure of the patron saint, Nuestra Señora de las Victorias, lies above the main gate, known as El Triunfo (The Triumph). There are wonderful panoramic views from the castle of the surrounding landscapes of the Extremadura.

⌐i⌐ *Plaza Mayor s/n*

BACK TO NATURE

The Parque Natural de Monfragüe lies to the northeast of Cáceres, and is a vast area of great rugged peaks, deep gorges and forests, watered by the River Tagus, which cuts right through it. The area is rich in flora and fauna and is a breeding ground for a great variety of birds. Among the many birds of prey that make their home here are the imperial eagle, black vulture, peregrine and several species of owl. Many animals, including deer, wild boar, moufflon and even the elusive Spanish lynx, live in the area.

FOR CHILDREN

Children can enjoy boating on the lakes in the region. A good choice would be the Embalse de Alcántara, which is northeast of Cáceres and provides facilities for various watersports.

▶ Take the **EX208** southeast.
At Zorita take the **EX102**
east to Guadalupe.

---

2 **Guadalupe,** Cáceres

The main attraction of
Guadalupe is the monastery, a
fortress-like structure of battlements and turrets in mellow
stone lying high up above the
little village of Guadalupe. The
monastery was originally built
by Alfonso XI for the
Hieronymites, who lived here
between the 14th and 19th
centuries. Since 1928 it has
been occupied by monks of the
Franciscan order. The church
contains the much-venerated
statue of the Black Virgin,
known as La Virgen Morena,
whose headdress is richly
encrusted with gems. The
sanctuary has long been an
important pilgrimage centre,
and religious festivals take place
here on 8 and 30 September
and 12 October, the day of La
Hispanidad (Day of the
Discovery of the Americas).

[i] *Plaza Mayor s/n*

▶ Rejoin the **EX102** and take
the **A5-E90** from Miajadas
southwest to Mérida.

3 **Mérida,** Badajoz

Important Roman remains are
the major attraction of Mérida.
The original town of *Augusta
Emerita* dates back to the 2nd
century AD and was named after
its founder, the governor
Augustus. It flourished under

*The Roman theatre at Mérida is
still used for performances*

the Romans and was then ruled
by the Moors between 713 and
1229, when it was taken by the
Catholic King Alfonso IX.

The Teatro Romano is most
impressive. The original theatre
was built by Agrippa, son-in-law
of Augustus, and rebuilt in the
2nd century BC, after it had
been destroyed by fire, with a
seating capacity for some 6,000
spectators. The theatre provides
a magnificent setting, and plays
are staged here in the summer.
The arena dates back to the 1st
century BC and it is believed the
chariot races that took place
here were watched by up to
14,000 people. Below the arena
are traces of the Casa Romana
del Anfiteatro (Patrician Villa),
with faintly visible signs of the
old pavements and parts of the
walls, showing mosaic decorations. The Museum of Roman
Art houses a fine collection of
Roman, Gothic and Moorish
objects, Roman sculptures,
mosaics, coins and pottery.

The Alcazaba was built by
the Moors in the 9th century on
an original Visigoth building,
later converted into a monastery.

Spanning the River
Guadiana, the Puente Romano
is an impressive structure

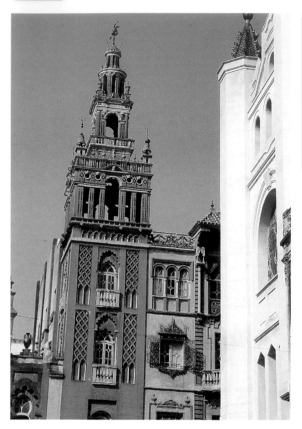

The Plaza de la Soledad in Badajoz, a frontier town which has endured battles and sieges in many wars

extending for 792m (866 yards) with 64 arches. The bridge is an important feature of Mérida, along with the Acueducto Romano, which is another outstanding structure. The bridge over the small River Albarregas is also Roman.

Mérida has a pretty main square, the Plaza de España, which is lined with arcades and overlooked by the Iglesia de Santa María (13th–15th century). To the northwest is the Arco de Trajano, a Roman triumphal arch, which stands 13m (43 feet) high and was once the town's north gate.

[i] *Avenida J Alvarez Saenz de Buruaga s/n*

▶ *Continue on the **A5-E90** west to Badajoz.*

4 Badajoz, Badajoz
Badajoz, capital of the province of the same name, is set on the banks of the River Guadiana, not far from the Portuguese border. It was called *Colonia Pacensis* by the Romans and received its present name from the Moors. A small Moorish kingdom was established here, until it fell to the Catholic King Alfonso IX of León in 1229.

FOR CHILDREN

The Roman ruins at Mérida bear no resemblance to a boring, dusty museum. Here you can really imagine gladiators fighting in the awesome amphitheatre.

Over the years its strategic position, so close to Portugal, caused the town to be involved in many bitter battles during the various European wars.

The town's focal point is the Plaza de España, which is overlooked by the 13th-century Gothic Catedral de San Juan (St John). It has a fortress-like tower and a 17th-century Renaissance façade and doorway. There are fine old tapestries in the sacristy and a splendid gold and silver monstrance on display in one of the chapels.

The town is overlooked by the old Moorish Alcazaba, from which there are good views. The 16th-century Palacio de la Diputación contained within the Alcazaba, now houses the Museo Arqueológico Provincial, which has an extensive collection of archaeological finds from the region. The Puente de Palmas is a 16th-century granite bridge with 32 arches over the River Guadiana.

[i] *Passaje de San Juan s/n*

▶ *Take the **EX100** north. Branch off on the **EX110** and travel north to Alburquerque.*

5 Alburquerque, Badajoz
A drive over the mountain pass of Los Conejeros will bring you to the village of Alburquerque, which is dominated by the remains of a massive 13th-century castle, once the scene of fierce fighting between the Portuguese and the Moors. A climb up to the castle ruins

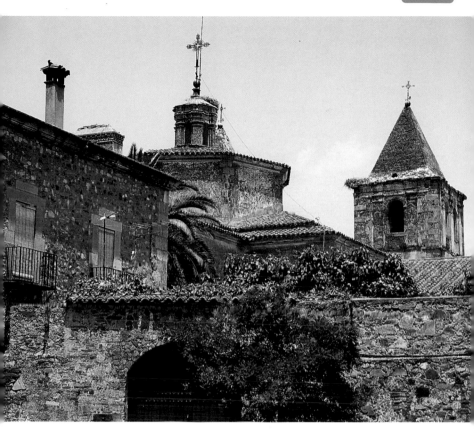

offers, as you would expect, fine
views of the surrounding countryside. The village down below
is surrounded by ancient walls
and well worth strolling around.
It has two interesting churches:
the 13th-century Gothic Iglesia
de Santa María del Mercado and
the parish church of San Mateo,
in the Gothic-Renaissance style.

▶ *Continue on the EX110 and
take a left turn to Valencia
de Alcántara.*

6 Valencia de Alcántara,
Cáceres
This little frontier town serves
as a customs post for travellers
to and from Portugal, 14km (8½
miles) away. It is a very pleasant
town, with old walls and the
ruins of a 13th-century Moorish
castle. Two churches of special
interest are the 13th-century
Iglesia de la Encarnación, which

has a very fine Gothic façade,
and the 16th-century Iglesia
de Nuestra Señora del Roca-
mador, whose Christ figure
has been ascribed to the artist,
Berruguete.

A number of dolmens have
been discovered in the area,
signifying the presence of
prehistoric man.

▶ *Take the N521 east and turn
left to Arroyo de la Luz.*

7 Arroyo de la Luz, Cáceres
On the way here you might like
to make a detour to Alcántara,
which features a famous Roman
bridge over the gorge of the
River Tajo. The bridge dates
back to AD 106 and is an
impressive structure of huge
dimensions.

The charming little town of
Arroyo de la Luz is an important
pottery centre for the region. Its

The Plaza San Jorge, Cáceres, a
town full of beautiful unspoilt
Gothic and Renaissance buildings

main building of interest is the
Iglesia de la Asunción, which
has a splendid Gothic portal and
contains a notable carved
retable, a work of the artist Luis
Morales, a native of Badajoz.

▶ *Rejoin the N521 and return
to Cáceres.*

SCENIC ROUTES

This region is an area of arid,
brown-coloured lands, with
bare rugged mountains and dry
valleys, combined with fertile
lands. One of the most sceni-
cally attractive areas is along
the C530 from Alburquerque
to Valencia de Alcántara.

Historical Cities
& Cathedrals

Salamanca has the oldest university in Spain and many lovely buildings of which those in the Plaza Mayor are among the most attractive, topped by the Ayuntamiento. From the left bank of the River Tormes there is a splendid view of the town across the Roman bridge.

2/3 DAYS • 579KM • 361 MILES

❶ Villanueva de Cañedo,
Salamanca

Make a short detour to visit the 13th-century Castillo del Buen Amor, an old fortified palace with large circular towers, now a hotel. It has an impressive interior with a fine Mudéjar coffered ceiling and inner patio.

▶ *Rejoin the **N630** and continue north to Zamora.*

❷ Zamora, Zamora

Zamora was long under Moorish domination, and was the scene of many battles between the Moors and the Christians, during which 'El Cid', conqueror of the Moors, played an important role. The cathedral stands near the right bank of the River Duero. It was built between 1151 and 1174 and is largely Romanesque, with a square tower and an impressive Byzantine-style cupola. Some splendid sculptures adorn the Puerta del Obispo (Bishop's Door). Inside, the aisles are Romanesque-Gothic. In the Capilla Mayor (Main Chapel) is a notable

RECOMMENDED WALKS

There are some beautiful areas for walking in the Sierra Peña de Francia, to the south of Salamanca. It offers superb mountain scenery, together with woods, lush green valleys and picturesque little villages dotted about the countryside. Much of the route follows the course of the River Duero, where you can take some time off and stroll along its banks. Around Tordesillas there are pleasant pathways along the river shaded by trees.

ⓘ *Casa de las Conchas, Rua Mayor*

▶ *From Salamanca take the **N630** north for 21km (13 miles) and branch right on to a private road, following signs for Villanueva de Cañedo.*

Top: the Ayuntamiento at Salamanca looks out over the famous Plaza Mayor. Right: the tower of the new cathedral

15th-century altarpiece and several impressive tombs. The cloister houses a museum that among other exhibits has a collection of 15th- to 17th-century Flemish tapestries.

The little 12th-century Iglesia de Santa Magdalena is a fine example of the Romanesque style of architecture that was most evident in Zamora in the 12th century. Sculpted *pasos* (or floats) which are paraded during Zamora's impressive Holy Week processions can be seen in the Museo de la Semana Santa. The 12th-century Iglesia de San Cipriano is noted for its finely decorated façade.

Standing on the Plaza Mayor are the 17th-century Ayuntamiento and the Gothic Iglesia de San Juan, which has attractive paintings around the altar. There is a good view of the town from the Puente Viejo (old bridge).

SCENIC ROUTES

Much of this itinerary offers interesting rather than spectacular scenery. One of the most attractive sections of the drive is between Zamora and Toro on the N122, which follows the course of the River Duero, offering pleasant views.

ℹ️ *Calle Santa Clara 20*

▶ *Take the N122 east. Join the A62-E80 at Tordesillas and continue northeast to Valladolid.*

3 **Valladolid,** Valladolid
The busy industrial town of Valladolid lies in the heart of the 'Meseta Central' plateau, in an area of flat landscapes. In the centre, near the Plaza Mayor, is the cathedral. This was started in 1580 on a grand scale by the renowned architect Juan de Herrera. Building continued in the 18th century under Alberto Churriguera, but the cathedral was never completed. Of special note is an impressive

16th-century high altar by the sculptor Juan de Juni.

Adjoining the cathedral is the Museo Episcopal, which contains religious relics, jewellery and a magnificent silver monstrance in the shape of a temple, made by the great Toledo craftsman, Juan de Arfe.

The former Colegio de San Gregorio (St Gregory's College) was built between 1488 and 1496. It has an Isabelline-Gothic façade carved with elaborate decorations including coats of arms. The Museo Nacional de Escultura Policromada on the first floor has an impressive collection of Spanish sculptures, including works by several of Spain's prominent 16th- and 17th-century artists.

Also worth a visit is the small Museo Oriental, which houses an attractive collection of art brought to Spain by missionaries from China and the Phillippines. The 12th- to 14th-century Iglesia de Santa María la Antigua is the oldest church in Valladolid and features a fine Romanesque tower. The 13th-century Iglesia de San Pablo has a superbly decorated façade, flanked by two quite simple towers. Valladolid university, a venerable institution founded in the 14th century, has a fine building which delights in a magnificent 18th-century baroque façade.

FOR HISTORY BUFFS

Literary experts might be interested in making a special visit to the Casa de Cervantes in Valladolid, away from the centre of town, where the famous author of *Don Quixote* lived between 1603 and 1606. The house has been well preserved, and contains a small museum where you can visit the room thought to have been the writer's study and look at one of his manuscripts on display.

SPECIAL TO...

The town of Valladolid is surrounded by an important wine-growing region, which stretches south towards Salamanca and takes in part of the province of León to the north. The best-known wines are those of La Nava, Roa and Peñafiel, which can be either red or white and tend to be fairly strong, and the heavy red wines of Toro which are grown further west. During the month of October you can make a little tour of the area, following the traditional 'Routes of the Wine'.

ℹ️ *Acera de Recoletos s/n*

▶ *Continue on the A62-E80. Branch off left on to the N611 to Palencia.*

4 **Palencia,** Palencia
The Gothic cathedral stands on the small square called Plaza Santa, just off the Plaza Mayor. It was built between 1321 and 1516 on the ruins of a Romanesque chapel erected by Sancho the Great. The interior is decorated in a mixture of Gothic, Isabelline, Plateresque and Renaissance styles. Some fine sculptures include works by Gil de Siloé and Simon of Cologne. The Capilla Mayor (main chapel) contains a magnificent main altarpiece with paintings by Juan of Flanders. The Chapel of the Holy Sacrament, behind the main chapel, features a notable retable by Valmaseda. Among many valuable objects in the Treasury is a beautiful 16th-century silver custodia by Juan de Benavente. A museum in the cloister contains an El Greco painting, together with other fine works of art and some 15th-century sculptures.

The 13th-century Iglesia de San Francisco has a sacristy with fine Mudéjar vaulting. The parish church of San Miguel (13th–14th century) is noted for

The 14th-century Santa Mariá Arch, gateway to Burgos, with the spire of the cathedral beyond

ℹ️ *Calle Mayor 105*

▶ *Leave southeast by the N610. Rejoin the A62-E80; head northeast to Burgos.*

5 Burgos, Burgos

Burgos is famed for its cathedral which is one of the largest and most impressive in Spain. The city was closely associated with the great Rodrigo Díaz de Vivar, better known as 'El Cid

its Romanesque portal and impressive tower. In the 16th-century Convento de Santa Clara (Convent of St Clare) is a reclining figure of Christ. Of special interest is the Capilla de San Bernardo (Chapel of St Bernard), where El Cid's marriage took place.

Campeador' (El Cid the champion). His body found a final resting place in the cathedral here in 1929.

The cathedral was founded by Ferdinand III in 1221, with a second phase of building in the 15th century, when its two tall pinnacles were added by John of Cologne. This imposing limestone structure has a richly decorated Gothic façade. In the transept is the tomb of

El Cid. His wife Ximena lies beside him. There is a fine 16th-century altarpiece in the Capilla Mayor and the finely carved choirstalls also date from the same century. The Capilla del Condestable (Constable Chapel) was designed by Simon de Cologne in 1482 in the Isabelline style. In the centre is an elaborately carved tomb of the Constable and his wife.

A number of beautifully designed chapels are placed around the interior of the cathedral. Of particular note are those of Santa Ana, whose magnificent retable includes the impressive Tree of Jesse, and the Capilla del Santo Christo, which contains a much venerated image of Christ. The 14th-century cloister contains an impressive figure of Christ at the Column by Diego de Siloé (16th-century). In the chapter house are some beautiful 15th- and 16th-century Flemish tapestries. Of special interest is the Capilla de Santa Caterina, which has some interesting historical documents, including the marriage contract of El Cid.

There are numerous monuments to visit in the city. The

Santa María Arch, built in the 14th century, is a masssive entrance gate originally part of the city walls. The 14th-century Iglesia de San Gil is noted for its pietà sculpture and magnificent 13th- to 14th-century altarpiece. The Gothic Iglesia de San Estéban has an impressive doorway and the 15th-century Iglesia de San Nicolás features a notable high altar and lovely vaulting. In the Plaza del General de Primo de Rivera stands an equestrian statue of the hero El Cid, brandishing his sword.

The 15th-century Casa del Cordón is the place where Christopher Columbus was received in 1496 by the Catholic monarchs Ferdinand and Isabella after returning from his second voyage across the Atlantic. King Philip I died here in 1506.

On the outskirts of town are two buildings of religious significance: the Real Monasterio de las Huelgas, (see the textile museum, Gothic cloister and figure of St James), and the Cartuja de Miraflores. Here you can see

Flowers along a little street in the village of Lerma

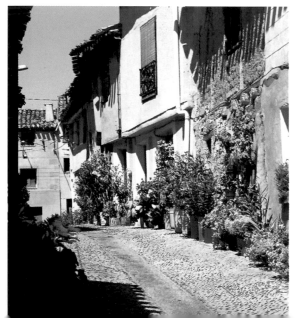

the resplendent tombs of King John and Isabella of Portugal and the Infante Alfonso, whose early death in 1468

FOR CHILDREN

To the Moors he was El Cid (Lord), to the Spaniards El Campeador (heroic warrior). The story of El Cid, a legend in Spain, is an exciting one. Born Rodrígo Díaz de Vivar, near Burrgos in 1043, he was a mercenary soldier fighting for the Christians and the Moors to earn money. Both he and his wife are buried in the cathedral in Burgos, but you can follow his story throughout the country. See his striking equestrian statue in the centre of Burgos.

8 Peñafiel, Valladolid
The splendid silhouette of the Castillo de Peñafiel rises high above the little village of the same name. Built in the 14th century, the castle has 12 round towers and an impressive keep. Other attractions in the village are the Plaza del Coso, where spectators at the bullfights used to watch from the balconies of the surrounding houses, and the 14th-century Iglesia de San Pablo (Church of St Paul), which features some fine Mudéjar architecture as well as Renaissance vaulting over the Capilla Infante (16th-century).

▶ Continue west on the **N122.**
At Valladolid take the **A62-E80** southwest to Tordesillas.

9 Tordesillas, Valladolid
In the monastery here, Juana la Loca (the Mad One), daughter of Ferdinand and Isabella and mother of Emperor Charles V, locked herself away after the death in 1506 of her husband Philip the Fair. She died here in 1555. The monastery, built between the 14th and 18th centuries, has some patios with Mudéjar decorations and a Gothic church with a 15th-century altar.

▶ Return to Salamanca on the **A62-E80.**

resulted in the succession to the throne of his sister, Queen Isabella the Catholic. Above the tombs of King John and Isabella rises a magnificent altarpiece by Gil de Siloé and Diego de la Cruz.

i Plaza Alonso Martínez 7

▶ Take the **A1-E05** to Lerma.

6 Lerma, Burgos
The 17th-century Palacio del Duque de Lerma (Ducal Palace) is one of several elegant mansions built during this period. Of interest is the tomb of Archbishop Cristóbal de Rojas of Sevilla which lies in the 17th-century Colegiata.

▶ Continue on the **A1-E05** south to Aranda de Duero.

Pottery is one of the local crafts in Salamanca; this market offers shoppers a tremendous selection of different shapes and sizes

7 Aranda de Duero, Burgos
The main attraction in Aranda de Duero is the late-Gothic Iglesia de Santa María la Real. Founded in the 15th century by Ferdinand and Isabella, its chief splendour is the magnificent Isabelline doorway with rich gilded decorations. Take a look, too, at the attractive little 13th-century Iglesia de San Juan and the Capilla de le Virgin de las Vinas, which is a popular pilgrimage centre.

i Plaza Mayor s/n

▶ Take the **N122** west to Peñafiel.

BACK TO NATURE

A regional road just after Lerma leads southeast to the ancient Monasterio de Santo Domingo de Silos, which offers an interesting visit. The monks here have made some highly successful recordings. A few miles further on is the Garganta de la Yecla (Yecla Gorges), a fascinating wonder of nature, consisting of a deep gash in the rocks, very narrow in places, with a little stream flowing between. You can follow the course of the gorge.

GREEN SPAIN

This region in the north of Spain consists of the Basque country (Euskadi), Cantábria, Asturias and Galicia. Although there are historical, cultural and administrative divisions, the area shares some common geographical factors. Spain's Atlantic seaboard is wetter than any other part of Spain, resulting in fresh green landscapes. To the north the Bay of Biscay, or 'Mar Cantábrico', has a magnificent coastline of rugged cliffs, inlets and sandy beaches. The Basque mountains start where the western Pyrenees end and give way to the Cordillera Cantábrica, which sweeps across the north. The Cordillera includes the Picos de Europa, and rises to more than 2,500m (8,000 feet). Galicia to the west has a distinctive coastline of rugged cliffs and fiord-like inlets known as the 'Rías Altas' in the north and the 'Rías Bajas' down the west.

The four areas have very different histories. The Basques were a strong, independent race, with a long history of seeking self-determination. Cantábria, further west, has a number of caves containing wall paintings that prove the presence of palaeolithic man. Asturias was once a separate kingdom, and played an essential part at the very beginning of the Reconquest. Galicia was occupied by the Celts as early as the 6th century BC. Santiago de Compostela, where the tomb of St James the Apostle (Santiago) was the goal of pilgrimages, led the development of the area from the 9th century. Galicians have their own language, Gallego, which bears some resemblance to Portuguese.

The Basque country has green pastures, maize-growing areas and fruit and walnut trees. Further south are vast plains with vineyards and cornfields. Cantábria is known for its dairy products, and Asturias is a cider-producing area. Fishing plays an important role in Galicia, and the region is famous for its seafood. In the Basque country many names are written first in Basque and then in Castilian. Galicia has a similar situation with its own language.

North and west Spain is green, the light is softer and old red-roofed houses line the village streets

Tour 22

Tucked away in the far north-western corner of Spain is Galicia, a little world of its own. Its jagged coastline of high cliffs and estuaries is reminiscent of the Norwegian fiords, and its countryside, climate and culture are far removed from the popular images of Spain. This tour is full of surprises, combining green hills, rivers and valleys, Roman towns and a spectacular coast interrupted by many picturesque fishing villages. The highlight is a visit to Spain's most important shrine, which has been the centre of pilgrimages for centuries. The town and its cathedral are among the most important and attractive monuments in the country.

Tour 23

This tour will delight anyone who enjoys spectacular mountain scenery. The route travels south from Oviedo into the Picos de Europa, making a stop in one of the major towns in the area, whose cathedral is known for its stained-glass windows. Following this are a number of visits to charming mountain towns. One of the most attractive parts of the tour is a trip to an important sanctuary in a secluded setting, surrounded by a magnificent panorama of green forested mountains. This is thought of as the birthplace of Christian Spain, as the first steps towards resistance to the Moorish occupation took root here. The tour rounds off with a drive along the northern coast and takes a look at the region's most important port.

Tour 24

Hills, valleys and remote rural villages form the background of this tour, which will appeal to those who love peace and quiet in beautiful surroundings. Exploration of the hinterland will take you through some isolated countryside. Delightfully unspoilt mountain villages dotted about the slopes will give you an insight into a way of life that has seen little change with the passage of time. The coastline here is softer than that of the neighbouring regions, and some of the seaside resorts are very picturesque, with attractive harbours, promenades and splendid sandy beaches. The famous prehistoric caves in the area are of great historical and cultural interest.

Tour 25

The Basque country is characterised in the north by the green landscapes of wooded hills and lush valleys. It has a rugged coastline with magnificent sandy beaches tucked in between spectacular cliffs. This itinerary includes some beautiful drives along the coast and stops in picturesque little resorts. A visit to Spain's busiest northern port provides a contrast to some of the typical small Basque mountain villages you will encounter in the interior of the country. The people and distinctive customs of the Basque country give the region an unmistakable character.

World of
Galicia

3 DAYS • 702KM • 435 MILES

The capital of Galicia, La Coruña was the starting point for King Philip II's 'invincible' Armada sent against England in 1588. The old town is an area of narrow cobbled streets and little squares with notable churches. The Torre de Hércules, a Celtic/Roman lighthouse, offers splendid views.

ⓘ *Casa Parades, Avenida la Marina*

▶ *From La Coruña take the **A6-E70** for 23km (14 miles) to Betanzos.*

La Coruña's harbour where up-to-date offices, traditional buildings and fishing boats rub shoulders

❶ **Betanzos,** La Coruña
Betanzos is a small town of great charm, with medieval walls and steep narrow streets, lined with attractive houses and balconies. It has several notable churches. The 14th to 15th-century Iglesia de Santa María del Azogue has an elegant façade and a fine Flemish altarpiece. The Monasterio de San Francisco was built in the 14th century, in the shape of a cross, by the Conde de Andrade, lord of Betanzos. In the church is his tomb, a vast sepulchre resting on a boar and a bear. Another notable church is the parish church of Santiago, rebuilt in the 15th century by the tailors' guild. Note the fine carving of St James, known as the Slayer of the Moors, over the doorway. Inside are several chapels, one of which contains an impressive retable in Isabelline style.

i *Calle Emilio Romay s/n*

▶ *Continue on the* **A6** *to Lugo.*

2 **Lugo,** Lugo

Massive great slate walls
surround the old Roman city of
Lugo. Originally a Celtic settlement, it became a city of some
importance under the Romans,
who called it *Lucus Augusti*.
Much of the old town was
destroyed by fire, first under
the Moors and then the
Visigoths, and it was the scene
of fierce battles during the
Napoleonic Wars. The *murallas*
(town walls) have a perimeter
of over 2km (1¼ miles). They
date back to the 2nd century AD

and were reinforced during the
14th century.

The Plaza de España is the
town's attractive main square. It
is lined with elegant buildings
and is enhanced by a fountain
in the centre, with a statue of
Hispaña. The Ayuntamiento on
the east side of the square has
an impressive rococo façade.

On the western side is the
cathedral. It was first erected in
the 12th century, with alterations and additions continuing
during the 15th and 18th
centuries. Parts of the building
show the Romanesque style,
with traces of French influences
related to the fact that Lugo was
on the route of the French
pilgrims going to Santiago.
Much of the cathedral is Gothic.
It has twin towers and an

impressive 18th-century façade.
Notable features inside are the
rococo altarpiece in the Capilla
Mayor, decorated choir-stalls
and a lovely 18th-century
Gothic cloister. In the south
ambulatory is the wooden
statue of the 'English' Virgin,
which was transported here
from St Paul's Cathedral,
London, during the 16th
century. The museum has a
collection of paintings and religious relics. Worth a visit is the
13th-century Iglesia de Santo
Domingo, which features some
fine Romanesque doorways and
an impressive retable. The
Museo Provincial displays some
interesting ceramics, coins and
regional handicrafts.

i *Plaza Mayor 27–29 (Galerías)*

Part of the Pilgrims' Route to
Santiago de Compostela

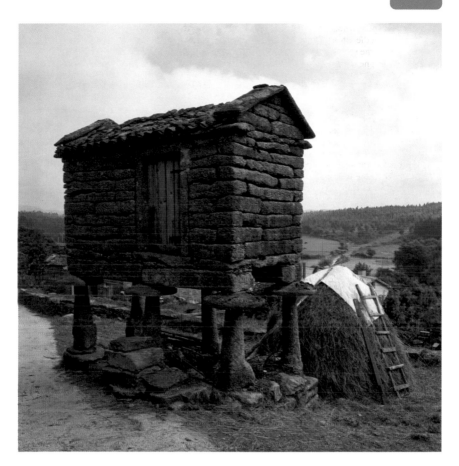

Characteristic grain store (hórreo)

▶ *Take the A6 southeast and after about 6km (4 miles) turn right on to the LU546 and go south to Monforte de Lemos, 65km (40 miles).*

3 Monforte, Lugo

The picturesque little village of Monforte is partly encircled by old ramparts and overlooked by a castle with a huge tower, which once belonged to the Counts of Lemos, hence the village's full name of Monforte de Lemos. Of major interest in the village is the Colegio de la Compañía (Jesuit College), whose church contains a beautiful 17th-century retable by Francisco Moure and three paintings by El Greco. Note, too, the fine 16th-century Renaissance doorways of the former Benedictine Monasterio de San Vicente del Pino.

▶ *Take the N120 southwest to Orense (Ourense).*

4 Orense/Ourense, Orense
Orense was founded by the Romans because of its thermal springs, around which the ancient town developed and

---

RECOMMENDED WALKS

Imagine yourself as a Roman sentry when you follow their route along the path round the top of the 3rd-century walls of Lugo. A walk along the ramparts also offers magnificent views of the surrounding countryside.

SPECIAL TO...

In Galicia you will see many stone buildings constructed on tall granite supports, with a saddle roof and a cross on top. These *hórreos* are mainly used to store maize and were built to protect the crops from humidity and vermin.
Between May and July the wild horses are rounded up in the mountains and brought to special corrals (*curros*) to be branded and have their manes and tails cut. This forms part of a rodeo-type festival known as La Rapa das Bestas (the marking of wild horses), held in towns throughout the region.

from which it got its name, *Aquae Urentes*. In the 6th and 7th centuries it was the seat of Suevian kings. The town suffered damage during the Moorish invasion in 716, but was built up again in the 10th century. Modern Orense is a busy commercial centre, but the old section of the town is delightful. The Palacio del Obispo (Bishop's Palace) stands on the corner of the Plaza Mayor and is noted for its attractive courtyard. This is now the Museo Arqueológico Provincial de Orense with items from prehistoric and Roman times, religious relics and a fine arts section (temporarily closed).

The Catedral de San Martín was first built between the 12th and 13th centuries and renovated in the 16th and 17th centuries after damage caused by wars and earthquakes. It is noted for its triple-arched portal, Pórtico del Paraíso (Paradise), which is richly decorated and preserves some of its original colouring. Note the large 16th-century Gothic retable and the carved choirstalls. An interesting item is the crucifix in the Capilla del Crucificado (Chapel of the Crucified Christ), said to have been found on the coast of western Galicia and brought here in 1330.

Take a look at the fine Gothic arches of the nearby Claustro de San Francisco.

The 13th-century Romanesque Iglesia de la Trinidad, located in the southern section of the town, features two large round towers and a fine Gothic doorway. The Puente Viejo (old bridge), which spans the River Miño, is an impressive structure, dating back to the 13th century. The little chapel in the nearby Campo de los Remedios contains a statue of the Virgen de los Remedios, to which pilgrimages are made.

i *Casa Legoeiro, Ponte Romana*

▶ *Take the* **N120,** *then the* **A52** *west to Vigo.*

5 Vigo, Pontevedra
Vigo is a major naval and fishing port, and one of Galicia's largest towns. Although it has Roman origins, its real growth began in the 16th century when trading links were established with America. During the 15th and 16th centuries it was constantly under threat of attack by English ships seeking to divest the Spanish fleets of their precious cargoes. In 1702 a returning Spanish fleet was virtually destroyed by English and Dutch seamen. Treasures of immense value were seized and the Spanish fleet never recovered from the attack.

Vigo is a pleasant town with old and new sections. The old part, the fishermen's quarters, called the Berbes, can be fun and there is plenty of lively action in the Pescadería (fish market) when business is on. A stroll along the Paseo de Alfonso XIII promenade offers a good view of the harbour. In the new town there are some attractive buildings around the Plaza de Compostela. There is a sweeping view of the town and bay from the Castro (castle) on top of the hill.

i *Calle Teófilo Llorente 8*

Vigo's statue celebrating the wild horses of Galicia

Granite is the building stone of the rocky west of Spain: here, elaborate granite turrets top a circular tower in Pontevedra

▶ *Head northeast towards Redondela. Turn left at the N550 and travel north to Pontevedra.*

6 Pontevedra, Pontevedra
This small provincial capital lies on the wide curve of the banks of the River Pontevedra. It has a bustling new town, and an old section that has changed little with time. The old port was known as *Pontis Veteris* (the old bridge) and parts of the old encirclement walls can still be seen.

The 18th-century Iglesia de la Peregrina (Pilgrimage), in the old quarter, is built in an unusual Italian-inspired baroque style. The Gothic Iglesia de Santa María la Mayor, built by the mariners' guild, has a lovely garden setting and is noted for its impressive baroque façade. The Museo de Pontevedra, housed in two 18th-century mansions, has a varied collection of items which includes treasures from the Celtic Bronze Age and works by

15th-century Spanish *primitives*, in addition to an interesting display of maritime exhibits.

ℹ️ *General Gutiérrez Mellado 1*

▶ *Head west for 35km (22 miles) to Isla de la Toja/A Toxa.*

7 Isla de la Toja/A Toxa, Pontevedra
This island has long had a reputation as the most exclusive summer resort in Galicia. It is linked to the mainland by a bridge. The neighbouring village of O Grove, back on the mainland, has an attractive little fishing harbour, known for its excellent shellfish.

▶ *Retrace the route for 5km (3 miles) from O Grove, then continue on the PO550 east then north to Cambados.*

8 Cambados, Pontevedra
Cambados is a pleasant little village by the sea. The manor house of El Pazo de Fefiñanes, which stands on the grandiose square of the Plaza de Fefiñanes, is a typical example of the Pazo style of architecture, a style unique to Galicia and popular with the nobility of the region in the 17th and 18th centuries. The 17th-century church in the square is built in a similar style to the manor.

▶ *Continue on the PO548 towards Padrón. Turn left on to the N550 just south of the town.*

9 Padrón, La Coruña
Padrón is the place where the legendary vessel carrying the Apostle St James landed. He is said to have preached Christianity in Spain for seven years before returning to Judaea. In the parish church by the bridge is the mooring stone of the boat. The 11th-century Colegiata de Santa María contains impressive tombs.

▶ *Take the N550 north to Santiago de Compostela.*

⑩ Santiago de Compostela, La Coruña

This is Spain's most famous pilgrimage centre, and the cathedral is the town's crowning glory. According to legend, the remains of the Apostle St James were found in 813 on the site of the present cathedral by the bishop of Iria Flavia, who was guided by a star. The name of Compostela is derived from Campus Stellae (Field of the Star). St James was made patron saint of Spain and by the mid-10th century masses of pilgrims were travelling from all over Europe, through France and along the north of Spain, to visit his shrine. The route they took subsequently became known as the Camino de Santiago (The Way to Santiago).

The cathedral, which stands on the Plaza del Obradoiro (or Plaza de España), dominates the whole town. It was built between 1060 and 1211, and is considered to be one of the finest achievements of Romanesque architecture. It is combined with a magnificent baroque façade from the 16th and 17th centuries. The richly carved decorations that adorn the west entrance are the work of the sculptor Fernando Casas y Novoa. A statue of St James stands high on the front gable between two imposing towers. Within the west front entrance is the magnificent Pórtico de la Gloria (Door of Glory), a masterpiece of 12th-century Romanesque work by Mateo. The interior is simple, the main focus being the Capilla Mayor. Above the high altar is a silver shrine with a richly decorated statue of St James, and below is the crypt, which contains the tombs of the Apostle and his two disciples, St Theodore and St Athanasius.

Other notable features are the beautiful wrought-iron grilles, the large Plateresque cloister and the finely carved Puerta de las Platerías (Goldsmith's Door). The museum and treasury contain some interesting religious items.

When in the cathedral ask about the Botafumeiro. This is a gigantic incense-burner that is normally kept in the library and brought out on feast days and special occasions. It is hung from the transept dome and is swung from side to side, higher and higher, by eight priests with ropes. This ceremony goes back to the time when large numbers of unwashed pilgrims descended on the cathedral to worship at the shrine of St James and some form of fumigation was necessary.

On the cathedral square are the elegant Renaissance Hostal de los Reyes Católicos, now a *parador* but originally founded by Fernando and Isabella as a hostel for poor pilgims; the handsome Palacio del Obispo (Bishop's Palace); and the 18th-century Ayuntamiento. Other places of interest in Santiago include the seminary of San Martín Pinario, which features an elegant doorway, and the twin-towered Convento de San Francisco. The 18th-century university is noted for its handsome classical façade.

ⓘ *Plaza de Galicia s/n*

▶ *Take the AC543 west to Noia.*

FOR CHILDREN

The Parque Infantil 'La Selva' in Santiago de Compostela is a small park with ramps to climb, a labyrinth to get lost in, chute rides and various amusements to keep the youngsters happy.

---

⑪ Noia, La Coruña

Noia (Noya) is a pleasant little village situated in a large bay, with a few churches and handsome mansions. A notable building is the Casa de los Churrachaos, formerly the home of the local feudal lords.

▶ *Take the AC550 northwest to Cée. Turn left on to the road to Cabo Fisterra.*

The stupendous Cathedral at Santiago de Compostela dominates the old quarter of the city

⑫ Cabo Fisterra, La Coruña

A most fitting end to this tour is a stop at Cabo Fisterra – 'end of the world' – to enjoy the dramatic setting of the lighthouse, poised on top of a great rock jutting out to sea. This is the most westerly point of Spain and was once the 'edge of the unknown'.

▶ *Return to La Coruña on the AC552, 115km (71 miles).*

SCENIC ROUTES

Galicia offers very attractive landscapes of green hills and valleys, with striking coastal scenery. One of the most beautiful parts of the tour is the drive from Santiago to Cabo Fisterra on the C550, where the coast of the Rías Bajas offers magnificent views of cliffs and inlets, wooded hills and sandy beaches.

The Green Belt
of Asturias

Oviedo, the major industrial centre of Asturias, developed in the 8th century as the capital city of the kingdom. In the old part of the town, visit the Gothic Basílica del Salvador (Cathedral) north of the Plaza Mayor. Its south tower rises 82m (270 feet) and offers a splendid view and the Capilla del Rey Casto is the pantheon of the Asturian kings. On Mount Naranco see the two Romanesque churches, successors to King Ramiro's 9th-century summer palace.

2 DAYS • 470KM • 292 MILES

ITINERARY

OVIEDO	▶	**León (121km-75m)**
LEÓN	▶	**Mansilla de las Mulas (17km-11m)**
MANSILLA DE LAS MULAS	▶	**Potes (127km-79m)**
POTES	▶	**Lebeña (10km-6m)**
LEBEÑA	▶	**Covadonga (77km-48m)**
COVADONGA	▶	**Cangas de Onís (11km-7m)**
CANGAS DE ONÍS	▶	**Gijón (78km-48m)**
GIJÓN	▶	**Oviedo (29km-18m)**

the old. It was the capital of the kingdom of León for a period between the 10th and 13th centuries, and fortification walls were built around the city by the Asturian kings. The year 1230 saw the unification of the kingdoms of León and Castile and a loss of status for León. In the Middle Ages it was one of the main staging points for pilgrims travelling to Santiago de Compostela.

The old quarters lead off from the Plaza Mayor, which is surrounded by attractive portals. The cathedral lies to the north of the square. It was built between the 13th and 14th centuries and is a remarkable work of Gothic architecture. The west façade is outstanding, with two great steeples and a central turreted gable, with a

large rose window and three ornately carved doorways. The cathedral is renowned for its superb stained-glass windows, the earliest of which date back to the 13th century and are to be seen in the central choir chapel and the rose windows in the west and north fronts. The Capilla Mayor has an impressive 15th-century Gothic altarpiece with a magnificent painting of the Entombment. The cloister is in the Plateresque style and has notable frescoes.

The Colegiata de San Isidoro dates back to the 12th century and forms part of the ancient ramparts. It features a huge Romanesque tower and

Left: maize drying. Below: a granary worker wearing the traditional special clogs

i Calle Marqués de Santa Cruz 1

▶ From Oviedo take the **AP66** then the **N630** to León.

❶ **León,** León
León lies at the confluence of two rivers, the Torío and Bernesga, and is known for its beautiful cathedral of Santa María de la Regla. As the centre of a thriving mineral industry, the town presents a sharp contrast between the new and

SCENIC ROUTES

This itinerary takes in the famous Picos de Europa, and most of the route passes through magnificent scenery. Between Oviedo and León (N630) the route becomes very attractive after Mieres, with superb views over the beautiful Cordillera Cantábrica (Cantábrian Mountains). The drive from Cistierna to Riaño on the N621 offers magnificent views and continues to Gijón through some of the most spectacular scenery of Asturias, with an outstanding stretch, known as the Cares Route, between Panes and Cangas de Onís.

From the little village of Potes you can explore the Picos de Europa

two impressive doorways. In the Capilla Mayor is a fine 16th-century altarpiece and the remains of St Isidore, to whom the church was dedicated.

A number of handsome buildings are located around the central Plazuela de San Marcelo, including the Ayuntamiento, a splendid building with twin towers.

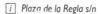 *Plaza de la Regla s/n*

▶ *Take the N601 southeast to Mansilla de las Mulas.*

2 Mansilla de las Mulas, León

Make a brief stop to look around this little village, which is surrounded by walls and has an attractive main square lined with arcades.

▶ *Take the N625, then the N621, northeast through Riaño to Potes.*

3 Potes, Asturias

Potes lies in a valley below the sharp peaks of the Picos de Europa. This little mountain village has great charm, with old wooden houses and a large 15th-century tower, which is now the town hall. It is an excellent centre for excursions into the mountains.

The Monasterio de Santo Toribio de Liébana, 3km (2 miles) west was founded by Franciscans, and became important in the following century when a piece of the True Cross was brought here from Jerusalem. This can be seen in a small chamber beyond the cloister. There is a fine view of Potes and the surrounding mountains from the end of the road.

From Potes make sure you visit Fuente Dé, situated 21km (13 miles) to the west. A road along the River Deva leads through forests and mountains to the Fuente Dé *parador*. Near by is the terminal of a cable-car that takes you up some 800m

Stork's nest on the tower of the Colegiata de San Isidoro in León

(2,625 feet) through magnificent scenery to the top of the rock. There are superb panoramic views from the lookout point here, called the Mirador del Cable, extending over the valley of the River Deva, the village of Potes and the central range of the Picos de Europa.

▶ *Continue on the N621 north to Lebeña, which is reached by bearing right off this road.*

RECOMMENDED WALKS

The Picos de Europa provides countless hikes and walks in beautiful surroundings. A drive south of Arenas de Cabrales brings you to Puente Poncebos, from which you can take a magnificent walk along the Cares Gorge. A pathway cut out from the rock takes you along the gorge, offering fantastic scenery and dizzy views of the swirling waters of the River Cares far below. You need a good head for heights. There are also some fine areas for walking in the beautiful oak forest, Bosque de Muniellos, or around the Lagos de Somiedo.

4 Lebeña, Asturias
The small Mozarab Iglesia de
Santa María de Lebeña lies at
the foot of steep cliffs, among
elegant poplars. It was built in
the 10th century and has been
well preserved. Note the fine
vaulting and horseshoe-shaped
arches, which bear finely carved
Corinthian capitals.

▶ *Rejoin and continue north on
the N621. At Panes take the
AS114 west and at Soto de
Cangas branch left on the
AS262 to Covadonga.*

5 Covadonga, Asturias
The sanctuary of Covadonga is
tucked away in a remote valley.
The setting is superb and the
place exudes an aura of mysti-
cism. The kingdom of Asturias
was founded in this region after
the defeat of Muslim forces in
722 by a Gothic nobleman
called Pelayo, who led the
Asturians to a resounding
victory against the Moors.

The sanctuary is dedicated
to the patron saint of Asturias, la
Virgen de las Batallas (Virgin of
the Battles). Pilgrimages are
made here on 8 September to
venerate her image, which
stands over the altar in the
Santa Cueva (Holy Cave).
Behind are the tombs of Pelayo,
who died in 737, his wife
Gaudiosa and King Alfonso I.

BACK TO NATURE

The Parque Nacional de 'Los
Picos de Europa' is a vast
region of great natural beauty,
known for its magnificent
forests. Watered by the rivers
Cares and Deje, the park contains the two glacier lakes,
Enol and Ercina. It is home to
wild cats, pole-cats, foxes,
wolves, badgers and chamois,
which inhabit the higher
slopes. Among the many different types of birds, you can see
various species of eagles,
owls and magpies, while the
rivers are full of a variety of
fish, which are preyed upon by
secretive otters.

The Basílica was erected at the
end of the 19th century in neo-
Romanesque style and features
two tall spires. The Tesoro de la
Virgen (Virgin's Treasury)
contains some fine treasures,
including a brilliant diamond-
studded crown.

🛈 *Plaza la Basílica*

▶ *Rejoin the AS114 and turn
west to Cangas de Onís.*

6 Cangas de Onís, Asturias
Once the Reconquest of Spain
had been started by the
Christians at the Battle of
Covadonga in 722, the court was
established at Cangas de Onís
and Asturias became known as a
symbol of the Christian resistance against the Moors. Some
elegant old mansions can still be
seen from those glorious times.
Of major interest is the 8th-
century Capilla de Santa Cruz,
which stands on a Celtic burial
mound. The old Puente
Romano (Roman bridge) spans
the gorge of the River Sella.

🛈 *Jardines del Ayuntamiento 2*

▶ *Take the N625 and at
Arriondas continue on the
AS260. On reaching the
N632 turn left to Gijón.*

An ancient bridge across the River
Sella at Cangas de Onís

7 Gijón, Asturias
Before arriving at Gijón you
might like to branch off at
Villaviciosa and take a short
detour along a lovely route to
the charming little fishing
harbour of Tazones.

Gijón is one of the most
important towns in Asturias,
with a busy port. It is situated
between two wide bays with the
old town built on an isthmus,
while the harbour stretches
away to the west. First Roman
and then Visigoth, the town was
known as *Gigia*. It was under
Moorish domination for a period
in the 8th century, after which it
was for a time residence of the
kings of Asturias. Charles V
built the harbour in 1522, and it
provided shelter for the ships of
the Spanish Armada. The
harbour was rebuilt in 1766 and
has since been enlarged several
times. The town was severely
damaged during fighting in the
Spanish Civil War. Much of it
was then rebuilt and has been
enlarged more recently, with the
result that Gijón is essentially a
modern town.

Gijón was the birthplace of
Gaspar Melchor de Jovellanos
(1744–1811), renowned in Spain

as a writer, statesman and economist. In 1794 he founded the Instituto Jovellanos as an institute for education in the natural sciences. This is located to the northeast of the town and now serves as the Provincial College of Industry and Nautical Science. His birthplace, Casa de Jovellanos (in the old part of town), has been restored and is now a museum with paintings by Asturian artists. Overlooking the Plaza del Marqués, near the port, the impressive Palacio de Revillagigedo (15th- to 16th-century), is now home to a contemporary arts centre for exhibitions, dance and drama.

The old fishermen's quarter, known as the Cimadevilla, is built up the slopes of the Santa Catalina hill. Here you will find an area of tiny, narrow streets, old houses, bars and lots of activity. There are fine views of the harbour and the mountains of the Picos de Europa from the top of the hill.

The port is very busy and has large docks that handle commercial business and passenger lines. The harbour has been considerably enlarged and extends to the west for several kilometres. Gijón is also a popular seaside resort. Its long sandy beach, Playa de San Lorenzo, is usually packed in summer.

i *Puerto Deportivo Dársena de Fomento 1*

▶ *Return to Oviedo southwest on the AS18.*

Scenes from the life of Christ on the altar of Oviedo cathedral

Landscapes of
Cantábria

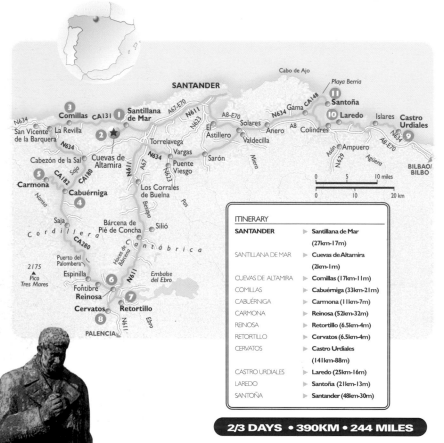

ITINERARY

SANTANDER	▶	**Santillana de Mar** (27km–17m)
SANTILLANA DE MAR	▶	**Cuevas de Altamira** (2km–1m)
CUEVAS DE ALTAMIRA	▶	**Comillas** (17km–11m)
COMILLAS	▶	**Cabuérniga** (33km–21m)
CABUÉRNIGA	▶	**Carmona** (11km–7m)
CARMONA	▶	**Reinosa** (52km–32m)
REINOSA	▶	**Retortillo** (6.5km–4m)
RETORTILLO	▶	**Cervatos** (6.5km–4m)
CERVATOS	▶	**Castro Urdiales** (141km–88m)
CASTRO URDIALES	▶	**Laredo** (25km–16m)
LAREDO	▶	**Santoña** (21km–13m)
SANTOÑA	▶	**Santander** (48km–30m)

2/3 DAYS • 390KM • 244 MILES

Santander's appeal lies mainly in its great sandy beaches and attractive setting, and its good nightlife in summer. It's rise to fame dates back to the early 20th century when it became a favourite resort of the Spanish royal family. The centre was largely rebuilt after being devastated by fire in 1941 and today Santander continues to thrive as a busy port and a popular resort. Its annual summer festival of song and dance adds prestige.

i Mercado del Este

▶ From Santander take the N611 southwest. Turn right on to the CA131 to Santillana de Mar.

❶ Santillana de Mar,
Cantábria

Santillana de Mar is an architectural delight, with beautiful mansions and churches, together with picturesque balconied houses and typical red-tiled roofs. Its little squares and old façades appear like stage settings from the past. Coats of arms on many façades relate to seamen of former times who returned from important voyages of discovery.

A focal point is the Plaza de Ramón Pelayo, which is lined with elegant buildings of the 14th to 16th centuries. The Romanesque Colegiata, one of the loveliest buildings, dates back to the 12th century with fine sculptures in the nave and aisle. The cloister contains a Renaissance alterpiece.

i Jesús Otero 20

▶ From Santillana take the road for 2km (1 mile) to the car-park of the Cuevas de Altamira (Caves of Altamira).

❷ Cuevas de Altamira,
Cantábria

The prehistoric wall paintings that were discovered in the Altamira Caves in the latter part of the 19th century are among the most significant in the world. For conservation reasons, however, the caves

Looking out over the red rooftops of Santillana de Mar

SPECIAL TO...

The festival of La Folia at San Vicente de la Barquera (west of Comillas) on the Sunday after Easter Involves decorated boats, music and celebrations.

---

are now closed to the public. You can visit the Neocueva, which is an exact reproduction of the original cave, and is now open to the general public, and see the workshop where techniques used in original cave paintings are still employed.

The Altamira caves have a depth of 270m (885 feet) and

are most impressive, containing paintings of animals that were hunted by palaeolithic man some 11,000 to 16,000 years ago. The paintings still retain their colours and reveal the unmistakable shapes of bison, deer and wild boars.

More prehistoric animal paintings can be seen in the caves of El Castillo and La Pasiega in Puente Viesgo, south of Torrelavega on the N623.

▶ *Rejoin the CA131 and continue west to Comillas, 17km (11 miles).*

3 Comillas, Cantábria
The little town of Comillas rises up a hill overlooking the sea. The resort has some elegant buildings and a pleasant beach. Of special note is the neo-classical Palacio del Marqués de Comillas, which stands in attractive gardens. In these is also a building known as 'El Capricho' (meaning 'the whim') designed by Antonio Gaudí, architect of the Templo de la Sagrada Familia and other distinctive buildings in Barcelona.

▶ *Take CA131 west to join the N634 and head southeast. Turn south at Cabezón de la Sal on CA180 to Cabuérniga, 33km (21 miles).*

4 Cabuérniga, Cantábria
Take a look round this little mountain town, capital of the valley, with its quaint houses and large wooden balconies.

▶ *Take the CA182 northwest for 11km (7 miles) to Carmona.*

5 Carmona, Cantábria
Carmona is another small village, typical of the area, where the pattern of life has seen little change from the old days. The detour is worthwhile, not only for a glimpse of this picturesque little place, with its Roman gateways and the Puerta de Córdoba, but also for its beautiful surroundings.

SCENIC ROUTES

The road from Cabuérniga to Reinosa travels through the beautiful Cordillera Cantábrica mountains on the CA280, over the passes of Puerto de Tajahierro and Palombera. The N611 from Cervatos up to Torrelavega follows a winding mountain road with many bends before passing through the dramatic Hoces de Bárcena gorge. The drive from Torrelavega on the N634 becomes very attractive again after Solares.

▶ *Return to Cabuérniga and take the CA280 south to Reinosa.*

6 Reinosa, Cantábria
Set high up in the valley of the River Ebro is the little mountain town of Reinosa which has some charming streets and is a popular summer resort.

▶ *Continue south on the N611. Shortly, turn left to Bolmir. East of Bolmir turn right to Retortillo, 6km (4 miles).*

7 Retortillo, Cantábria
Stop here to see the Roman ruins of *Juliobriga*, just outside the village. You can get a good idea of the layout of this fortified village from the bell tower of the ruined church.

RECOMMENDED WALKS

There are plenty of places for walking in the Cordillera Cantábrica. The village of Fontibre (northwest of Reinosa) is a good base for a number of walks, with marked trails you can take in various directions. The Valle de Campo is a beautiful area of poplar trees and lush vegetation, where you will find the source of the Ebro, one of Spain's most important rivers.

▶ *Return by the same route to the N611. Turn left and drive south to Cervatos, just off the road.*

8 Cervatos, Cantábria
The major feature of interest in this small village is the 12th-century Romanesque Colegiata, notable for the carvings that adorn the frieze above the door. Look for the figures of the three monkeys shown covering their ears, eyes and mouth, signifying prudence and wisdom in the beliefs of eastern cultures.

▶ *Take the N611 north. Before Torrelavega take the N634 east to Castro Urdiales.*

9 Castro Urdiales, Cantábria
This attractive little fishing port has been a much-visited summer resort for a long time,

and its popularity dates back to Roman times.

The Gothic Iglesia de Nuestra Señora de la Asunción features an impressive Puerta del Perdón. Visit also the Castillo of Santa Ana (now a lighthouse), the medieval fortress and the Roman bridge.

▶ *Take the coastal road **N634** west to Laredo.*

10 Laredo, Cantábria

The little town of Laredo lies to the east of the wide bay of Santoña. With its pleasant villas and splendid beach it is a popular seaside resort. The old part of the town is picturesque, with some handsome old buildings and cobbled streets. There are ruins of two former monasteries in Laredo, as well as a 13th-century church.

▶ *Continue west on the coastal road and turn right at Cicero for the 5km (3 miles) to Santoña.*

11 Santoña, Cantábria

To the west of the bay is the port of Santoña on a peninsula beneath a steep rock. The town was fortified in earlier times – Napoleon is said to have had plans to conquer it. The Romanesque Colegiata was built between the 12th and 13th centuries. About 2km (1¼ miles) away is the splendid beach of Berria.

▶ *Take the **CA148** southwest to Gama and rejoin the **N634** back to Santander.*

Journey's end for these old fishing boats. Left: the Virgin del Mar ocean beach close to Santander

Exploring the
Basque Country

2 DAYS • 358KM • 222 MILES   San Sebastián (Donostia in Basque) is the provincial capital of Guipúzcoa. The elegant buildings along the promenade are a reminder of the 19th century, when San Sebastián was Spain's most fashionable resort. The Alameda del Boulevard is a lively area of restaurants and shops, while to the west is the busy fishing harbour.

ITINERARY

SAN SEBASTIÁN	▶ Zarautz (26km-16m)
ZARAUTZ	▶ Getaria (4km-2m)
GETARIA	▶ Zumaia (6km-4m)
ZUMAIA	▶ Ondarroa (23km-14m)
ONDARROA	▶ Lekeitio (12km-7m)
LEKEITIO	▶ Gernika-Lumo (23km-14m)
GERNIKA-LUMO	▶ Bilbao (35km-22m)
BILBAO	▶ Vitoria-Gasteiz (66km-41m)
VITORIA-GASTEIZ	▶ Salvatierra (25km-16m)
SALVATIERRA	▶ Tolosa (61km-38m)
TOLOSA	▶ Fuenterrabía/Hondarribia (52km-32m)
FUENTERRABÍA/ HONDARRIBIA	▶ San Sebastián (25km-16m)

i Calle Reina Regente 3

▶ From San Sebastián take the N1 south. Turn right on to the **N634** to Zarautz, 26km (16 miles).

❶ Zarautz, Guipúzcoa
You may like to make a quick stop en route in the picturesque little fishing port of Orio, which lies along the bank of an estuary.

The old harbour at Zarautz (Zarauz in Basque) is backed by the tall Monte de Santa Barbara. It has a splendid beach and is a popular summer resort. Places of major interest are the Gothic/baroque Iglesia de Santa María, the Iglesia de San

---

SCENIC ROUTES

The Cornisa Cantábrica (Cantabrian Corniche) is a magnificent stretch between Zarautz, Getaria and Zumaia on the N634. A zigzagging road follows the coast, offering magnificent views. From Zumaia the drive continues along the coast, on the G1638, with beautiful views, to Lekeitio. The N1 offers some scenic parts after Alsasua, with excellent views over the Puerto de Otzaurte, and there is more beautiful scenery between Tolosa and San Sebastián.

The lovely horseshoe-shaped beach at fashionable San Sebastián is popular with the Spanish

Francisco and the hermitages of San Pelayo and San Pedro. The Torre Lucea and the 15th-century Palacio del Marqués de Narros are also impressive. Zarautz was once an important shipyard. It was here that the *Victoria* was built, between 1519 and 1522, to carry Juan Sebastián Elcano, companion of Magellan, around the world.

i Nafarroa Kalea 23

▶ Continue on the **N634** for 4km (2 miles) to Getaria.

2 Getaria, Guipúzocoa

There is some magnificent scenery as you approach Getaria and a fine view down over the pretty little fishing village which stands on a promontory. The Gothic parish church of San Salvador overlooks the harbour, and has underground tunnels linking the two. Over the breakwater is the little fortified Isla San Anton (known as the 'Ratón de Getaria', mouse of Getaria, for reasons unknown), which rises up steeply to a lighthouse. It offers a rewarding view of the area. The Ayuntamiento contains frescoes describing the voyage around the world of the navigator, Juan Sebastián Elcano, who was born here.

▶ *Continue west for 6km (4 miles) to Zumaia (Zumaya).*

3 Zumaia, Guipúzcoa

Nestling at the foot of the Monte Santa Clara hill is Zumaia, another delightful little resort with a charming harbour and attractive houses.

The Museo de Zuloaga, formerly a monastery, was founded by the great painter Ignacio Zuloaga, and has a superb collection of paintings by Spain's most famous painters including Zuloaga, El Greco and Goya.

▶ *Follow the **N634** and continue along the **GI638** to Ondarroa.*

4 Ondarroa, Vizcaya

You are now in the neighbouring province of Vizcaya. The resort of Ondarroa is set in a bay that is protected by low hills. The town encompasses a combination of attractive old cottages and more modern blocks. It has a sandy beach and a pleasant harbour with lively fishermen's quarters. A Roman bridge, the Puente Romano, spans the river.

▶ *Continue on the same road northwest for 12km (7 miles) to Lekeitio (Lequeitio).*

5 Lekeitio, Vizcaya

Lekeitio is another popular seaside resort of attractive houses and a good beach, which separates the resort area from the fishing port. The 16th-century Iglesia de Santa María is a fine example of Vizcayan Gothic architecture. Narrow cobbled streets lead down to the old part of town. The palaces of Abaróa and Uribarren are particularly elegant buildings.

▶ *Take the **BI2238** west for 23km (14 miles) to Gernika-Lumo.*

6 Gernika-Lumo, Vizcaya

The famous painting, *Guernica*, by Pablo Picasso is a reminder of the terrible event that took place here in 1937 during the Spanish Civil War, when German aircraft bombed the town, killing a large number of people. The town was devastated, but has been rebuilt in the traditional style. Originally displayed in the Museum of Modern Art in New York, Picasso's painting was returned to Spain and now hangs in the Centro de Arte Reina Sofía, in Madrid, together with all the preliminary sketches.

Gernika's former Parliament building, the Casa de Juntas, contains a striking stained-glass window depicting historic scenes. In the adjoining court-

yard you can see the stump of the town's old oak tree, revered as a symbol of Basque independence. In the Middle Ages officials were elected beneath its branches. Near by is a monument commemorating the 1937 attack on the town.

Some 5km (3 miles) north the Cuevas de Santimamiñe wall paintings, believed to date back some 13,000 years, were discovered in 1917.

ⓘ *Artekale 8*

▶ *Take the **BI635** south and join the **N634** west to Bilbao (Bilbo).*

FOR CHILDREN

Children might enjoy a trip on the funicular railway Funicular de Artxanda. This departs from Plaza Funicular and ascends to the village of La Reinata, Monte Archanda, which offers a sweeping view of Bilbao's old dockyards. Many horse-riding excursions into the countryside are available, catering for adults and children. Contact the tourist office in Bilbao for information on the various riding centres to be found in the region.

The rivers of the Basque country end in picturesque harbours like this one at Ondarroa

Two other museums are also worth a visit; the Museo Vasco, for its collection of tombs, arms and carvings, and, over in the new town, the Museo de Bellas Artes, which features works by famous Dutch and Spanish painters of the 15th and 16th centuries.

You can also enjoy a stroll through Bilbao's lively old quarter (Casco Viejo) where the attractively arcaded square (Plaza Nueva) and the Gothic Catedral de Santiago feature among its attractions.

[i] *Plaza del Ensanche 11*

▶ *Return east along the **N634** and take the **N240** south-east for 66km (41 miles) to Vitoria-Gasteiz.*

8 Vitoria-Gasteiz, Alava
Vitoria is the capital of Alava, and of the Basque Country, as well as being the seat of a bishop. A focal point of the old town is the Plaza de la Virgen Blanca, which is surrounded by houses and balconies typical of Vitoria. In the centre is an imposing monument commem-

7 Bilbao (Bilbo), Vizcaya
Bilbao is the capital of the Basque province of Vizcaya and its largest port. Although essentially an industrial town, Bilbao is now home to an outstanding attraction, the Guggenheim Museum. The museum houses an important collection of 20th-century European and American art, including works by Matisse, Brancusi, Modigliani, Picasso, Ernst, Miró and Dalí. Attention is also drawn to the spectacular design of the complex itself, a brilliant creation of gleaming shapes and forms by the Canadian-born architect Frank Gehry.

RECOMMENDED WALKS

Many areas all over the region offer splendid walks, and information is available from the local tourist offices.
In Bilbao a short walk is a climb up the hill from behind the church of San Nicolás de Bari, which brings you to the Gothic-style Begoña Basilica. It was built in 1588 and is the place of worship of Begoña, the patron saint of Bilbao. A *romería* is held here on the first Saturday after 15 August.

SPECIAL TO...

The national sport of the Basque country is *pelota* (also known as *jai-alai*). There are variations, but basically this is a type of ballgame played between four men in a court called a *frontón*, using scoop rackets and a small, hard ball which travels at tremendous speed. The sport is supposed to be the fastest in the world. Each town and village has a court and a team.
The Basque country has its own folklore, including the unusual *aurresku*, a war-like dance, and the *ezpata dantza*, a sword dance, accompanied by flutes and a drum.

orating Wellington's victory over the French at the battle of Vitoria in 1813. Overlooking the square is the 14th-century Iglesia de San Miguel. A stone image of the Virgen Blanca (White Virgin), patron saint of the city, can be seen in a niche on the outside portal. Inside is a fine 17th-century altarpiece by Juan de Velázquez and Gregorio Hernández. The Catedral de Santa María was built between the 14th and 15th centuries in the shape of a Latin cross and is noted for its richly decorated triple-arched tympanums. An impressive *Assumption* can be seen in one of the side chapels. Look out also for a bullfighting scene carved on one of the pillar's capitals.

In the Plaza Santo Domingo near by is the Museo de Arqueología (Archaeological Museum), which displays objects from the Celtiberian and Roman times, among other items. The 14th-century parish church of San Pedro features a fine doorway and impressive sculpted tombs of the Alava family. From the middle of the 15th century, Vitoria was a centre for craftsmen who worked predominantly in the wool and iron trades. The Portalon, built in wood and

BACK TO NATURE

There is an area of great natural beauty in the province of Alava, north of Vitoria, around three artificial lakes. Embalse de Urrunaga (Lake Santa Engracia) is situated along the road from Bilbao to Vitoria. On the slopes of the mountain are the Cuevas de Mairelegorreta, which are well worth a visit. Embalse de Albiña (Lake Albina), east of the N240, lies at the entrance to the Aramayona valley. Further south is Embalse de Ullívari (Lake Ullívari), which stores water in the Gamboa canyon. The lake offers watersports and fishing.

brick, is a remaining example of one of the many trading houses of the medieval and Renaissance times. Other attractive areas are the Plaza del Machete and the Cuchillería (street of cutlery), where you will find the 16th-century Casa del Cordón, noted for its fine Gothic ceiling, and the Bedaña Palace, a 16th-century mansion with a magnificent façade. The new cathedral of María Immaculada, which was consecrated in 1969, has been built in a rather unusual neo-Gothic style.

The industrial town of Tolosa is set amongst the Basque hills

[i] *Plaza General Loma s/n*

▶ *Take the NI to Salvatierra.*

9 Salvatierra, Alava
The little town of Salvatierra was founded by Alfonso X in 1256. It still preserves its medieval streets and parts of the old defensive walls. Its two main churches, those of San Juan and Santa María, have a somewhat fortress-like appearance.

▶ Follow the **NI** *east and then north to Tolosa.*

10 Tolosa, Guipúzcoa

Tolosa was capital of the province of Guipúzcoa for a period in the middle of the 19th century and is now a thriving industrial town (known for the *boinas*, or Basque beret). There are Roman antiquities and ancient buildings of the Templars.

▶ *Continue on the **NI** north, bypassing the centre of San Sebastián, and then east. Turn off north for Fuenterrabía.*

11 Fuenterrabía/ Hondarribia, Guipúzcoa

This little town was a stronghold over a long period of time and consequently the scene of many battles. It is now a popular seaside resort. The remains of its ancient walls are preserved as a national monument and the 12th-century Palacio del Rey Carlos V (now a *parador*) was built as a defence against pirate raids.

There are some lovely views from these ancient walls. Other buildings worth taking a look at are the 16th-century Iglesia de Santa María (mainly Gothic with Renaissance influences), and the 17th-century Ayuntamiento.

A short drive up to the ridge of Monte Jaizquíbel leads to the Santuario de Nuestra Señora de Guadalupe which offers fine views.

▶ *Rejoin the **NI** back to San Sebastián.*

MOTORING IN SPAIN

ACCIDENTS

Road users involved in an accident should mark the presence of their vehicle by placing a warning triangle in front of and behind and try to move it to the hard shoulder or lay-by. The police should be contacted if the accident has resulted in serious casualties. SOS telephone posts are normally available on motorways only. Other roads are patrolled by traffic police. See also **warning triangles**.

BREAKDOWNS

If your car breaks down try to move it to the side of the road, or to a position where it will obstruct the traffic flow as little as possible.

Switch on your hazard warning lights and place a warning triangle at the appropriate distance on the road behind. Bear in mind the prevailing road conditions and, if near or on a bend, the triangle should be placed where it is clearly visible to following traffic.
See also **warning triangles**.

CAR HIRE

If you are not taking your own car, you can make arrangements to hire before departure. Many package holidays include car hire as an option. The main car hire companies are represented in Spain.

If you rent when you get to Spain, look for local firms in the telephone book under *Alquiler de coches* or *Automóviles alquiler*.

To rent a car you need your driver's licence – an international driver's permit is often more useful – and money, or a credit card, for the deposit. If you are leaving cash, the deposit can be quite a significant amount.

There may be a minimum age (often 21, sometimes higher) and a requirement that you have been driving for at least a year with a full licence. Some firms may also impose a maximum age limit.

CHILDREN

Children under the age of 12 are not permitted to travel as front-seat passengers unless using a suitable restraint system. *Note* under no circumstances should a rear-facing restraint be used in a seat with an airbag.

CRASH (SAFETY) HELMETS

Crash helmets are compulsory for motorcyclists.

DIMENSIONS AND WEIGHT RESTRICTIONS

Private cars and towed trailers or caravans are restricted to the following dimensions: height – 4m; width to 2.5m; length – 12m. The maximum permitted overall length of private vehicle/trailer or caravan combination is 12m. Trailers with an unladen weight in excess of 750kg must have an independent braking system.

DOCUMENTS

Licences issued by European Union countries are acceptable (for UK and Republic of Ireland driver's licences should be of the pink EU-type). Visitors from other countries should have an international driving licence, which should be obtainable from the motoring organisations in their home countries.

The minimum age at which visitors from the UK or Republic of Ireland may use a temporarily imported motor-cycle (over 75cc) or car is 18. The holder of an older all green UK licence (in Northern Ireland any licence issued before 1 April, 1991) should consider exchanging it for a new style licence if time allows to avoid any local difficulties. Alternatively these older licences may be accompanied by an IDP (International Driving Permit).

Note The licence of a Spanish driver who needs glasses to drive is endorsed accordingly. Such drivers must carry a spare pair of glasses in their vehicle. It is strongly recommended that visiting motorists should do the same to avoid any misunderstanding with the local authorities. You also require the vehicle's registration document, plus a letter of authorisation from the owner, if not accompanying the vehicle, and the current insurance certificate (a green card, obtainable from your insurance company, is recommended). You are required to display a nationality plate or sticker on the vehicle.

DRINKING AND DRIVING

The laws in Europe regarding drinking and driving are strict and the penalties are severe. The best advice is, as at home, if you drink don't drive.

DRIVING CONDITIONS

Driving is on the right. Tolls are charged on some of the motorways. The surfaces of the main roads vary, but are generally good. Secondary roads are often rough, winding and may be encumbered by slow horse-drawn traffic.

In the Basque area, local versions of place-names appear on signposts together with the national version. In winter snowfalls frequently close many of the roads across the Pyrenees.

Tele Ruta (freephone 900 123505) offers a recorded information service in Spanish on the best routes, roadworks etc.

FUEL

You will find comparable grades of petrol in Spain, with familiar brand names along the main routes. It is wise to keep the tank topped up, particularly in remote areas.

Remember when calculating mileage per litre (gallon) that the extra weight of a caravan or roof rack increases the petrol consumption. It is best to use a locking filler cap.

INSURANCE
Comprehensive insurance, which covers you for some of the expenses incurred after a breakdown or an accident, is strongly advised.

LIGHTS
Full headlights are prohibited in built-up areas. Motorcyclists must use dipped headlights during the day. A replacement set of bulbs is required.

MOTORING CLUB
The Real Automóvil Club de España (RACE), which has its headquarters at Calle Isaac Newton, Technological Park of Madrid, 28760 Madrid tel: 915 94 72 78, fax: 915 94 73 19, is associated with local clubs in a number of provincial towns. The office hours of the RACE in Madrid are 8.30–5.30 Monday–Thursday and 8.30–2.30 Friday during the summer (15 June–15 September), and for the rest of the year 8.30–5.30 Monday–Friday.

PARKING
Car parks are called *aparcamientos* in Spanish and are usually signposted in cities and towns with a large white P on a blue background. In larger towns and cities, a car park may be the only, and the best, option as street parking can be a real problem and restrictions are not always easy to understand.
• Street parking is generally on a meter, usually limited to two hours, and expensive for a longer stay.
• Carry coins to feed the meters.
• Free on-street parking may be found further from a town centre, but always check for restrictions usually mounted on lampposts.
• Never leave anything of value visible in the car, especially if parking on back streets.
• City car parks are often located underground, accessed via ramps that can be narrow and steep.
• Charges vary widely from city to city and from one car park to another in the city. A general guideline is that the nearer to

the historical area they are, the more expensive they become.

POLICE
There are three different police organisations in Spain dealing with different aspects of public order.

Policía Municipal whose main responsibility is urban traffic, are the local police. They are identifiable by their blue uniforms and white checked bands on their vehicles. Policía Nacional, who wear grey uniforms and berets, deal with law and order and national security. Crimes should be reported to the police station (*comisaría*). Guardia Civil, who are responsible for border posts, policing country areas and the coast and highway patrols, wear olive green uniforms. There are also special Basque police in the Basque country, recognisable by their red berets.

ROADS
The surfaces of the main roads vary, but are good. The roads are winding in many places, and at times it is not advisable to exceed 48–56kph (30–35mph). Secondary roads are often rough and you can come across some unexpected bad patches. Look out for the sign '*carretera en mal estado*' ('road in poor condition').

Spain has a good network of motorways and dual carriageways. About half of these are toll roads (*autopistas*) and the rest are free (*autovías*).

Emergency telephones are located at regular intervals on all Spanish motorways and dual carriageways.

Unfamiliar Road Signs
Aduana Customs
Alto! Pare Stop
Altura máxima Maximum height
Autovía Motorway
Calzada Deteriorada Bad road
Carretera cortada Road closed
Ceda el Paso Give way
Cuidado Caution
Curva Peligrosa Dangerous bend
Despacio Slow
Desviacion/Desvio Diversion

Direccion Unica One way
Entrada Entry
Estacionamiento de Automoviles Car-park
Estacionamiento Prohibido No parking
Obras Road works
Paso Prohibido No entry
Peatones Pedestrians
Peligro Danger
Prohibido adelantar No overtaking
Salido Exit
Zona peatonal Pedestrian zone

ROUTE DIRECTIONS
The following abbreviations are used as prefixes to identify Spanish roads.
A for *Autopistas* and *Autovías*
C for *Comarcal*
N for *Nacional*

SEAT BELTS
Seat belts are compulsory for the driver and front passenger. Middle- and rear-seat passengers must use seat belts if the vehicle is fitted with them.

SPEED LIMITS
Built-up areas 50kph (31mph). Other roads 90kph (55mph) or dual carriageways and roads with overtaking lanes 100kph (62mph). Motorways 120kph (74mph).

TOLLS
Tolls are payable on many motorways (*autopistas*) in Spain. Tickets are issued on entry, and payment varies according to distance and type of vehicle.

WARNING TRIANGLES
In the event of accident or breakdown, the use of two warning triangles is compulsory for vehicles over 3,500kg (3 tons, 8cwt, 100lb) and passenger vehicles with more than nine seats (including the driver's). These must be placed on the road 50m (55 yards) in front of and behind the vehicle and be visible from at least 100m (110 yards). It is required that all vehicles (except those with two-wheels) carry triangles to avoid any misunderstandings with the local authorities.

ACCOMMODATION AND RESTAURANTS

On the following pages is a selection of hotels (◇) which can be found along the routes of each tour, along with suggestions for restaurants (⦿) where you can take a break.

Hotel Prices
The hotels listed are grouped into three price categories based on a nightly rate for a double room with breakfast:
€ up to €80
€€ €80–140
€€€ over €140

Restaurant Prices
The restaurants are also in three price categories, based on a three-course meal with house wine, for one person. Some are located in the hotels listed:
€ up to €15
€€ €15–30
€€€ over €30
Unless otherwise stated, restaurants are open daily for lunch and dinner.

TOUR 1
BARCELONA, Barcelona
◇ **Astoria €€€**
París 203, 08036 Barcelona
(tel: 932 09 83 11);
www.derbyhotels.es
117 rooms.
◇ **Claris €€**
Carrer de Pau Claris 150, 08009 Barcelona
(tel: 934 87 62 62);
www.derbyhotels.es
124 rooms.
◇ **Continental €€**
Rambla de Canaletes 138, 08002 Barcelona
(tel: 933 01 25 70);
www.hotelcontinental.com
35 rooms.
◇ **Husa Oriente €€€**
Ramblas 45, 08002 Barcelona
(tel: 933 02 25 58);
www.husa.es/hoteloriente
142 rooms.
⦿ **Agut d'Avignon €€€**
Trinitat 3, 08002 Barcelona
(tel: 933 02 60 34)
Traditional Catalan dishes.

⦿ **La Bombeta €€**
Carrer de La Maquinista 3, 08003 Barcelona
(tel: 933 19 94 45)
Seafood in a fishermen's bar.
⦿ **Los Caracoles €€**
Escudellers 14, 08080 Barcelona
(tel: 933 02 31 85).
Classic Catalan dishes.
⦿ **L'Illa de Gràcia €**
Carrer de Sant Domènec 19, 08012 Barcelona
(tel: 932 38 02 29)
Simple healthy food.

MONTSERRAT, Barcelona
◇ **Abat Cisneros €€**
Plaça del Monestir, 08199 Montserrat
(tel: 938 77 77 01)
56 rooms.

CARDONA, Barcelona
◇ **Parador de Cardona €€**
Castell de Cardona s/n, 08261 Cardona
(tel: 938 69 12 75);
www.parador.es
54 rooms.

TOUR 2
BARCELONA, Barcelona
◇ **Mesón de Castilla €€**
Valldonzella 5, 08002 Barcelona
(tel: 933 18 21 82);
www.mesoncastilla.com
57 rooms.
◇ **San Agustí €€**
Plaça de San Agustín 3, 08001 Barcelona
(tel: 933 18 16 58);
www.hotelsa.com
75 rooms.
⦿ **Els Quatre Gats €€**
Montsió 3-bis, 08002 Barcelona
(tel: 933 02 41 40)
Closed Aug.
Traditional Catalan dishes.

TOSSA DE MAR,
Girona/Gerona
◇ **Diana €**
Plaza de Espanya 6, 17320 Tossa de Mar
(tel: 972 34 18 86);
www.diana-hotel.com
21 rooms.

◇ **Pensión Cap d'Or €**
Passeig de Vila Vella 1, 17320 Tossa de Mar
(tel: 972 34 00 81)
Closed Nov–Mar.
11 rooms.

GIRONA, Girona/Gerona
◇ **Condal €**
Joan Maragall 10, 17002 Girona
(tel: 972 20 44 62).
38 rooms.
◇ **Peninsular €**
Avenida Sant Francesc 6, 17001 Girona
(tel: 972 20 38 00);
www.novahotels.com
45 rooms.
⦿ **Albereda €€**
Albereda 7, 17002 Girona
(tel: 972 22 60 02)
Ampurdan cuisine.
⦿ **Casa Marieta €**
Plaça Independencia 5–6, 17001 Girona
(tel: 972 20 10 16)
Traditional Catalán cooking in modern surroundings.

FIGUERES, Girona/Gerona
◇ **Hotel President €**
Avenida Salvador Dali 82, 17600 Figueres
(tel: 972 50 17 00);
www.hotelpresident.info
80 rooms.

TOUR 3
BARCELONA, Barcelona
◇ **Turin €€€**
Carrer Pintor Fortuny 9–11, 08001 Barcelona
(tel: 933 02 48 12);
www.hotelturin.com
100 rooms.
⦿ **7 Portes €€**
Passeig Isabel II 14, 08003 Barcelona
(tel: 933 19 30 33)
Rice dishes.

SITGES, Barcelona
◇ **El Cid €**
Sant José 39 bis, 08870 Sitges
(tel: 938 94 18 42)
76 rooms.

🍽 **Fragata €€**
Paseo de la Ribera 1, 08870
Sitges
(tel: 938 94 10 86)
Seafood dishes.
🍽 **La Masia €€**
Paseo Vilanova 164–166,
08870 Sitges
(tel: 938 94 10 76)
*Catalan and regional
specialities.*

TARRAGONA, Tarragona
◇ **Astari €€**
Via Augusta 95–97, 43003
Tarragona
(tel: 977 23 69 00);
www.hotelastari.com
83 rooms.
◇ **Lauria €**
Rambla Nova 20, 43003
Tarragona
(tel: 977 23 67 12);
www.hlauria.es
72 rooms.
◇ **Núria €€**
Via Augusta 145, 43003
Tarragona
(tel: 977 23 50 11);
www.hotelnuria.es
57 rooms.
🍽 **Merlot €€**
Cavallers 6, 43003 Tarragona
(tel: 977 22 06 52)
*Closed Sun, Mon lunch, 1–15 Feb.
Mediterranean cuisine.*

**TOUR 4
VALENCIA,** Valencia
◇ **Ad Hoc Monumental €€**
Boix 4, 46003 Valencia
(tel: 963 91 91 40);
www.adhochoteles.com
28 rooms.
◇ **Sorolla €€**
Convento Santa Clara 5, 46002
Valencia
(tel: 963 52 33 92);
www.hotelsorolla.com
58 rooms.
🍽 **Bodega Montaña €**
José Benlliure 69, 46011
Valencia
(tel: 963 67 23 14)
*Popular, characterful tapas bar
and long wine list.*
🍽 **El Gourmet €€**
Marti 3, 46005 Valencia
(tel: 963 95 25 09)
Closed Holy Week, Aug and Sun.

BENIDORM, Alicante
◇ **Canfali €€**
Plaza de San Jaime 5, 03500
Benidorm
(tel: 965 85 08 18)
38 rooms.
🍽 **I Fratelli €€**
Calle Dr. Orts Llorca 20,
03500 Benidorm
(tel: 965 85 39 79)
Italian/international cooking.
🍽 **La Lubina €**
Avenida de Bilbao 3, 03500
Benidorm
(tel: 965 85 30 85)
*Closed Dec–Feb. Sea bass (la
lubina) is the speciality dish here.*

**TOUR 5
ALICANTE,** Alicante
◇ **Melía Alicante €€€**
Plaza Puerta del Mar, 03002
Alicante
(tel: 965 20 50 00);
www.solmelia.com
545 rooms.
◇ **Tryp Ciudad de Alicante
€€**
Gravina 9, 03002 Alicante
(tel: 965 21 07 00);
www.solmelia.com
70 rooms.
🍽 **Dársena €€**
Marina Deportiva, Muella 6,
03002 Alicante
(tel: 965 20 75 89)
Mediterranean cuisine.
🍽 **Restaurant El
Jumillano €€**
César Elhuezabal 64, 03001
Alicante
(tel: 965 21 29 64)
Excellent local recipes.

ELCHE/ELX,
Alicante
◇ **Huerto del Cura €€**
Porta de la Morera 14, 03203
Elche
(tel: 966 61 00 11);
www.huertodelcura.com
83 rooms.
🍽 **Mesón el Granaino €€**
Josep Maria Buch 40, 03201
Elche
(tel: 966 66 40 80)
*Closed Holy Week, Sun, 2 weeks Aug.
Andalucian cuisine.*

MURCIA, Murcia
◇ **Arco de San Juan €€**
Plaza Ceballos 10, 30003 Murcia

(tel: 968 21 04 55);
www.arcossanjuan.com
100 rooms.
◇ **NH Rincón de Pepe €€**
Calle de Apóstoles 34, 30001
Murcia
(tel: 968 21 22 39);
www.nh-hotels.com
148 rooms.
🍽 **Rocío €€**
Batalla de las Flores, 30008
Murcia
(tel: 968 24 29 30)
*Good value, good quality Murcian
dishes.*

**TOUR 6
PALMA,** Mallorca
◇ **Gran Meliá Victoria €€€**
Avenida Joan Miró 21, 07014
Palma
(tel: 971 73 25 42);
www.solmelia.com
171 rooms.
◇ **Palacio Casa Galesa €€€**
Carrer Miramar 8, 07001 Palma
(tel: 971 71 54 00);
www.palaciocasagalesa.com
12 rooms.
◇ **San Lorenzo €€€**
Carrer Sant Lorenc 14, 07012
Palma
(tel: 971 72 82 00);
www.hotelsanlorenzo.com
12 rooms.
🍽 **Casa Eduardo €€**
Muelle Viejo s/n, 07012 Palma
(tel: 971 72 11 82)
Closed Sun, Mon. Seafood dishes.
🍽 **La Bóveda €€**
Carrer de la Botería 3, 07012
Palma
(tel: 971 71 48 63)
*Closed Sun.
Good Spanish staples and tapas.*

PEGUERA, Mallorca
◇ **Bahía €**
Avinguda Peguera 81, 07160
Peguera
(tel: 971 68 61 00);
www.hotelbahia.com
52 rooms.

DEIÀ, Mallorca
◇ **Costa d'Or €€€**
Lluch Alcari s/n, 07179 Deià
(tel: 971 63 90 25);
www.hoposa.es
Closed Nov–Apr.
42 rooms.

Restaurant Jaime €€€
Carrer Arxiduc Lluis Salvador
24, 07179 Deià
(tel: 971 63 90 29)
*Closed Mon. Fresh fish, home-
made desserts.*

PORT DE POLLENÇA,
Mallorca
Sis Pins €€€
Avinguda Anglada Camarasa 77,
07470 Port de Pollença
(tel: 971 86 70 50)
51 rooms.

TOUR 7
ALMERÍA, Jaén
Torreluz III €€
Plaza Flores 3, 04001 Almería
(tel: 950 23 43 99);
www.torreluz.com
Also €.
102 rooms.
**Rincón de Juan Pedro
€€€**
Calle Federico de Castro 2,
04003 Almería
(tel: 950 23 58 19)
*Traditional lunch, international
dinner.*

MOJÁCAR, Almeria
Parador de Mojácar €€
04638 Playa de Mojácar
(tel: 950 47 82 50);
www.parador.es
98 rooms.

ÚBEDA, Jaén
Hotel la Paz €
Calle Andalucía 1, 23400 Úbeda
(tel: 953 75 21 40);
www.hotel-lapaz.com
40 rooms.
Parador de Úbeda €€€
Plaza Vázquez Molina 1, 23400
Úbeda
(tel: 953 75 03 45);
www.parador.es
Also €€.
36 rooms.

TOUR 8
MÁLAGA, Málaga
Los Naranjos €€
Paseo de Sancha 3, 29016
Málaga
(tel: 952 22 43 16);
www.hotel-losnaranjos.com
41 rooms.

**Parador de Málaga-
Gibralfaro €€€**
Castillo de Gibralfaro, 29016
Málaga
(tel: 952 22 19 02);
www.parador.es
38 rooms.
Casa Pedro €€€
Calle Quitapeñas 121, 29017
Málaga
(tel: 952 29 00 13)
Fresh seafood with sea views.
El Chinitas €€
Moreno Monroy 4, 29015
Málaga
(tel: 952 21 09 72)
Meat and fish dishes.

NERJA, Málaga
Balcón de Europa €€
Paseo Balcón de Europa 1,
29780 Nerja
(tel: 952 52 08 00);
www.hotelbalconeuropa.com
111 rooms.
Parador de Nerja €€€
Almuñecar 8, 29780 Nerja
(tel: 952 52 00 50);
www.parador.es
96 rooms.
Casa Luque €€
Plaza Cavana 2, 29780 Nerja
(tel: 952 52 10 04)
Gourmet tapas and wines.

GRANADA, Granada
Alhambra Palace €€€
Plaza Arquitecto Garcia de
Peredes 1, 18009 Granada
(tel: 958 22 14 68);
www.h-alhambrapalace.es
136 rooms.
Dauro II €€
Navas 5, 18009 Granada
(tel: 958 22 15 81)
48 rooms.
Macía Plaza €
Plaza Nueva 4, 18010 Granada
(tel: 958 22 75 36);
www.maciahoteles.com
44 rooms.
Cunini €
Plaza Pescadería 14, 18001
Granada
(tel: 958 25 07 77)
Closed Sun and Mon evening.

TOUR 9
MÁLAGA, Málaga
Don Curro €€
Sancha de Lara 7, 29015 Málaga
(tel: 952 22 72 00);

www.hoteldoncurro.com
118 rooms.
Antonio Martín €€€
Plaza del la Malagueta, 29016
Málaga
(tel: 952 22 73 98)
Malagan and Andalucian cuisine.

TORREMOLINOS, Málaga
Hotel Cervantes €€
Las Mercedes s/n, 29620
Torremolinos
(tel: 952 38 40 33);
www.hotasacervantes.com
397 rooms.
Miami €
Aladino 14, 29620 Torremolinos
(tel: 952 38 52 55);
www.residencia-miami.com
14 rooms.
Frutos €€€
Avenida Riviera 80, Los Alamos
Torremolinos, 29620
Torremolinos
(tel: 952 38 14 50)
Top-quality Spanish cuisine.

MIJAS, Málaga
TRH Mijas €€
Urbanización Tamisa 2, 29650
Mijas
(tel: 952 48 58 00);
www.trhhoteles.com
204 rooms.
Mirlo Blanco €€
Plaza de la Constitución 2,
29650 Mijas
(tel: 952 48 57 00)
Basque and international dishes.
**Restaurante El
Padrastro €€**
Paseo del Compás 22, 29650
Mijas
(tel: 952 48 50 00)
*International cooking with
panoramic views.*

MARBELLA, Málaga
Andalucia Plaza €€€
Apartado 21, 29600 Nueva
Andalucia, Marbella
(tel: 952 81 20 00);
www.h10hotels.com
400 rooms.
El Fuerte €€
Avenida El Fuerte, 29602
Marbella
(tel: 952 92 00 00);
263 rooms.
Hostal El Castillo €
Plaza San Bernabé 2, 29600
Marbella

(tel: 952 77 17 39);
www.hotelcastillo.com
26 rooms.

Gran Plaza Apartments €€€
Plaza de los Naranjos, 29600
Marbella
(tel: 952 82 48 60)
Andalucian cuisine.

PUERTO BANÚS, Málaga
Pyr Marbella €€
Avenida Rotary Internacional,
29660 Puerto Banús
(tel: 952 81 73 53);
www.hotelpyr.com
319 rooms.

Antonio €€€
Muelle Rivera, 29660 Puerto
Banús
(tel: 952 81 35 36)
Seafood dishes.

La Caracola Del Puerto €€
Muelle Benabola 5, 29660
Puerto Banús
(tel: 952 81 16 84)
Closed Tue. Mediterranean cuisine.

RONDA, Málaga
Hotel Don Miguel €€
Plaza de España 4, 29400 Ronda
(tel: 952 87 77 22);
www.dmiguel.com
30 rooms.

Parador de Ronda €€€€
Plaza de España, 29400 Ronda
(tel: 952 87 75 00);
www.parador.es
78 rooms.

Reina Victoria €€
Paseo Dr. Fleming 25, 29400
Ronda
(tel: 952 87 12 40);
www.hotelhusareina
victoriaronda.com
89 rooms.

Tragabuches €€€
Calle José Aparicio 1, 29400
Ronda
(tel: 952 19 02 91)
Modern Spanish/Andalucian.

**TOUR 10
SEVILLA,** Sevilla
Bécquer €€€
Calle Reyes Católicos 4, 41001
Sevilla
(tel: 954 22 89 00);
www.hotelbecquer.com
139 rooms.

Hostal Goya €
Mateus Gago 31, 41004 Sevilla
(tel: 954 21 11 70);
www.hostalgoyasevilla.com
19 rooms.

Hotel Amadeus €€
Calle Farnesio 6, 41004 Sevilla
(tel: 954 50 14 43);
www.hotelamadeussevilla.com
14 rooms.

Casa Robles €€
Calle Álvarez Quintero 58,
41004 Sevilla
(tel: 954 56 32 72)
Andalucian cuisine.

CARMONA, Sevilla
Parador de Carmona €€€
Alcázar s/n, 41410 Carmona
(tel: 954 14 10 10);
www.parador.es
63 rooms.

CÓRDOBA, Córdoba
Hotel Conquistador €€€
Magistral González Francés
15–17, 14003 Córdoba
(tel: 957 48 11 02);
www.hotelconquistadorcordoba.
com
129 rooms.

Mezquita €€
Plaza Santa Catalina 1, 14003
Córdoba
(tel: 957 47 58 85)
21 rooms.

NH Amistad Córdoba €€€
Plaza de Maimónides 3,
14004 Córdoba
(tel: 957 42 03 35);
www.nh-hotels.com
84 rooms.

El Churrasco €€
Romero 16, 14003 Córdoba
(tel: 957 29 08 19)
Closed Aug.
Local cuisine.

Mesón el Burlaero €€
Calle de la Hoguera 5, 14003
Córdoba
(tel: 957 47 27 19)
Mediterranean and Andalucian.

**TOUR 11
SEVILLA,** Sevilla
Hostería del Laurel €€
Plaza de los Venerables 5,
41004 Sevilla
(tel: 954 22 02 95);
www.hosteriadellaurel.com
22 rooms.

Murillo Hotel €
Calle Lope de Rueda 7–9,
41001 Sevilla
(tel: 954 21 60 95);
www.hotelmurillo.com
57 rooms.

Rio Grande €€
Calle Betis, 41010 Sevilla
(tel: 954 27 39 56)
Andalucian classic.

HUELVA, Huelva
Los Condes €
Alameda Sundheim 14,
21003 Huelva
(tel: 959 28 24 00)
54 rooms.

Portichuelo €
Gran Via 1, 21003 Huelva
(tel: 959 24 57 68)
*Closed Sun in summer; Sun dinner
rest of year.*
Andalucian cuisine.

**TOUR 12
SEVILLA,** Sevilla
Simón €€
García de Vinuesa 19, 41001
Sevilla
(tel: 954 22 66 60);
www.hotelsimonsevilla.com
29 rooms.

Taberna del Alabardero €€
Calle Zaragoza 20, 41001 Sevilla
(tel: 954 50 27 21)
Modern dishes and alfresco dining.

**ARCOS DE LA
FRONTERA,** Cádiz
**Parador de Arcos de la
Frontera €€**
Plaza del Cabildo, 11630 Arcos
de la Frontera
(tel: 956 70 05 00);
www.parador.es
24 rooms.

CÁDIZ, Cadiz
Parador Hotel Atlántico €€
Duque de Nájera 9, 11002
Cádiz
(tel: 956 22 69 05);
www.parador.es
76 rooms.

Achuri €€
Calle Plocia 15, 11006 Cádiz
(tel: 956 25 36 13)
Basque and Andalucian seafood.

JEREZ DE LA FRONTERA, Cádiz
◊ **Ávila €**
Calle Ávila 3, 11140 Jerez de la Frontera
(tel: 956 33 48 08)
33 rooms.
◊ **Montecastillo Resort €€€**
Carretera de Jerez a Arcos, Km 9-Junto al C1, 11406 Jerez de la Frontera
(tel: 956 15 12 00);
www.montecastillo.com
220 rooms and villas.
◊ **Serit €€**
Higuera 7, 11402 Jerez de la Frontera
(tel: 956 34 07 00);
www.hotelserit.com
35 rooms.
🍴 **Gaitán €€**
Gaitán 3, 11403 Jerez de la Frontera
(tel: 956 34 58 59)
Closed Sun dinner. Traditional Spanish and Portuguese cooking.

TOUR 13
ZARAGOZA, Zaragoza
◊ **Husa Via Romana €€**
Don Jaime I 54–56, 50001 Zaragoza
(tel: 976 39 82 15);
www.hotelramiroizaragoza.com
66 rooms.
◊ **Ramiro I €€**
Calle Coso 123, 50001 Zaragoza
(tel: 976 29 82 00);
www.hotelhusaviaromana.com
104 rooms.
🍴 **La Mar €€**
Plaza Aragon 12, 50004 Zaragoza
(tel: 976 21 22 64)
International dishes, mainly fish and seafood.

CALATAYUD, Zaragoza
◊ **Calatayud €**
Carretera Madrid-Barcelona, Km.237, 50300 Calatayud
(tel: 976 88 13 23)
78 rooms.
◊ **Hospederia Mesón de La Dolores €**
Plaza de Mesones 4, 50300 Calatayud
(tel: 976 88 90 55);
www.mesonladolores.com
34 rooms.
◊ **Husa Monasterio Benedictino €€€**
Plaza San Benito s/n,

50300 Calatayud
(tel: 976 89 15 00)
35 rooms.

NUÉVALOS/PIEDRA, Zaragoza
◊ **Monasterio de Piedra €€€**
50210 Nuévalos
(tel: 902 19 60 52);
www.monasteriopiedra.com
60 rooms.

TOUR 14
HUESCA, Huesca
◊ **Pedro I de Aragón €€**
Avenida del Parque 34, 22003 Huesca
(tel: 974 22 03 00);
www.gargallo-hotels.com
129 rooms.
◊ **San Marcos €**
San Orencio 10, 22002 Huesca
(tel: 974 22 29 31);
www.hotelsanmarcos.es
27 rooms.
🍴 **Las Torres €€**
Calle María Auxiliadora 3, 22003 Huesca
(tel: 974 22 82 13)
Closed Sun. Innovative regional cuisine.

JACA, Huesca
◊ **Conde Aznar €€**
Paseo Constitución 3, 22700 Jaca
(tel: 974 36 10 50);
www.condeaznar.com
Also 🍴 **€€.**
Closed Wed, except winter.
24 rooms.

TOUR 15
PAMPLONA, Navarra
◊ **Residencia Eslava €€**
Plaza Virgen de la O 7, 31001 Pamplona
(tel: 948 22 22 70)
28 rooms.
🍴 **Erburu €€**
San Lorenzo 19–21, 31001 Pamplona
(tel: 948 22 51 69)
Closed Mon & second half Jul.

OLITE, Navarra
◊ **Parador de Olite €€**
Plaza de los Teobaldos 2, 31390 Olite
(tel: 948 74 00 00);
www.parador.es
43 rooms.

TUDELA, Navarra
◊ **Tudela Bardenas €€**
Avenida Zaragoza 60, 31500 Tudela
(tel: 948 41 08 02);
www.tudelabardenas.com
46 rooms.

TARAZONA, Zaragoza
◊ **Brujas de Bécquer €**
Carretera Zaragoza s/n 30, 50500 Tarazona
(tel: 976 64 04 04)
56 rooms.

LOGROÑO, La Rioja
◊ **Murrieta €€**
Marqués de Murrieta 1, 26005 Logroño
(tel: 941 22 41 50);
www.hotelmurrietalogrono.com
104 rooms.
◊ **NH Logroño €**
Avenida Club Deportivo 98, 26007 Logroño
(tel: 941 51 92 70);
www.nh-hoteles.com
83 rooms.
🍴 **Asador La Chata €€**
Carnicerias 3
(tel: 941 25 12 96), 26001 Logroño
Regional wood-roasted meat dishes.
🍴 **Cachetero €€**
Laurel 3, 26001 Logroño
(tel: 941 22 84 63)
Regional cuisine with original touches.

TOUR 16
MADRID, Madrid
◊ **Anaco €€**
Tres Cruces 3, 28013 Madrid
(tel: 915 22 46 04);
www.anacohotel.com
39 rooms.
◊ **Hostal Nuevo Gaos €€**
Calle Mesonero Romanos 14, 28013 Madrid
(tel: 915 32 71 07)
23 rooms.
🍴 **Botín €€**
Cuchilleros 17, 28005 Madrid
(tel: 913 66 42 17)
Suckling pig and other roast meats are the speciality.

TOLEDO, Toledo
◊ **El Cardenal €€**
Paseo de Recaredo 24, 45003 Toledo

(tel: 925 22 49 00)
27 rooms.
◇ **Imperio €**
Calle de las Cadenas 5, 45005
Toledo
(tel: 925 22 76 50)
21 rooms.
◇ **Maria Cristina €€**
Marqués de Mendigorría 1,
45003 Toledo
(tel: 925 21 32 02)
74 rooms.
◇ **Santa Isabel €**
Calle Santa Isabel 24, 45002
Toledo
(tel: 925 25 31 20)
24 rooms.
◎ **Hierbabuena €€**
Callejón de San José 17, 45003
Toledo
(tel: 925 22 39 24)
*Closed Sun evening. Imaginative
seasonal cuisine.*

ARANJUEZ, Madrid
◇ **Hotel Castilla €**
Carretera Andalucía 98, 28300
Aranjuez
(tel: 918 91 26 27)
17 rooms.
◎ **Casa Pablo €€**
Almibar 42, 28300 Aranjuez
(tel: 918 91 14 51)
*Unpretentious Spanish food in
city centre.*

CHINCHÓN, Madrid
◇ **Hotel Nuevo Chinchón
€**
Urbanización Nuevo
Chinchón, 28370 Madrid
(tel: 918 94 05 44);
www.hotelnuevochinchon.com
17 rooms.
◇ **Parador de Chinchón €€**
Avenida Generalísimo 1,
Chinchón, 28370 Madrid
(tel: 918 94 08 36);
www.parador.es
38 rooms.

TOUR 17
MADRID, Madrid
◇ **Hostal la Macarena €**
Cava de San Miguel 8, 28005
Madrid
(tel: 913 65 92 21)
25 rooms.
◇ **Hostal la Perla
Asturiana €**
Plaza de Santa Cruz 3, 28012
Madrid

(tel: 913 66 46 00);
www.perlaasturiana.com
30 rooms.
◇ **Inglés €€**
Echegaray 8, 28014 Madrid
(tel: 914 29 65 51)
58 rooms.
◎ **Café de Oriente €€€**
Plaza de Oriente 2, 28013
Madrid
(tel: 915 41 39 74)
Café/restaurant with refined cuisine.

ALCALÁ DE HENARES,
Madrid
◎ **Hostería del Estudiante
€€**
Calle Colegios 3, 28801 Alcalá
de Henares
(tel: 918 88 03 30)
*Ample Castillian cuisine and
local wines.*

CUENCA, Cuenca
◇ **Hotel Residencia Figón
de Pedro €**
Calle Cervantes 17, 16004
Cuenca
(tel: 969 22 45 11)
28 rooms.
◇ **Leonar de Aquitania €€**
Calle San Pedro 60, 16001
Cuenca
(tel: 969 23 10 00)
49 rooms.
◇ **Parador de Cuenca €€**
Subida a San Pablo s/n, 16001
Cuenca
(tel: 969 23 20 20);
www.parador.es
Also ◎ **€€/€€€.**
63 rooms.
◎ **Casa Marlo €€€**
Colón 41, 16002 Cuenca
(tel: 969 21 11 73)
*Mediterranean regional
cooking.*

TOUR 18
MADRID, Madrid
◇ **Bauzá Hotel €€€**
Calle de Goya 79, 28001 Madrid
(tel: 914 35 75 45);
www.hotelbauza.com
167 rooms.
◇ **Francisco I €€**
Arenal 15, 28013 Madrid
(tel: 915 48 02 04);
www.hotelfrancisco.com
58 rooms.

◇ **Me Madrid Reina Victoria
€€€**
Plaza de Santa Ana 14, 28012
Madrid
(tel: 917 01 60 00);
www.solmelia.com
195 rooms.
◎ **Las Cueves de Luis
Candelas €€**
Cuchilleros 1, 28005 Madrid
(tel: 913 66 54 28)
Traditional Castillian cuisine.

EL ESCORIAL, Madrid
◇ **Hostal Cristina €**
Juan de Toledo 6, 28200 San
Lorenzo de El Escorial
(tel: 918 90 19 61);
www.hotelmirandasuizo.com
16 rooms.
◇ **Miranda Suizo €€**
Calle Floridablanca 18, 28200
San Lorenzo de El Escorial
(tel: 918 90 47 11)
52 rooms.

ÁVILA, Ávila
◇ **El Rastro €**
Plaza del Rastro 1, 05001 Ávila
(tel: 920 21 12 18)
10 rooms.
◇ **Hostería Bracamonte €€**
Bracamonte 6, 05001 Ávila
(tel: 920 25 12 80)
22 rooms.
◇ **Parador de Ávila €€**
Marqués Canales de Chozas 2,
05001 Ávila
(tel: 920 21 13 40);
www.parador.es
61 rooms.
◎ **Copacabana €€**
Calle San Millán 9, 05001
Ávila
(tel: 920 21 11 10)
*Fresh Castillian food in friendly
atmosphere.*

TOUR 19
MADRID, Madrid
◇ **Liabeny €€€**
Salud 3, 28013 Madrid
(tel: 915 31 90 00);
www.hotelliabeny.com
220 rooms.
◇ **Residencia Lisboa €**
Ventura de la Vega, 17, 28014
Madrid
(tel: 914 29 46 76);
www.hostallisboa.com
27 rooms.

🍽 **Casa Paco** €€
Puerta Cerrada 11, 28005
Madrid
(tel: 913 66 31 66).
Closed Sun, Aug.

SEGOVIA, Segovia
◇ **Infanta Isabel** €€
Plaza Mayor 12, 40001 Segovia
(tel: 921 46 13 00);
www.hotelinfantaisabel.com
39 rooms.
◇ **Los Arcos** €€
Paseo de Ezequiel González 26,
40002 Segovia
(tel: 921 43 74 62)
59 rooms.
◇ **Los Linajes** €€
Dr Velasco 9, 40003 Segovia
(tel: 921 46 04 75)
55 rooms.
◇ **Parador de Segovia** €€
Carretera Valladolid, La Lastrilla
s/n, 40003 Segovia
(tel: 921 44 37 37);
www.parador.es
113 rooms.
🍽 **Casa Duque** €€
Cervantes 12, 40001 Segovia
(tel: 921 46 24 87).
*Roasts are the speciality at the oldest
restaurant in Segovia.*
🍽 **José María** €€€
Calle Cronista Lecea 11,
40001 Segovia
(tel: 921 46 60 17)
*Tapas bar and traditional
restaurant.*

TOUR 20
CÁCERES, Cáceres
◇ **Extremadura** €€€
Avenida Virgen de Guadalupe
28, 10001 Cáceres
(tel: 927 62 96 39);
www.extremadurahotel.com
152 rooms.
◇ **Meliá Cáceres** €€€
Plaza San Juan 11, 10003
Cáceres
(tel: 927 21 58 00);
www.solmelia.com
86 rooms.
◇ **Parador de Cáceres** €€€
Calle Ancha 6, 10003 Cáceres
(tel: 927 21 17 59);
www.parador.es
Also 🍽 €€.
20 rooms.

TRUJILLO, Cáceres
◇ **Las Cigueñas** €€
Avenida de Madrid s/n,
Carretera N-V, 10200 Trujillo
(tel: 927 32 12 50)
78 rooms.
◇ **Parador de Trujillo** €€
Calle de Santa Beatriz de Silva,
10200 Trujillo
(tel: 927 32 13 50);
www.parador.es
Also 🍽 €€.
48 rooms.

GUADALUPE, Cáceres
◇ **Hospedería del Real
Monasterio** €
Plaza Juan Carlos 1, 10140
Guadalupe
(tel: 927 36 70 00);
www.monasteriorguadalupe.com
47 rooms.
◇ **Parador de Guadalupe**
€€€
Marqués de la Romana 12,
10140 Guadalupe
(tel: 927 36 70 75);
www.parador.es
Also 🍽 €€.
41 rooms.

MÉRIDA, Badajoz
◇ **Nova Roma** €€
Suárez Somonte 42, 06800
Mérida
(tel: 924 31 12 61)
55 rooms.
◇ **Parador de Mérida** €€
Plaza de la Constitución 3, 06800
Mérida
(tel: 924 31 38 00);
www.parador.es
Also 🍽 €€.
79 rooms.
◇ **Tryp Medea** €€€
Avenida de Portugal s/n, 06800
Mérida
(tel: 924 37 24 00);
www.solmelia.com
126 rooms.

BADAJOZ, Badajoz
◇ **Husa Río** €€
Avenida Adolfo Díaz Ambrona
13, 06006 Badajoz
(tel: 924 27 26 00);
www.husa.es
101 rooms.

◇ **Husa Zurbarán** €€€
Paseo Castelar s/n, 06001
Badajoz
(tel: 924 00 14 00);
www.hotelzurbaran.com
215 rooms.
◇ **Lisboa** €€
Calle Augusto Vázquez 2, 06006
Badajoz
(tel: 924 27 29 00);
www.hotellisboabadajoz.es
176 rooms.

TOUR 21
SALAMANCA, Salamanca
◇ **Gran Hotel** €€€
Plaza Poeta Iglesias 3, 37002
Salamanca
(tel: 923 21 35 00);
www.helcom.es/granhotel
136 rooms.
◇ **Monterrey** €€€
Azafranal 21, 37001 Salamanca
(tel: 923 21 44 00);
www.helcom.es/monterrey
143 rooms.
◇ **Parador de Salamanca**
€€€
Teso de la Feria 2, 37008
Salamanca
(tel: 923 19 20 82);
www.parador.es
Also 🍽 €€.
108 rooms.
🍽 **La Olla** €€
Plaza del Peso 8, 37001
Salamanca
(tel: 923 26 85 54)
Castillian cuisine.

ZAMORA, Zamora
◇ **Hostería Real de Zamora**
€
Cuesta de Pizarro 7, 49027
Zamora
(tel: 980 53 45 45);
www.hosteriasreales.com
26 rooms.
◇ **Parador de Zamora** €€€
Plaza de Viriato 5, 49001 Zamora
(tel: 980 51 44 97);
www.parador.es
Also 🍽 €€/€€€.
52 rooms.

VALLADOLID, Valladolid
◇ **Felipe IV** €€
Calle de Gamazo 16, 47004
Valladolid
(tel: 983 30 70 00);
www.hfelipeiv.com
131 rooms.

◇ **Imperial** €€
Calle del Peso 4, 47001
Valladolid
(tel: 983 33 03 00);
100 rooms.
◇ **Olid Meliá** €€€
Plaza San Miguel 10, 47003
Valladolid   •
(tel: 983 35 72 00);
www.solmelia.com
211 rooms.
◇ **Parque** €€
Joaquin Garcia Morato 17, 47007
Valladolid
(tel: 983 22 00 00);
www.hotelparque.com
185 rooms.
◎ **El Figón de Recoletos** €€
Acera de Recoletos 3, 47004
Valladolid
(tel: 983 39 60 43)
Closed 20 Jul–12 Aug, Sun eve.

BURGOS, Burgos
◇ **España** €€
Paseo del Espolón 32, 09003
Burgos
(tel: 947 20 63 40);
www.hotelespana.net
69 rooms.
◇ **Mesón del Cid** €€
Plaza Santa María 8, 09003
Burgos
(tel: 947 20 87 15);
www.mesondelcid.es
55 rooms.
◇ **Norte y Londres** €€
Plaza de Alonso Martínez 10,
09003 Burgos
(tel: 947 26 41 25);
www.hotelnorteylondres.com
50 rooms.
◎ **Casa Ojeda** €€/€€€
Calle Vitoria 5, 09004 Burgos
(tel: 947 20 90 52)

TOUR 22
A CORUÑA, La Coruña
◇ **España** €
Juana de Vega 7, 15004 La
Coruña
(tel: 981 22 45 06);
www.hotespa.com
84 rooms.
◇ **Finisterre** €€€
Paseo del Parrote 2, 15001
La Coruña
(tel: 981 20 54 00);
www.worldhotels.com
92 rooms.

◇ **Hotel Riazor** €€
Avenida de Pedro Barrie de la
Maza 29, 15004 La Coruña
(tel: 981 25 34 00)
174 rooms.
◎ **El Coral** €€
Callejón de la Estacada 9, 15004
La Coruña
(tel: 981 20 05 69)
*Galician dishes prepared with
distinction.*

LUGO, Lugo
◇ **Gran Hotel Lugo** €€€
Avenida Ramón Ferreiro 21,
27002 Lugo
(tel: 982 22 41 52),
www.gh-hoteles.com
167 rooms.
◇ **Méndez Núñez** €
Reiña 1, 27002 Lugo
(tel: 982 23 07 11);
www.hotelmendeznunez.com
70 rooms.

PONTEVEDRA, Pontevedra
◇ **Parador de Pontevedra**
€€€
Barón 19, 36002 Pontevedra
(tel: 986 85 58 00);
www.parador.es
Also ◎ €€/€€€.
47 rooms.
◇ **Rías Bajas** €€
Daniel de la Sota 7, 36001
Pontevedra
(tel: 986 85 51 00);
www.hotelriasbajas.com
100 rooms.
◇ **Virgen del Camino** €€
Virgen del Camino 55, 36001
Pontevedra
(tel: 986 85 59 00);
www.hotelvirgendelcamino.com
53 rooms.

**SANTIAGO DE
COMPOSTELA,** A Coruña
◇ **Hesperia Gelmírez** €
Hórreo 92, 15702 Santiago de
Compostela
(tel: 981 56 11 00);
www.hesperia.com
138 rooms.
◇ **Hostal Giadás** €
Plaza del Matedero 2, 15703
Santiago de Compostela
(tel: 981 58 70 71)
8 rooms.

◇ **Parador Hostal de los
Reyes Católicos** €€€
Placa do Obradoiro 1, 15705
Santiago de Compostela
(tel: 981 58 22 00);
www.parador.es
136 rooms.
◇ **Husa Universal** €€
Plaza de Galicia, 2, 15706
Santiago de Compostela
(tel: 981 58 58 00);
www.hotelhusauniversal.com
54 rooms.
◎ **Don Gaiferos** €€
Rúa Nova 23, 15705 Santiago de
Compostela
(tel: 981 58 38 94)
*Closed Sun dinner. First-class
savoury Galician cooking.*

TOUR 23
OVIEDO, Asturias
◇ **De La Reconquista** €€€
Gil de Jaz 16, 33004 Oviedo
(tel: 985 24 11 00);
www.hoteldelareconquista.com
142 rooms.
◇ **La Gruta** €€
Alto de Buenavista, s/n, 33006
Oviedo
(tel: 985 23 24 50)
105 rooms.

LEÓN, León
◇ **Guzmán El Bueno** €
López Castrillón 6, 24003 León
(tel: 987 23 64 12)
No credit cards.
26 rooms.
◎ **Restaurante El Palomo**
€€
Calle Escalerilla 8, 24003 León
(tel: 987 25 42 25)
Typical Leónese dishes.

GIJÓN, Asturias
◇ **Hernán Cortés** €€
Fernández Vallín 5, 33205 Gijón
(tel: 985 34 60 00);
www.hotelhernancortes.es
53 rooms.
◇ **Parador de Gijón** €€€
Parque de Isabel la Católica,
33203 Gijón
(tel: 985 37 05 11);
www.parador.es
40 rooms.
◎ **El Puerto** €€€
Claudio Alvargonzález, Gijón
(tel: 985 34 90 96)
Closed Sun evening & Holy Week.

CANGAS DE ONIS,
Asturias
◇ **Hotel Aultre Naray €€**
Peruyes 335 Cangas de Onis
(tel: 985 84 08 08);
www.aultrenaray.com
10 rooms.
◎ **El Molín de la Pedrera €€**
Rio Güeña 2, 33550 Cangas de
Onis
(tel: 985 84 91 09).
Asturian cuisine based on fresh local produce.

TOUR 24
SANTANDER, Cantabria
◇ **Abba Santander €€**
Calderón de la Barca 3, 39002
Cantabria
(tel: 942 21 24 50);
www.abbasantanderhotel.com
32 rooms.
◇ **Ciudad de Santander €€€**
Menéndez Pelayo 13–15, 39006
Santander
(tel: 942 31 99 00);
www.nh-hotels.com
62 rooms.
◎ **Zacarías €€**
General Mola 41, 39004
Santander
(tel: 942 21 23 33)
A wide range of Cantabrian and seafood dishes.

SANTILLANA DEL MAR,
Cantabria
◇ **Parador de Santillana
€€€**
Plaza de Ramón Pelayo 8, 39330
Santillana de Mar
(tel: 942 81 80 00);
www.parador.es
28 rooms.

LAREDO, Cantabria
◇ **El Ancla del Laredo €€**
Calle González Gallego 10,
39770 Laredo
(tel: 942 60 55 00);
www.hotelelancla.com
32 rooms.

◇ **Ramona €**
Alameda de José Antonio 4,
39770 Laredo
(tel: 942 60 71 89)
16 rooms.
◎ **Camarote €€**
Avenida Vitoria, 39770 Laredo
(tel: 942 60 67 07)
Seafood specialist.

TOUR 25
SAN SEBASTIÁN, Guipúzcoa
◇ **Abba de Londres y de
Inglaterra €€€**
Zubieta 2, 20007 San Sebastián
(tel: 943 44 07 70);
www.abbalondreshotel.com
148 rooms.
◇ **Mercure Monte Igueldo
€€**
Paseo del Faro 134, Monte
Igueldo, 20008 San Sebastián
(tel: 943 21 02 11);
www.mercure.com
125 rooms.
◇ **Niza €€**
Zubieta 56, 20007 San Sebastián
(tel: 943 42 66 63);
www.hotelniza.com
41 rooms.
◎ **Juanito Kojua €€**
Portu 14, 20003 San Sebastián
(tel: 943 42 01 80)
Seafood restaurant in the old town.

BILBAO, Vizcaya
◇ **Barcelo Hotel Avenida
€€€**
Zumalacárregui 40, 48007 Bilbao
(tel: 944 12 43 00);
www.bchoteles.com/avenida
189 rooms.
◇ **Carlton €€€**
Plaza Federico Moyua 2, 48009
Bilbao
(tel: 944 16 22 00);
www.aranzazu-hoteles.com
148 rooms.

◇ **Ercilla €€€**
Ercilla 37–39, 48011 Bilbao
(tel: 944 70 57 00);
www.hotelercilla.es
346 rooms.
◎ **Zortziko €€€**
Alameda de Mazarredo 17,
48001 Bilbao
(tel: 944 23 97 43)
Closed Sun evening. One of the top basque country establishments.

VITORIA-GASTEIZ, Alava
◇ **Hotel Dato €**
Calle Eduardo Dato 28, 01005
Vitoria-Gasteiz
(tel: 945 14 72 30);
www.hoteldato.com
14 rooms.
◇ **Parador Argómaniz €€€**
Carretera N-1, Km 363 (15km
from Vitoria), 01192 Vitoria-
Gasteiz
(tel: 945 29 32 00)
53 rooms.
◎ **El Portalón €€**
Correría 151, 01001 Vitoria-
Gasteiz
(tel: 945 14 42 01)
Basque cooking with fresh fish.

**FUENTERRABÍA/
HONDARRIBIA,** Guipúzcoa
◇ **Husa Jauregui €€**
Zuloaga 5, 20280 Fuenterrabía
(tel: 943 64 14 00);
www.husa.es
53 rooms.
◇ **Parador de Hondarribia
€€€**
Plaza de Armas 14, 20280
Fuenterrabía
(tel: 943 64 55 00);
www.parador.es
36 rooms.

PRACTICAL INFORMATION

TOUR INFORMATION

The addresses, telephone numbers and opening times of the attractions mentioned in the tours, including the telephone numbers of the Tourist Information Centres are listed below tour by tour.

TOUR 1

[i] Plaça de Catalunya 17- S, Barcelona.
Tel: 932 85 38 34.

[i] Avenida Valls d'Andorra 33, La Seu d'Urgell.
Tel: 973 35 15 11.

[i] Querol 1, Puigcerdà.
Tel: 972 88 05 42.

[i] Plaça de l'Ajuntament 3, Ribes de Freser.
Tel: 972 72 77 28.

[i] Plaça de l'Abat Oliba s/n, Ripoll.
Tel: 972 70 23 51.

[i] Palau de l'Abadia 9, Sant Joan de les Abadesses.
Tel: 972 72 05 99.

[i] Plaça d'Espanya 1, Camprodón.
Tel: 972 74 00 10.

[i] Hospici 8, Olot.
Tel: 972 26 01 41.

[i] Ciutat 4, Vic.
Tel: 938 86 20 91.

1 Montserrat
Monestir de Montserrat
Sierra de Montserrat.
Tel: 938 77 77 66 (Basílica).
www.abadiamontserat.net.
Open daily 7.30am–7.30pm (8.30pm Jul–Sep).

2 Cardona
Colegiata de Sant Vincenc
Castillo de Cardona.
Tel: 938 68 41 69.
Open Tue–Fri 10–1.30, 3–5.30 (6.30 Jul–Sep), Sat–Sun 11–1.

3 Solsona
Museu Diocesano y Comarcal
Palau Episcopa.
Tel: 973 48 21 01.
Open Tue–Sat 10–1, 4–6 (10–1, 4.30–7 May–Sep), Sun 10–2.

4 La Seu d'Urgell
Museu Diocesà
Plaça del Degenat.
Tel: 973 35 32 42.
Open Jul–Sep, Mon–Sat 10–1, 4–7; Oct–May, Mon–Sat 12–1, 4–6, Sun 10–1.

7 Ripoll
Monestir de Santa Maria
Plaça Abat Oliba.
Tel: 972 70 02 43.
Open daily 8–1, 3–7; cloisters open daily 10- 1, 3–7.

8 Sant Joan de les Abadesses
Sant Joan de les Abadesses
Tel: 977 72 00 13.
Open Mar–Apr & Oct, daily 10–2, 4–6; May–Jun & Sep 10–2, 4–7; Jul–Aug 10–7; Nov–Feb 10–2 (also 4–6 Sat, Sun).

10 Olot
Museu Comarcal de la Garrotxa
Carrer Hospici 8.
Tel: 972 27 91 30.
Open Mon–Sat 11–2, 4–7.

Jardí Botànic and Casal dels Volcans
Avinguda Santa Coloma de Farners.
Tel: 972 26 62 02.
Open daily in winter 10–2, 5–6 (to 7pm in summer).

11 Vic
Museu Episcopal
Adjoining cathedral.
Tel: 938 85 64 52.
Open Apr–Sep, Tue–Sat 10–7; Oct–Nov, Tue–Fri 10–1, 3–6, Sat 10–7, Sun 10–2.

Back to nature
Parc Natural del Cadi-Moixeró
Information Centre.
Tel: 938 24 41 51.

TOUR 2

[i] Passeig de Gracia 107, Barcelona.
Tel: 932 38 80 91.

[i] Plaça Catalunya 21, Blanes.
Tel: 972 33 03 48.

[i] Avenida del Pelegrí 25, Edificio Terminal, Tossa de Mar.
Tel: 972 34 01 08.

[i] Plaça Mercat 28, Sant Felio de Guíxols.
Tel: 972 82 00 51.

[i] Passeig del Mar 22, Palamós.
Tel: 972 60 05 00.

[i] Plaça de la Iglesia s/n, Palafrugell.
Tel: 972 61 18 20.

[i] Plaça del Castell, La Bisbal d'Empordà.
Tel: 972 64 51 66.

[i] Rambla de la Llibertat 1, Girona.
Tel: 972 22 65 75.

[i] Plaça del Sol, Figueres.
Tel: 972 50 31 55.

[i] Plaça de la Llibertat 1, Besalú.
Tel: 972 59 12 40.

[i] Passeig Industria 25, Banyoles.
Tel: 972 57 55 73.

5 Tossa de Mar
Museu Municipal
Plaça Roig y Soler 1.
Tel: 972 34 01 08.
Open Tue–Sat 10–2, 4–6, Sun 10–2.

8 Girona
Museu d'Art
Pujada de la Catedral.
Tel: 972 20 38 34.
Open Tue–Sat 10–6 (to 7pm Mar–Sep), Sun 10–2

Banys Àrabs
Tel: 972 21 32 62
Open Mon–Sat 10–2 (to 7pm Apr–Sep), Sun 10–2.

9 Empúries
The Site
Tel: 972 77 02 08.
Open daily 10 -6 (to 8pm Jun–Sep).

10 Figueres
Museu de l'Empordà
Rambla 1.
Tel: 972 50 23 05.
Open Tue–Sat 11–7, Sun 11–2.

Teatre-Museu Dalí
Plaça Gala i Salvador Dalí. Tel: 972 51 18 00;
www.dali-estate.org
Open Tue- Sat 11 -7, Sun 11–2.

11 Besalú
Monestir de Sant Pere
El Prat de Sant Pere.
Tel: 972 59 12 40 (tourist office).
Contact tourist office for opening times.

12 Banyoles
Museu Arqueològic Comarcal
Plaxa de la Font.
Tel: 972 57 23 61.
Open Tue–Sat 10.30–1, 2–6.30, Sun 10.30–2.

Back to nature
Jardí Botànic de
Marimurtra
Blanes.
Tel: 972 33 08 26.
*Open Jun–Sep, daily 9–8;
Oct–May 9–6.*

For children
Water World
Carretera de Vidreres,
km 1.2, Lloret de Mar.
Tel: 972 36 86 13;
www.waterworld.es
*Open mid-May to 30 Sep,
10–6.*

Back to nature
Jardín Botánico de Cap
Roig
Castell Cap Roig. Calella
de Palafrugell.
Tel: 972 61 45 82.
*Open summer, daily 9–8
(6pm in winter).*

For children
Museu de Joguets
La Rambla, Figueres.
Tel: 972 50 45 85.
*Open Mon–Sat 10–6, Sun
11–2 (Oct–Jun closed
Mon).*

TOUR 3
---

i Plaça de Catalunya
17–S, Barcelona.
Tel: 932 85 38 34.

i Sínia Morera 1, Sitges.
Tel: 938 95 50 04.

i Passeig del Carme
(Parc de Ribes Roges),
Vilanova i la Geltrú.
Tel: 938 15 45 17.

i Fortuny 4, Tarragona.
Tel: 977 23 34 15.

i Plaça del Carrilet,
Tortosa.
Tel: 977 44 96 48.

i Calle Mayor 31 bis,
Lleida (Lérida).
Tel: 973 70 03 19.

1 Sitges
Museu del Cau Ferrat
Carrer del Fonollar.
Tel: 938 94 03 64.
Open Tue–Fri 9.30–2,

*3.30–6 (mid-Jun to Sep
9.30–2, 4–7), Sun 10–3
year round.*

2 Vilanova i la Geltrú
Museu Romàntic Casa
Papiol
Calle Major 32.
Tel: 938 93 03 82
*Guided tours Tue–Fri
9.30–1.15, 4–5.15, Sat
10–1, 4–5, Sun 10–1.*

Biblioteca Museu
Balaguer
Avinguda Victor Balaguer
s/n.
Tel: 938 15 42 02.
*Open Mon–Fri 9.30–2,
Wed 9.30–7.*

4 Tarragona
Museu Nacional
Arqueològic
Plaça del Rei 5.
Tel: 977 23 62 06.
*Open Jun–Sep, Mon–Sat
10–8 (Oct–May, 10–1.30,
4–7), Sun 10–2 year round.*

Museu y Necrópolis
Paleocristina
Anevida Ramon y Cojal
80.
Tel: 977 23 62 09.
*Open Tue–Sat 9.30–8.30,
Sun 10–2.*

8 Lleida
Museu de la Paeria
Plaza Paeria 1.
Tel: 973 70 03 93.
*Open Mon–Sat 11–1, 5–8,
Sun 11–2.*

**9 Monestir de
Poblet**
Plaça Corona d'Aragó,
Poblet.
Tel: 977 87 02 54.
*Guided tours Mon–Sat
10–12.30, 3–6, Sun
10.30–12.30, 3–5.30.*

**11 Monestir Santes
Creus**
Santes Creus.
Tel: 977 63 83 29.
*Open Tue–Sun 10–1,
3–5/6.*

Special to...
Museu del Vi (Wine
Museum)
Plaça Jaume 1, Vilafranca
del Penedès.
Tel: 938 90 05 82.
*Open Tue–Sat 10–2, 4–7,
Sun 10–2.*

For children
Port Aventura
Autovía Salou/Vila–Seca
Km2.
Tel: 977 77 90 90;
www.portaventura.com
*Open mid-Mar to mid-Jun,
10–7/8; high season daily
10am–midnight (Nov, Dec
weekends only).
Closed last week Dec.*

Back to nature
Parc Natural del Delta de
l'Ebre
Information Centre
Tel: 977 48 96 79.

TOUR 4
---

i Calle de la Paz 48,
Valencia.
Tel: 963 98 64 22.

i Plaza Cronista
Chabret, Sagunto.
Tel: 962 66 22 13.

i Carrer del Riu 38,
Cullera.
Tel: 961 72 09 74.

i Avenida Marqués del
Campo s/n, Gandía.
Tel: 962 87 77 88.

i Plaza Oculista Buigues
9, Dénia.
Tel: 966 42 23 67.

i Plaza de la Iglesia 6,
Jávea (Xàbia).
Tel: 965 79 43 56.

i Avenida Ejércitos
Españoles 44, Calp/Calpe.
Tel: 965 83 69 20.

i Avenida Martínez
Alejos 16, Benidorm.
Tel: 965 85 13 11.

i San Llorenç 2, Alcoy.
Tel: 965 53 71 55.

i Calle Alameda Jaime 1
50, Xátiva.
Tel: 962 27 33 46.

1 Sagunto
Teatro Romano
Sagunto.
Tel: 962 66 22 13.
*Open Tue–Sat 10–6 (to
8pm in summer), Sun 10–2.*

4 Gandía
Palacio Ducal
Signposted from the
centre of Gandía.
Tel: 962 87 14 65.
*Guided tours Tue–Sun
10–2, 3.30–7.*

10 Alcoy/Alcoi
Casal de Sant Jordi
Calle San Miguel 62.
Tel: 965 54 08 12.
*Open Tue–Fri 11–1,
5.30–7, Sat–Sun
10.30–1.30.*

11 Xátiva (Játiva)
Museo Municipal
Uphill from the Almeda
Jaume I.
Tel: 962 27 65 97.
*Open Tue–Sun 10–2, 4–8;
mid-Jun to mid-Sep 10–2,
6–10.*

Back to nature
L'Albufera
Visitors Centre.
Tel: 961 62 73 45.
Open 9–2, 4–5.30.

For children
Safari Park Vergel
Between Ondarra and
Oliva.
Tel: 965 75 02 85.
Open daily 10–5.30/6.30.

For children
Terra Mítica
Camino al Moralet, s/n.
Tel: 965 00 47 43.
*Open late Apr–end May,
Sep to mid-Dec, 10–8;
Jun–Aug 10am–midnight;
Nov, Dec weekends only.*

TOUR 5
---

i Rambla Méndez
Núñez 23, Alicante.
Tel: 965 20 00 00.

ⓘ Parque Municipal,
Elche/Elx.
Tel: 966 65 81 95.

ⓘ Francisco Die 25,
Orihuela.
Tel: 965 30 27 47.

ⓘ Plaza Julián Romea 4,
Murcia.
Tel: 902 10 10 70.

ⓘ Lope Gisbert 12,
Lorca.
Tel: 968 46 61 57.

ⓘ Plaza Toneleros,
Mazarrón.
Tel: 968 59 44 26.

ⓘ Plaza Almirante
Bastarrache s/n,
Cartagena.
Tel: 968 50 64 83.

❶ Elche/Elx
Museo Arqueológico
Tel: 965 45 36 03.
*Open Tue–Sat 10–1.30,
4.30–8, Sun 10.30–1 30.*

Huerto del Cura
Tel: 965 45 19 36.
*Open daily 8–8 (to 9pm
Aug); Sep–Dec 7–6.*

❸ Murcia
Museo Salzillo
Plaza San Agustín.
Tel: 968 29 18 93.
*Open Tue–Sat 10–2, 4–8,
Sun 10–2.
Closed Jul–Aug Sat Sun*

❹ Alhama de Murcia
Museo de la Huerta
Alcantarilla.
Tel: 968 89 38 66.
*Open Tue–Fri 10–8,
Sat–Sun 10–1.30.*

For history buffs
Santuario de la
Fuensanta
Tel tourist office: 968 22
05 59.

Back to nature
Parque Natural de Sierra
Espuña.
Tel: 968 42 54 55.
Open 9–1, 4–6.30.

TOUR 6

ⓘ Plaça de la Reina 2,
Palma.
Tel: 971 71 22 16.

ⓘ Canonge Oliver 10,
Port de Sóller.
Tel: 971 63 30 42.

❷ Valldemossa
Cartoixa Reial
Tel: 971 61 21 06.
*Open Mar–Oct, Mon–Sat
9.30–6.30 (to 4 Nov–Feb),
Sun 10–1.*

❺ Monestir de Lluc
Monestir de Lluc
Tel: 971 87 15 25.
Open daily 10–1, 2.30–5.

❽ Coves d'Artà
Tel: 971 84 12 93.
*Guided tours daily 10–5.30;
Jul–Sep 10–7 (last visit of
the day 30 minutes before
closing time).*

❾ Manacor
Museo Arqueológico
Torre dels Enegistes,
Carretera Cales de
Mallorca, s/n.
Tel: 971 84 30 65.
Open Tue, Wed, Thu 9–1.

⓫ Coves del Drac
Porto Cristo.
Tel: 971 82 07 53.
*Guided tours daily 10–5.30;
Apr–Oct 10–5.*

Castell de Bellver
West of Avinguda Joan
Miró, Palma.
Tel: 971 73 06 57.
*Open Mon–Sat
8.15am–8.30pm, Sun
10–7.*

For children
Marineland
Calle Garcilaso de la Vega,
Costa d'en Blanes, Calvia.
Tel: 971 67 51 25;
www.marineland.es
*Open Apr–Sep, Mon–Fri
9.30–4.30, Sat–Sun
9.30–5; Oct–Mar 9.30–5.*

TOUR 7

ⓘ Parque de Nicolás
Salmerón Esq Martínez
Campos, Almería.
Tel: 950 27 43 55.

ⓘ Plaza Nueva s/n,
Mojácar.
Tel: 950 61 50 25.

ⓘ St Martinez Falero 11.
Cazorla.
Tel: 953 70 01 25.

Aqualand
Carretera Cala Figuera–
Magalluf, Costa de Calvia.
Tel: 971 13 08 11;
www.aqualand.es/magaluff
Open May–Oct, daily 10–6.

Aqualand
Autovía Palma–El Arenal,
Km 15.
Tel: 971 44 00 00;
www.aqualand.es/elarenal
*Open mid-May to Oct daily
10–5 (Jul–Aug to 6pm).*

Aqualandia
Carretera Palma, Alcudia,
Km 25.
Tel: 971 51 12 28.
Open May–Oct daily 10–6.

Acuario de Mallorca
Near the Coves del Drac.
Tel: 971 82 09 71.
*Open Mar–Oct, daily 11–5;
Nov–Feb, daily 11–3.*

Autosafari Park
Carretera
Portocristo–Son Servera,
Km 5.
Tel: 971 81 09 09.
*Open daily 10–4 (to 7pm
Apr–Sep).*

For history buffs
Casa Museu Fray Junípero
de la Serra
Carrer de Junípero Serra,
Petra.
Tel: 971 56 11 49.
Visits by arrangement.

Back to nature
Parc Natural Mondragó
Santanyi.
Tel: 971 18 10 22.
*Open summer daily 9–5;
winter 9–4.*

ⓘ Plaza Baja del Marqués
4, Úbeda.
Tel: 953 750 897.

ⓘ Avenida Mariana
Pineda s/n, Guadix.
Tel: 958 69 95 73.

❻ Vélez Blanco
Cueva de los Letreros
Vélez Blanco.
Tel: 950 41 53 54.
*Open year round. Free
access.*

Back to nature
Parque Natural de Cabo
de Gata-Nijar
Tel Information Centre:
950 16 04 35.

Back to nature
Parque Natural de
Cazorla
Carretera del Tranco, Km
18. Torre de Vinagre Visitor
Centre.
Tel. 953 71 30 40.

TOUR 8

ⓘ Pasaje de Chinitas 4,
Málaga.
Tel: 952 21 34 45.

ⓘ Puerta del Mar 2,
Nerja.
Tel: 952 52 15 31.

ⓘ Avenida Europa
(Palacete I a Najarra),
Almuñécar.
Tel: 958 63 11 25

ⓘ Corral del Carbón,
Plaza Mariana Pineda 10
Bajo, Granada.
Tel: 958 24 71 28

ⓘ Plaza San Sebastian 7,
Antequera.
Tel: 952 70 25 05.

❷ Nerja
Cuevas de Nerja
4km (2.5 miles) east of
Nerja.
Tel: 952 52 95 20.
*Open daily 10–2,
3.30–6.30.*

□6□ Granada
Alhambra and Generalife
Tel: 902 44 12 21;
www.alhambra-
patronato.es
Open Mar–Oct 8–8;
Nov–Feb 8–6. Floodlit visits
summer Tue, Thu, Sat
10–11.30; winter Fri, Sat
8–9.30.

Catedral
Granka 5, Capilla Real.
Tel: 958 22 29 59.
Open Mon–Sat
10.30–1.30, 4–7, Sun 4–7.

**Museo Provincial de
Bellas Artes**
Palacio Carlos V.
Tel: 958 22 48 43.
Open daily 10–7.30;
shorter hours in winter.

Museo de la Alhambra
Palacio Carlos V.
Tel: 958 22 75 27.
Open summer daily 9–8;
winter 9–6.

Museo Arqueológico
Carrer del Darro 41.
Tel: 958 22 56 03.
Open Wed–Sat 9–6, Sun
9–2.30, Tue 2.30–6.

□8□ Antequera
**Los Dólmenes (Dolmen
Caves)**
1km (0.5 miles) east of
Antequera.
Tel: 952 70 25 05.
Open Mon–Sat 9–6, Sun
9.30–2.30.

For children
**Parque Acuático
Aquavelis**
Urb. el Tomillar-Carr. Vélez.
Tel: 952 54 27 58.
Open Jun–Sep daily 10–6.

For history buffs
**Museo Federico García
Lorca**
Fuente Vaqueros.
Tel: 958 51 64 53.
Open Jul–Aug Tue–Sun
10–1, 5–7 (4–6pm
Oct–Mar).

□□□ **TOUR 9** □□□

□i□ Pasaje de Chinitas 4,
Málaga.
Tel: 952 21 34 45.

□i□ Plaza Rlas Infante 1,
Torremolinos.
Tel: 952 37 95 12.

□i□ Avenida Antonio
Machado 10,
Benalmádena-Pueblo.
Tel: 952 44 12 95.

□i□ Plaza de la Virgen,
Mijas.
Tel: 952 48 59 00.

□i□ Avenida Jesús Santos
Rein 6, Fuengirola.
Tel: 952 46 76 25.

□i□ Glorieta de la
Fontanilla, Marbella.
Tel: 952 77 14 42.

□i□ Plaza de España 1,
Ronda.
Tel: 952 87 12 72.

For history buffs
Cuevas de la Pileta
20km (12.5 miles) south-
west of Ronda.
Tel: 952 16 73 43.
Open daily 10–1, 4–6. Visits
by previous arrangement
only.

Special to...
Museo Taurino
Calle Virgen de la Paz,
Ronda.
Tel: 952 87 41 32.
Open daily 10–6 (to 8pm
in summer). Closed day of
bullfight and day before.

For children
Tivoli World
Carretera de Benalmá-
dena, Arroyo de la Miel.
Tel: 952 57 70 16;
www.tivoli.es
Open May–Oct, daily
4pm–1am (Jun–Aug
6pm–2am); Nov–Apr, Sat,
Sun 12–8.

Sea Life Benalmádena
Puerto Deportivo,
Benalmádena.
Tel: 952 56 01 50;

www.sealifeeurope.com
Open Mon–Fri 10–6,
Sat–Sun 10–8.

Jardín de las Aguilas
Castilo dc Aguilas,
Benalmádena Pueblo.
Tel: 952 56 82 39.
Open daily. Performances
subject to weather.

Aqualand
Carretera de Circun-
valación, Torremolinos.
Tel: 952 38 88 88;
www.aqualand.es/
torremolinos
Open May–Oct, daily 10–6.

Selwo Aventura
Autovía Costa del Sol, Km
162.5, Las Lomas del
Monte.
Tel: 902 19 04 82;
www.selwo.es
Open daily 10–6 (10–8
Jul–Aug).

□□□ **TOUR 10** □□□

□i□ Avenida de la
Constitución 21B, Sevilla.
Tel: 954 22 14 04.

□i□ Calle del Río 33,
Priego de Córdoba.
Tel: 957 70 06 25.

Sevilla
Reales Alcázares
Plaza del Triunfo s/n,
Sevilla.
Tel: 954 50 23 23.
Open Apr–Sep, Tue–Sat
9.30–7, Sun 9.30–5;
Oct–Mar, Tue–Sat 9.30–6,
Sun 9.30–2.30.

□1□ Carmona
**Musaeo de la Necrópolis
Romana**
Avenida Jorge Bonsor 9.
Tel: 954 14 08 11.
Open Tue–Fri 10–2, 4–6.

□3□ Córdoba
Mezquita–Catedral
Torrijos s/n, Córdoba.
Tel: 957 47 05 12.
Open Jan, Dec, Mon–Sat
10–6.30 (Feb, Nov to 6;
Mar, Jul–Oct to 7; Apr–Jun
to 7.30, Sun 2–7 (also Sun
am for services).

Museo Arqueológico
Plaza Jerónimo Páez.
Tel: 957 47 40 11.
Open Wed–Sat 9–8.30, Tue
2.30 –0.30, Sun 9–2.30.

Museo de Bellas Artes
Plaza del Potro.
Tel: 957 47 33 45.
Open Wed–Sat 9–8.30, Tue
2.30–8.30, Sun 9–2,30.

Museo Municipal Taurino
Plaza Maimónides, 5.
Tel: 957 20 10 56.
Open Tue–Sat 10–2,
4.30–6.30, Sun 9.30–2.30.
Closed Mon.

**□5□ Priego de
Córdoba**
**Museo Casa Natal de
Niceto Alcalá Zamora**
Río 33.
Tel: 957 70 06 25.
Open Mon–Sat 10–1.

□9□ Osuna
Museo Arqueológico
Torre del Agua.
Tel: 954 81 12 07.
Open daily, summer
10–1.30, 5–7; winter
11–1.30, 3.30–6.30.

For children
Aquopolis
Avenida del Deporte-
Sevilla-Este.
Tel: 954 40 06 22;
www.aquopolis.es
Open mid-May to Sep.

Aquasierra
Villafranca de Córdoba.
Tel: 957 19 06 99;
www.aquasierra.es
Open Jun–Sep only.

□□□ **TOUR 11** □□□

□i□ Avenida de la
Constitución 21B, Sevilla.
Tel: 954 22 14 04.

□i□ Avenida de Alemania
12, Huelva.
Tel: 959 25 74 03.

□2□ Itálica
Roman Ruins
9km (5.5 miles) northwest
of Sevilla on N630.
Tel: 955 99 73 76.

Open Tue–Sat 9–5.30, Sun 10–4; Apr–Sep 8.30–8.30, Sun 9–3.

[5] Zalamea la Real
Minas de Ríotinto
Plaza del Museo s/n, Mines del Río Tinto.
Tel: 959 59 00 25.
Museum open 10.30–3, 4–7 (to 8pm in summer).

[8] Huelva
Museo Provincial
Calle Alameda Sundheim 13.
Tel: 959 65 04 24.
Open Tue–Sat 9–8.30; Sun 9–2.30.

[9] Monasterio de la Rábida
4km (2.5 miles) southwest of Palos de la Frontera.
Tel: 959 35 04 11.
Open daily, summer 10–1, 4–7; winter 10–1, 4–6.

Back to nature
Parque Nacional de Coto Doñana
Reception and Interpretation Centre.
Tel: 959 44 23 40.
Pre-booked guided tours only. Summer 8–8; winter 9–7.

For children
Carabelas Quay
Huelva.
Tel: 959 53 05 97.
Open Jun–Sep, Tue–Sun 11–8; Oct–Mar, Tue–Sun 11–5.

TOUR 12

[i] Avenida de la Constitución 21B, Sevilla.
Tel: 954 22 14 04.

[i] Paseo de Canlejas, Cádiz.
Tel: 956 24 10 01.

[i] Calle Luna 22, El Puerto de Santa María.
Tel: 956 54 24 13.

[i] Alameda Cristina, Jerez de la Frontera.
Tel: 956 33 11 50.

[6] Cádiz
Museo de Cádiz
Plaza de la Mina s/n.
Tel: 956 20 33 68.
Open Tue 2.30–8.30, Wed–Sat 9–8.30, Sun 9–2.30.

Torre de Poniente
Plaza Catedral.
Tel: 956 28 61 54.
Open mid-Jun to mid-Sep 10–8; mid-Sep to mid-Jun 10–7.

[11] Jerez de la Frontera
Alcázar
Calle Alameda Vieja.
Tel: 956 33 34 99.
Open Mon–Sat 10–6, Sun 10–3.

For children
Real Escuela Andaluza de Arte Ecuestre
Avenida Duque de Abrantes s/n, Jerez de la Frontera.
Tel: 956 31 96 35.
Guided tours including a visit to facilities and training sessions Mon, Wed, Fri 11–12.30. Weekly performances Tue, Thu at noon (also Tue Mar–Oct).

TOUR 13

[i] Plaza del Pilar s/n, Zaragoza.
Tel: 976 39 35 37.

[i] Plaza del Fuerte, Calatayud.
Tel: 976 88 63 22.

[i] Calle Catedral 5, (Albarracín).
Tel: 978 71 02 51.

[i] Glorieta Pío XII, Torreón de la Zuda, Teruel.
Tel: 902 47 70 00.

[i] Calle Mayor, 1, Alcañiz.
Tel: 978 83 12 13.

[2] Monasterio de Piedra
3.2km (2 miles) from Nuévalos.
Tel: 976 84 90 11.
Open daily 9–6.

For history buffs
Casa–Museo de Goya
Fuendetodos.
Tel: 976 14 38 30.
Open Tue–Sun 11–2, 4–7.

Recommended walks
National Game Reserve Montes Universales
Tel tourist office: 978 71 02 51.

TOUR 14

[i] Plaza de la Catedral 1, Huesca.
Tel: 974 29 21 70.

[i] Avenida Regimiento de Galicia, 2–local 1, Jaca.
Tel: 974 36 00 98.

[1] Castillo de Loarre
Northeast of Ayerbe.
Tel: 619 30 74 80.
Open mid-Mar to mid-Oct Tue–Sun 10–1.30, 4–7 (also Mon Jul, Aug); mid-Oct to mid-Mar 11–2, 4–5.30.

[4] San Juan de la Peña
Monasterio
4km (2.5 miles) from Santa Cruz de los Seros.
Tel: 947 35 51 19;
www.monasteriosanjuan.com
Open mid-Mar to May, Sep to mid-Oct daily 10–2, 4–7; Jun 10–2.30, 4–8; Jul–Aug 10–2.30, 3.30–8; Nov to mid-Mar 11–2, 4–5.30.

[5] Jaca
Museo Diocesano
Housed in the cathedral.
Tel: 974 36 18 41.
Open daily 9–1.30, 5–8

[6] Sabiñánigo
Museo Etnológico de Artes Populares
Sabiñánigo.
Tel 974 48 42 61.
Open Apr–Sep Tue–Sat 10.30–1.30, 4–7; Jul–Aug daily 10.30–1.30, 5–9; Oct, Mar Tue–Sat 10.30–1.30, 3.30–6.30; Sun 10.30–3.30, 4–7 year round.

[9] Parque Nacional de Ordesa y Monte Perdido
2km (1.2 miles) northeast of Brotó. Visitors' centre.
Tel: 974 24 33 61;
www.ordesa.net

TOUR 15

[i] Calle Eslava 1, Pamplona.
Tel: 848 42 00 00.

[i] Rua Mayor 1, Olite.
Tel: 948 74 17 03.

[i] Juicio 4, Tudela
Tel: 948 84 80 58.

[i] Plaza de San Francisco 1, Tarazona.
Tel: 976 64 00 74.

[i] Medinaceli 2, Soria.
Tel: 975 21 20 52.

[i] Paseo del Espolón s/n, Logroño.
Tel: 941 29 12 60.

[i] San Nicolás 1, Estella.
Tel: 948 55 63 01.

[4] Olite
Castillo de los Reyes de Navarra
Tel: 948 74 00 35.
Open Oct–Apr 10–2, 4–6; May–Sep 10–2, 4–7 (8 Jul–Aug).

[8] Soria
Monasterio de San Juan de Duero
Soria (just outside centre).
Tel: 975 22 13 97.
Open Jul–Aug daily 10–2, 5–8; Sep–Jun 10–2, 4–7.

Ruinas de Numancia
8km (5 miles) north of Soria.
Tel: 975 21 20 52.
Open Apr–Sep Tue–Sat 10–2, 4–8; Sep–Mar 10–2, 4–6; Sun 10–2 year round.

Special to...
The *Sanfermines* (Fiesta of San Fermín)
Held from 6–14 July.

TOUR 16

i Plaza Mayor 3, Madrid.
Tel: 915 88 16 36.

i Puerta de Bisagra s/n,
Toledo.
Tel: 925 22 08 43.

i Plaza San Antonio 9,
Aranjuez.
Tel: 918 91 04 27.

2 Toledo
Museo de Santa Cruz
Calle Miguel Cervantes 3.
Tel: 925 22 14 02.
*Open Mon–Sat 10–6.30,
Sun 10–2.*

Hospital de Tavera
Calle Cardenal Travera 2
Tel: 925 22 04 51.
*Guided tours Tue–Sun
10.30–1.30, 3–5.30.*

Casa y Museo de El
Greco
Calle Samuel Leví 3.
Tel: 925 28 42 25.
*Open Mon–Sat 10–7, Sun
10–3.*

Alcázar
Cuesta de Carlos V.
Tel: 925 22 16 73.
*Currently can only be
viewed from the outside.*

4 Aranjuez
Palacio Real
Plaza Parejas.
Tel: 918 91 03 05.
*Guided tours Apr–Sep
10–6.15; Oct–Mar, Tue–Sun
10–5.15.*

Casa del Labrador
Jardin del Principe, Calle
de la Rcina.
Tel: 918 91 13 44.
*By prior arrangement
Apr–Sep 10–6.15;
Oct–Mar, Tue–Sun 10–6.15.*

For children
Trena de la Fresa
Tel: 902 228 822.
*Open mid-Apr to mid-Oct
Sat–Sun.*

Warner Bros Movie
World
Carretera M301 Km
15.500, San Martín de la
Vega.
Tel: 918 21 12 34;
www.warnerbrospark.com
*Open Apr–Jun mid-Sep to
end Sep Mon–Thu 10–8,
Fri–Sun 10–12. Closed Aug
to mid-Sep, Oct–Mar.*

TOUR 17

i Plaza Mayor 69,
Madrid.
Tel: 915 88 29 00.

i Plaza de los Santos
Niños, Alcalá de Henares.
Tel: 918 81 06 34.

i Plaza de los Caídos 6,
Guadalajara.
Tel: 949 21 16 26.

i Gonzalez Palencia 2-
bajo. Cuenca.
Tel: 969 17 88 00.

1 Alcalá de Henares
Museo Casa Natal de
Cervantes
Calle Mayor.
Tel: 918 89 96 54.
Open Tue–Sun 10–6.

2 Guadalajara
Palacio del Infantado
Plaza de los Caídos 1.
Tel: 949 21 33 01.
Open Tue–Sat 10–2 , 4–7.

5 Cuenca
Museo de Arte Abstracto
Español
Calle Canónigos.
Tel: 969 21 29 83;
www.march.es/cuenca
*Open Tue–Fri 11–2, 4–6,
Sat 11–2, 4–8, Sun
10–2.30.*

Museo Diocesano
Avenida Obispo Valero.
Tel: 969 22 42 10.
*Open Tue–Sat 11–1.30,
4.30–6.30, Sun 1.30 (winter
shorter hours).*

7 Belmonte
Castillo de Belmonte
Belmonte.
Tel: 967 17 00 08.
*Open daily 10–1, 4–7
(summer 10.30–1, 4–7).*

**9 Parque
Arqueológico de
Segóbriga**
Centro de Interpretacion,
Cuenca.
Tel: 629 75 22 57.
*Open Apr–Oct Tue–Sun 10–
9; Nov–Mar Tue–Sun 10–8.*

10 Uclés
Monasterio de Uclés
Tel: 969 13 50 58.
*Open Apr–Oct Mon–Fri
9–6, Sat–Sun 10–6;
Nov–Mar Mon–Fri 9–8,
Sat–Sun 10–8.*

Recommended
walks
Serranía de Cuenca
La Ciudad Encantada,
35km (22 miles) north of
Cuenca.
Tel: 969 23 21 19;
www.safarimadrid.com
Open daily 9am–sunset.

TOUR 18

i Plaza Mayor 69,
Madrid.
Tel: 915 88 29 00.

i Grimaldi 4, El Escorial.
Tel: 918 90 53 13.

i Plaza de Pedro Dávila
4, Ávila.
Tel: 920 21 13 87.

i Carretera Salamanca,
Béjar.
Tel: 923 40 30 05.

i Ronda Palenque,
2 Centro de Promoción
de la Artesanía, Talavera
de la Reina.
Tel: 925 72 14 54.

**1 Valle de los
Caídos**
Valle de los Caídos.
Tel: 918 90 56 11.
*Basilíca and La Cruz open
Tue–Sun 10–5 (Apr–Sep
10–6.30).*

2 El Escorial
Monasterio de El Escorial
Calle Juan du Barbón y
Battemberg.
Tel: 918 80 59 02.
*Open Tue–Sun 10–5 (to
6pm Apr–Sep).*

6 Béjar
Palacio Ducal
Plaza Mayor s/n.
Tel tourist office: 923 40
30 05.
*For opening times contact
tourist office.*

**8 Monasterio de
Yuste**
1.8km (1 mile) from
Cuacos de Yuste.
Tel: 927 17 21 30.
*Guided tours: Apr–Oct,
Mon–Sat 9.30–12.30.*

For children
Safari Madrid
Aldea del Fresno, near
Navalcarnero (Madrid).
Tel: 918 62 23 14;
www.safarimadrid.com
Open daily 10.30–dusk.

TOUR 19

i Plaza Mayor 69,
Madrid.
Tel: 915 88 29 00.

i Plaza Mayor 10,
Segovia.
Tel: 921 46 03 34.

1 El Pardo
Palacio Real El Pardo
Calle Manuel Alonso s/n.
Tel: 913 76 15 00.
*Guided tours Mon–Sat
10.30–5, Sun 10–1.30;
Apr–Sep, Mon–Sat
10.30–6, Sun 9.30–1.30.*

**3 Manzanares el
Real**
Castillo de los Mendoza
Manzanares el Real.
Tel: 918 21 71 91;
www.manzanareselreal.
org
*Open Tue–Sun 10–1.30,
3–6 (10–7 in winter).*

[i] Tourist Information Centre
[12] Number on tour

Practical • Information

[5] El Paular
Monasterio de Santa Maria de El Paular
El Paular.
Tel: 918 69 14 25;
www.monasterioelpaular.com
Call for times.

[6] La Granja
Palacio
La Granja.
Tel: 921 47 00 19.
Open Apr–Sep, Tue–Sun 10 6; Oct–Mar, Tue–Sat 10–1.30, 3–5, Sun 10 2.

[7] Segovia
Alcázar
Plaza del Alcázar
Tel: 921 46 07 59.
Open Apr–Sep daily 10–7; Oct–Mar Mon–Thu 10–6, Fri–Sun 10–7.

For children
Parque del Ríofrío
10km (6 miles) south of Segovia.
Tel: 921 47 00 19 (Palacio de Ríofrío).
Open Tue–Sat 10 1.30, 3–5, Sun 10–2.

TOUR 20

[i] Plaza Mayor 3, Cáceres.
Tel: 927 01 08 34.

[i] Plaza Mayor s/n, Trujillo. Tel: 927 32 26 77.

[i] Plaza Mayor s/n, Guadalupe.
Tel: 927 15 41 28.

[i] Avenida J Alvarez Saenz de Buruaga s/n, Mérida.
Tel: 924 00 97 30.

[i] Passaje de San Juan s/n, Badajoz.
Tel: 924 22 49 81.

[1] Trujillo
Palacio de los Duques de San Carlos
Plaza Mayor.
Tel tourist office: 927 32 26 77.
Open Mon–Sat 10.30–1, 4.30–6.30, Sun 10.30–1.

Palacio de Orellana–Pizarro
Plaza de Don Juan Tena
Tel tourist office: 927 32 26 77.
For opening times contact the tourist office.

[2] Guadalupe
Monasterio de Guadalupe
Plaza de Guadalupe.
Tel: 927 36 70 00;
www.monasterioguadalupe.com
Guided tours daily 9.30–1, 3.30–6.30.

[3] Mérida
Teatro Romano and Anfiteatro
Mérida.
Tel: 924 31 25 30;
www.merida.es
Open Jul to mid-Sep daily 9.30 1.45, 4–6.15; mid-Sep to Jun 9.30–1.45, 4–6.15.

Museo de Arte Romano
Tel: 924 31 19 12;
www.museoarteromano.mcu.es
Open Tue–Sat 10–2, 4–9, Sun 10–2.

Alcazaba
Tel: 924 00 34 38.
Same opening times as for Teatro Romano and Anfiteatro (see above).

[4] Badajoz
Museo Arqueológico Provincial
Plaza José Alvarez y Saenz de Buruaga.
Tel: 924 00 19 08.
Open Tue–Sun 10–3.

Back to nature
Parque Natural de Monfragüe
Tel: 927 19 91 34.

TOUR 21

[i] Casa de las Conchas, Rua Mayor, Salamanca.
Tel: 923 26 85 71.

[i] Calle Santa Clara 20, Zamora.
Tel: 980 53 18 45.

[i] Acera de Recoteros s/n, Valladolid.
Tel: 983 35 18 01.

[i] Calle Mayor 105, Palencia.
Tel: 979 74 00 68.

[i] Plaza Alonso Martínez 7, Burgos.
Tel: 947 20 31 25.

[i] Plaza Mayor s/n, Aranda de Duero.
Tel: 947 20 31 25.

[2] Zamora
Museo Catedrálico
Cathedral.
Tel: 980 53 18 02.
Open Tue–Sun 10–2, 5–8.

Museo de la Semana Santa
About 1km (0.5 miles) northeast of old town, Zamora.
Tel: 980 53 27 95.
Open Mon–Sat 10–2, 5–8, Sun 10–2.

[3] Valladolid
Museo Nacional de Escultura Policromada
Colegio de San Gregorio, Calle Cadenas de San Gregorio.
Tel: 983 25 03 75.
Open Tue–Sat 10–2, 4–6, Sun 10–2.

Museo Oriental
Paseo de Filipinos 7.
Tel: 983 30 68 00.
Open Mon–Sat 4–7, Sun 10 2.

[4] Palencia
Museo
Cathedral Cloister, Plaza Santa.
Tel: 979 70 13 47.
Open Mon–Sat 10.30–1.30, 4–6 (7.30 Jul–Sep), Sun 11.15–1.

[5] Burgos
Catedral de Burgos
Plaza Santa Maria s/n.
Tel: 947 27 39 50.
Open Mon–Sat 9.30–1, 4–7, Sun 9.30–11.45, 4–7.

Real Monasterio de las Huelgas
Calle Compás de Adentro.
Tel: 947 20 16 30.
Guided tours Tue–Sat 10–1.15, 4–5.15 (5.45 Sat), Sun 10.30–2.15.

Cartuja de Miraflores
Carretera de San Pedro Cardeña, 4km (2.5 miles) southeast of Burgos.
Tel 947 20 31 25.
Open Mon–Sat 10.15–3, 4–6, Sun 11.20–12.40.

[9] Tordesillas
Monasterio de Santa Clara
Tordesillas.
Tel: 983 77 00 71.
Guided tours Tue–Sat 10.30–1.15, 4 5.15 (Apr–Sep, Tue–Sat 10–1, 3.30–6.30), Sun 10.30–1.30, 3.30–5.30.

For history buffs
Casa de Cervantes
Calle del Rastro s/n, Valladolid.
Tel: 983 30 88 10;
www.museocasacervantes.mcu.es
Open Tue–Sat 9.30–3.30, Sun 10–3.

Back to nature
Monasterio de Santo Domingo de Silos
Tel: 947 39 00 49.
Open Tue–Sat 10–1, 4.30–6 (Sun 4.30–6).

TOUR 22

[i] Casa Paredes, Avenida La Marina 18, La Coruña.
Tel: 981 18 43 44.

[i] Calle Emilio Romay s/n, Betanzos.
Tel: 981 77 36 93.

[i] Plaza Mayor 27–29 (Galerías), Lugo.
Tel: 982 23 13 61.

[i] Casa Legoeiro, Ponte Romana s/n, Orense.
Tel: 988 37 20 20.

Practical • Information

[i] Calle Teófilo Llorente 8, Vigo.
Tel: 986 22 47 57.

[i] General Gutiérrez Mellado 1, Pontevedra.
Tel: 986 85 08 14.

[i] Plaza de Galicia, Santiago de Compostela.
Tel: 981 57 39 90.

[2] Lugo
Museo Provincial de Lugo
Plaza de la Soledad.
Tel: 982 24 21 12.
Open Sep–Jun Mon–Fri 10.30–2, 4.30–8.30, Sat 4.30–8.30; Jul, Aug Mon–Fri 11–2, 5–8, Sat 10–2.

[4] Orense/Ourense
Catedral de San Martín
Plaza del Trigo 1.
Tel: 988 22 09 92.
Open daily 7.45–1.30, 4.30–8.30.

[6] Pontevedra
Museo de Pontevedra
Calle Pasantería 10.
Tel: 986 85 14 55.
Open Jun–Sep, Tue–Sat 10–2.15, 5–8.45; Oct–Mar, Tue–Sat 10–2, 4–7; Sun all year 11–2.

Back to nature
Parque de Ancares
Tel tourist office: 982 23 13 61.

For children
Parque Infantil 'La Selva'
Fernando III El Santo 33, Santiago de Compostela.
Tel: 981 59 77 22.
Open daily 4.30–9.

TOUR 23

[i] Calle Marqués de Santa Cruz 1, Oviedo.
Tel: 985 22 75 86.

[i] Plaza de la Regla s/n, León.
Tel: 987 29 21 89.

[i] Plaza la Basílica, Covadonga.
Tel: 985 84 60 35.

[i] Jardines del Ayuntamiento 2, Cangas de Onís.
Tel: 985 84 80 05.

[i] Puerto Deportivo Dársena de Fomento, Gijón.
Tel: 985 34 60 46.

[1] León
Colegiata Real de San Isidoro
Plaza de San Isidoro 4
Tel: 987 87 50 88.
Open Sep–Jun Mon–Sat 10–1.15, 4–6.30, Sun 10.30–1; Jul–Aug Mon–Sat 9–8, Sun 9–2.

[3] Potes
Monasterio de Santo Toribio de Liébana
3km (2 miles) west of Potes.
Tel: 942 73 05 50.
Open daily 10–1, 4–7.

[5] Covadonga
La Santa Cueva (Holy Cave)
Tel tourist office: 985 84 60 35.
Open daily 9–7.30.

Back to nature
Parque Nacional de los Picos de Europa
Tel: 985 84 86 14.

TOUR 24

[i] Mercado del Este, Santander.
Tel: 942 31 07 08.
[i] Jesús Otero 20, Santillana de Mar.
Tel: 942 81 82 51.

[2] Cuevas de Altamira
3km (2 miles) from Santillana del Mar.
Tel: 942 81 81 02.
Open May–Oct Tue–Sat 9–8, Sun 9.30–3; Oct–Apr Tue–Sat 9.30–6.

TOUR 25

[i] Calle Reina Regente 3, San Sebastián.
Tel: 943 48 11 66.

[i] Nafarroa Kalea 23, Zarautz.
Tel: 943 83 09 90.

[i] Artekale 8, Guernica-Lumo.
Tel: 946 25 58 92.

[i] Plaza del Ensanche 11, Bilbao.
Tel: 944 79 57 60.

[i] Plaza General Loma s/n, Vitoria-Gasteiz.
Tel: 945 16 15 98.

[3] Zumaia
Museo de Zuloaga
Behind the beach across the river.

Tel: 943 86 23 41
Open Apr to mid-Sep, Wed–Sun 4–8.

[6] Gernika-Lumo
Casa de Juntas
Calle Karmelo Etxegarai.
Tel: 946 25 11 38.
Open daily 10–2, 4–6 (7 in summer).

[7] Bilbao (Bilbo)
Museo Guggenheim
Avenida Abandoibarro 2.
Tel: 944 35 90 80;
www.guggenheimbilbao.es
Open Tue–Sun 10–8.

Museo Vasco
Plaza Miguel Unamuno 4.
Tel: 944 15 54 23;
www.euskal-museoa.org
Open Tue–Sat 11–5, Sun 11–2.

Museo de Bellas Artes
Plaza del Museo 2.
Tel: 944 39 60 60.
Open Tue–Sat 10–8, Sun 10–2.

[8] Vitoria-Gasteiz
Museo de Arqueología
Correría, 116.
Tel: 945 18 19 18;
www.museobilbao.com
Open Tue–Fri 10–2, 4–6.30, Sat 10–2, Sun 11–2.

For children
Funicular de Artxanda
Plaza Funicular s/n.
Tel: 944 45 49 66.

For information on Equestrian Centres: Tel tourist office: 943 86 23 41, Apr to mid-Sep.

INDEX

Index & Acknowledgements

The Automobile Association
would like to thank the following libraries and photographers for their help in the preparation of this book:

PICTURES COLOUR LIBRARY 63b, 64/5; **SPECTRUM COLOUR LIBRARY** 21b, 26, 38, 78, 96, 145, 151, 150/1, 154/5, 156/7.
The remaining pictures are held in the Association's own library (AA WORLD TRAVEL LIBRARY) and were taken by:
P BAKER 7, 34, 35a, 35b, 36/7, 37, 39a, 39b, 152; M CHAPLOW 4, 27, 44/5, 44, 45, 77, 118/19, 122/3; S L DAY 2; J EDMANSON 6, 25, 28/9, 30, 31a, 31b, 32, 33, 47, 50b, 51, 52/3, 55, 56, 57, 58, 59, 62, 68b, 73a, 99, 100, 101, 102, 103, 104, 105, 106, 106/7, 108, 113, 115, 116, 120, 121, 124, 125; P ENTICKNAP 8, 9, 10a, 10b, 12/13, 14, 15, 16/17, 17, 18, 19, 20, 21a, 22/3, 48, 80, 81, 82/3, 83, 84/5, 85, 86/7, 87, 88, 89, 90, 91, 923/3, 93, 94, 95, 110, 110/11, 117, 126, 127a, 127b, 129, 130/1, 130, 132, 134, 135, 137, 138, 139, 140/1, 141, 143a, 143b, 144/5, 146, 147, 148; M JOURDAN 133, 136, 149, 153; A MOLYNEUX 40, 60, 61, 64; J POULSEN 49a, 53, 54; D ROBERTSON 41, 42, 43, 46/7, 49b, 50a, 63a, 66, 67, 68a, 69, 70, 71, 72, 73b, 74, 75; R STRANGE 97, 98, 109; J A TIMS 114, S WATKINS 79.

Author's acknowledgements:
Mona King thanks the following for their help: Turespaña, Madrid; TurMadrid, Madrid; Turismo de Sevilla, Sevilla and The Spanish Tourist Office, London.

Contributors
Verifier: Apostrophe S **Original copy editor:** Helen Douglas-Cooper **Indexer:** Marie Lorimer

Atlas

A Coruña/
La Coruña
182-183

Santander

Bilbao/
Bilbo

186

Donostia/
San Sebastián

184-185

Burgos

Pamplona/
Iruña

F

Valladolid

Salamanca

Zaragoza

187 **188-189**

190-191

192-193

MADRID

Barcelona

AND

P

194-195

196-197

198-199

Valencia

Palma de
Mallorca

Menorca

Córdoba

Eivissa

Mallorca

Sevilla/
Soville

200-201

Granada

Alacant/
Alicante

Formentera

Cádiz

202-203

Cartagena

Málaga

GB

MA

DZ

Toll free motorway	Regional road	International boundary
Toll motorway	Local road	National park, natural reserve
Interchange/ restricted interchange	Secondary road	⊕ International airport
$ Service area	▼ 63 ▼ Distance in kilometres	Panoramic view
= 2009 = Motorway under construction (opening year)	Scenic route	León Town or place of great tourist interest
Motorway in tunnel	Railway and tunnel	Mérida Interesting town or place
National road	Dénia Ferry route and destination	Almería Other tourist town or place

914.604
S

Spain's best-loved
driving tours